Planetary Gardener

Life First

Gilles Clément et Coloco —
Nicolas Bonnenfant, Miguel Georgieff, Pablo Georgieff

Civic city. Lars Müller Publishers

Contents

p. 006 **1.** Putting *Life* first

p. 014 **2.** Adopting the viewpoint of the *Planetary gardener*

p. 044 **3.** Acting now

Engagement
3.A Asfalto mon Amour, Lecce
3.B Le Cloître Workshops, Le Cloître-Saint-Thégonnec
3.C Happy Garden, Aubervilliers
3.D The Punk Gardens, Montholon
3.E Lago Bullicante, Rome

Dynamics
3.F The Transformer, Saint-Nicolas-de-Redon
3.G R-Urban, Colombes, Gennevilliers
3.H Vive les Groues, Nanterre
3.I Biodiversity School, Boulogne-Billancourt
3.J GardeNation, Paris

Strategies
3.K Base 217, Le Plessis-Pâté / Brétigny-sur-Orge
3.L The Edges of Girona, Girona
3.M Parc du Peuple de l'herbe, Carrières-sous-Poissy
3.N The Aire, the River and its Double, Geneva
3.O Aldeia Maracanã - Rio de Janeiro

Territories
3.P Ingenious Landscapes, across the Planetary Garden
3.Q Cerros Isla, Santiago de Chile
3.R Underwater Landscape Plan, the Calanques National Park
3.S A Primary Forest for the Future, Western Europe
3.T Le Potager des Autres, Potager du Roi, Versailles

p. 544 **4.** *Engage* with the living world

A *manifesto* for prioritizing the living world

At the back of *Le Potager du Roi* (*The King's Kitchen Garden*) in Versailles, over the span of a year, the Others' Kitchen Garden came to life – tended by those who care about the future of our planet, not just in thought and words, but also in action. That's why *La Préséance du vivant* (*Life Takes Precedence*) exhibition at the Landscape Biennale curated by Gilles Clément and Coloco (Pablo Georgieff, Miguel Georgieff, Nicolas Bonnenfant) couldn't be limited to showcasing past achievements; it had to provide a similarly experimental environment.

Set up according to a framework and a schedule, the temporary garden had migrated from other projects and, enhanced by its stay on the royal grounds, moved on to new destinations. The large enclosing wall served for documenting on–site activity, with human activities recorded alongside those of other life forms. This new perspective on humanity's relationship with all other species, endangered or not, aligned well with the contemporary landscape approach central to both the exhibition and this book.

Acknowledging the creator's political responsibility in all aspects of their work resonates deeply with our design ethos. So, it made perfect sense to include this book in the research series Design2context/Civic city that explores the role of design in fostering a more equitable, less selfish, and, above all, less destructive world. Just like the exhibition, this book is divided into three major parts: one deals with understanding the living world based on current scientific data; the next one illustrates *La Préséance du vivant* (*Life Takes Precedence*) concept through a varied selection of landscape–related experiments, while the final part revisits the concepts and tools developed by Gilles Clément and Coloco to inspire action.

Wearing multiple hats, we were involved in conceiving and designing the exhibition as integral designers], while as Civic city, we had the opportunity to host a 24–hour Life First (Vivants d'abord) stream, bringing together individuals from around the world who approach landscape environments with similar societal awareness. It therefore felt right to continue this pursuit of understanding by putting together a book that would show our world through the eyes of the landscape designer. It's interesting to compare this viewpoint with that of other creative disciplines. The traveling exhibition Climate Care, first presented in Vienna's Museum für angewandte Kunst (MAK) and designed by us, showcased the approach of urban planners and architects based on similar scientific considerations; the book Financing Our Common Future, also published by Lars Müller, explains the perspective of the economists attuned to ecology. We believe that, in the face of blindness and other forms of denial, this effort of designing information and creating awareness deserves a guidebook and a manifesto that calls on everyone to participate in saving life – not only by planting, but also by stripping the asphalt off our environment.

Read and enjoy.

Ruedi and Vera Baur, Civic city

1. Putting *Life* first

Putting Life first can be defined in three ways :

A survival instinct

It expresses itself through alarm cries. We must collectively realize that putting Life first is crucial, or else we will destroy it through greed, carelessness, or ignorance!

A way of paying attention

It expresses itself through questioning. Let's engage all our senses and get amazed; let's take the time needed to coexist on the same land. Let's enhance the ancestral knowledge about the living world and relearn everything related to life. How can we reinvent our relationship with living beings, based on new intentions?

A code of conduct

It expresses itself through commitments. Let's change the way we work and consume. We should no longer finance misguided projects or teach harmful techniques that destroy the planet. Let's stop practices that reduce the space available for living beings.

In the garden, we invent by doing, then record the transformations of the site using a notation system. Putting Life first becomes central, like a kind of musical key that allows us to perform the garden's score together.

Daring to change our view of landscape

"Throughout its evolution, the city has been organized around the criteria that prioritized convenience for just one kind of living being: the humans. If we try to imagine a city developing in a way that regards the entire living world as a complex and interdependent whole, we can fundamentally shift the principles of urban planning."

Coloco and Gilles Clément, 2013
the opening lines of 55 000 hectares of Nature,
a study commissioned by Bordeaux Métropole

Taking Responsibility for a Fertile Future

War is raging on Earth. Control over natural resources, ownership of arable land, and command over trade routes have long been the pillars of empire–building.

Private property, the foundation of capitalism, has extended to life itself. Genetically modified, life is now protected by international intellectual property rights, resulting in financial gains. This applies to seeds as well as animals, and the possibility of genetically modified and patentable humans is a technological reality with frightening prospects for market approval. Between genetic editing and technological implants, what will remain of our human–ness? It's for humanity to decide, as nearly anything is possible today. Is this the next stage of Homo sapiens' evolution, as some predict? The lack of global governance on this critical matter is alarming.

Nevertheless, we will likely still need to maintain our vital functions biologically. For this, we will continue to rely on our planet's biosphere for quite some time – because, despite our marvelous technology, we still don't know how to produce food from solar energy as plants do, forming the foundation of the entire terrestrial food chain.

Water, mining deposits, and fossil fuel reserves are now largely privatized worldwide. Few governments or local authorities are able to preserve them as public assets, and even fewer as communal resources. Land use is controlled almost everywhere, and where it isn't, strong pressures exist to make these lands profitable. Considered unproductive by the economic system, keeping these lands as biodiversity reserves is weighed against economic losses. In some cases, multinational corporations received financial compensation from governments for not being able to exploit the land.

Meanwhile, life keeps inventing new things – in a radical otherness that doesn't care about money or power. Living organisms are born, grow, and create links of cooperation and competition unique to each ecosystem. They all die eventually, and their bodies go back into the endless cycle of life; decomposed by saprophytes, they become available for future living beings. Life on Earth is by far the most complex phenomenon we know in the Universe, the only one that resists entropy. The vast amounts of knowledge we accumulate daily only highlight how much we do not know – and keep opening up new fascinating areas of research.

At the same time, each of us has a unique experience of what it means to be alive. We humans have consciousness and speech, allowing us to share our emotions, viewpoints, and struggles. We also have opposable thumbs, a brilliant evolutionary invention that allows us to physically engage in transforming the world. When we pick up a pickaxe and start a garden, our act becomes a commitment to the future.

Let's not forget, however, that ages ago, other cultures – the Australian Aborigines or the Amazonian peoples, for example – saw their environment, particularly their landscapes, as a living system made up of relationships and stories, where the individual made no sense without their genealogy, and where non–humans were considered equal to humans. Plants were seen as capable of teaching, mountains of dreaming, and animals as having eternal souls... Primitive nonsense! European monarchical capitalism couldn't care less about this knowledge. Evangelizing the barbarians, slaughtering them to take their lands, and granting those lands to the nobility so they could make them productive with slave labor – that was the agenda of the time. Before the factory, the plantation was the economic model of nascent capitalism. What remains of pre–colonial Americas, Africa, or Asia is a fraction of the irreplaceable, millennia–old knowledge of these peoples. This knowledge detailed their relationships with the living world, allowing them to sustain balance within their ecosystems, and connected them to their origins through mythical stories that gave meaning to the existence of every living being. It's hard to say the same for the Capitalocene. Who today can think in terms of millennia or even centuries?

Trying to imagine the next ten years causes profound anxiety, and it's easier today to picture the end of the world than the end of capitalism. Shifting it towards a fertile model of planetary scale is our main contemporary challenge. Thousands of smaller alternative projects and committed corporate policies are already making changes, but major nations are stuck in agreements that mostly go nowhere.

We have come to realize that Gaia, a living meta–organism that creates its own conditions for habitability, disregards borders: currents, clouds, seeds, birds, and even poisons and radioactive elements ignore them alike. The future of our environment is clearly uncertain, and the fate of our societies can keep us awake at night. The efforts made by political forces to protect life clash with powerful industrial and financial lobbies whose agenda is to maximize short–term profits, no matter the cost. Dazed by the recent media spotlight on climate change and its more visible consequences, we carry on with our compulsive consumer lives. Unable, for now, to turn political ecology into an alternative governing force, we fluctuate between identitarian closure and neoliberal globalism, mixed into toxic cocktails that vary based on country or region.

The drive to survive, which we share with all living things, can lead us to actions beyond our imagination.

Hope is the fuel for resistance; it is renewable and non-polluting. Hope burns inside each of us, and the only time we can act is now!

Hope can sometimes manifest through violent clashes, for it's hope that drives the people chaining themselves to trees and declaring they are ready to die in order to protect trees from chainsaws. Or those throwing cakes at artworks in museums to draw media attention to mass extinction. Or others, who protest all over the world, from Rio to Brussels, from Kinshasa to Geneva, and from Jakarta to New York, against government climate inaction – and who are getting legally condemned for this as repeat offenders.

This book is dedicated to the environmental activists murdered around the world – over two hundred in Brazil alone in 2022 – and to the last remaining representatives of the thousands of species that disappear forever, year after year... We will never forget you. But hope also shows in small everyday gestures, from the kids who stop, mesmerized, to watch a millipede, to the grandparents who, in their twilight years, still plant trees for future generations to enjoy.

It's hope, again, that led us to make landscaping our profession, accepting to face technical, regulatory and political challenges on the ground, in order to enable and support life. This profession, both poetic and diplomatic, has only recently become part of planning procedures. It exists in just a few countries, in different forms and backed by remarkable histories, sometimes seen as a break from architecture, sometimes as part of agronomy.

The landscapist tries to get a message across to political leaders and the public, to draw attention to what we are doing to our cities, our countryside, and our forests. A message of warning, for sure, but one that is supported by concrete proposals for rethinking the place of life in view of the rampant artificialization of the world. Planned or not, living on Earth will require us to deal with multiple conflicts, from managing migrations to controlling urban sprawl, and from producing food to preserving major climate regulation mechanisms. We have no choice but to prepare ourselves for the world to come, the one we will bequeath to our descendants.

Imagining new relationships with living things

Putting Life First is a call to collectively reflect on our capacity for action. As curators of the Landscape Biennial in Versailles in 2022, we brought to the fore the responsibilities inherent to our profession, as well as its capacity to adapt to current challenges. We showcased a series of projects in progress, signaling the changes that are already at work. These exploratory projects suggest a series of approaches allowing us to imagine new futures. The exhibition, and the resulting publication, are an invitation to get involved at all levels. Landscape architects, and all other actors engaged in land use planning, need to anticipate, support, and enable these changes to keep our shared Planetary Garden livable. And this challenge is not for professionals only: on spaceship Earth, there are no passengers, for each of us is a member of the crew.

Collective awareness of our impact on the biosphere is obviously growing. We are increasingly concerned about the origin of our food, and the carbon footprint of our construction practices and our travel. On the other hand, the logic of profit, population trends, and geopolitical conflicts are increasing the pressure on our biosphere – that fine layer, no more than twenty kilometers deep, between the ocean floor where microplastic particles settle, and the atmosphere boundaries, beyond which more and more space junk accumulates in Earth's orbit. Overlapping the biosphere is the technosphere: from the ocean depths where massive cables carry the Internet to the geostationary orbits now colonized by private satellites.

From repeated warnings of climate experts to multifaceted reflections of contemporary philosophers, thinkers stress the urgency to imagine new relationships with other forms of life.

But in the real world, in places where we actually live, reactions are slow to take shape, stuck in the cautiousness of political calculations and the difficulty of revising our models of desire along with their destructive side effects.

And it's not just land use planning: all disciplines are being shaken up by the issue of life, as demonstrated by the 108 experts from around the world invited to take part in our 24-hour event in Versailles. We need to harness all known approaches, from life sciences to shamanic traditions, in order to reconfigure our relationships with the living world. Let's consider each piece of land as a fragment of the Planetary Garden – and act accordingly, as gardeners!

Changing our cultural model

From the tenet of Putting Life first emerges a new framework that turns land use planners into custodians of the planet's fertility, because every square meter counts. This approach begins with an invitation to "adopt the viewpoint of the Planetary gardener," which is the name of the first chapter of this book. Advances in biology have helped us understand that we, humans, are made up of billions of other microscopic living beings, and our bodies themselves contain multiple ecosystems whose balance affects our health. We need to take our bodies back and take care of them daily. "Reclaim your body!" says a graffiti we recently saw. Seen this way, humans are no longer disconnected from their environment, and are not only individually responsible for their own health, but also, collectively, for the health of Gaia.

To make this possible, we should start by looking at the Planetary Garden with sympathy and curiosity. We should ask questions about it, and perhaps even try to establish communication with non-humans so we could understand how they express their vital drive, what are the dangers they are facing and the situations in which they thrive and flourish. With this in mind, our book seeks to bring the idea of Putting Life first to an audience wider than the participants of the Landscape Biennial. We are thinking of those who choose to take a different route: students, activists, and everyone else who has realized that a lifestyle shift is necessary.

Sharing individual stories of different gardens, their successes and struggles, we create a valuable collection of testimonials. There is no recipe or foolproof method for making a project work – only a series of experiences which, when networked together, sketch out possible alternatives.

Putting Life first points out that we are looking at landscapes as dynamic situations, both in terms of aesthetics and representation. To expand our concept of landscape, we need to transform how we view our own species and what a shared living environment can be. Since the concept of the Garden in Motion was first introduced in 1985 in an article named "La friche apprivoisée!" ("The Tamed Wasteland!"), a breakthrough has taken place: landscape also entails the appreciation of wild grass at the foot of a tree, which made it possible to gradually stop the use of phytosanitary products in public spaces. All of this implies tolerance of the spontaneous expressions of life, requiring a balance between humility and ambition.

Our cultural model is evolving, which is a challenge for most professions that have inherited practices from other, obsolete visions. Gardeners often fall into this category. They are told they need to change, but it's hard to adapt to the profound, ever-changing considerations of recent years. However, if a setting is aesthetically attractive, it offers a gateway through our senses. Numerous initiatives have proven this possible and stimulating. This work is essential because it's not just about letting things grow; it's also about letting them live. We work in very local ways that stem from the understanding of species' communities and of the interactions that humans, intentionally or not, have with them.

So let's take a stand in the fight against the models that kill, and welcome the prospect of a different aesthetic. This is difficult to achieve in an increasingly artificialized environment and within the short time we have before exceeding planetary limits. The twenty experiences shared in this book point to possible ways forward, addressed not only to land use professionals, but also to the general public who can appreciate other forms and timelines of relationships with living things. In so doing, we hope to find the inspiration it takes to become, each in our own capacity, the Planetary gardeners.

The garden thus becomes a place of resistance, a refuge for our non-human family. Anyone with a piece of land or a planter on their balcony can contribute: the surface area of private gardens in France is much larger than that of protected natural areas. We can also reclaim public spaces in various ways, from engaging in rebellious acts like guerrilla gardening to obtaining official permits to plant. Therefore, we resolutely need artists, scientists, and policymakers working together to explore new models. At the same time, we should use popular ecology to spread knowledge widely, so that the expertise on living beings extends beyond the specialists who have mastered Latin nomenclature. Farmers, especially in less industrialized countries, still possess the knowledge and practices of a much more energy-efficient world.

We should be equally concerned about introducing our children to the diversity and dynamics of life. It's crucial to offer them places to learn and experiment – places where they can connect with a physical, tactile, and sensual world, far from the virtual worlds of video games and social media. For how can we learn to appreciate diversity if we are becoming more and more illiterate about it?

Lulled by the clamor or climate alarms, our kids are far from naïve. With unsettling sincerity, they hit us with that fundamental question: "But if we know, why aren't we doing anything?" As parents and educators, we try to explain the complexity of the contemporary world and highlight all that is actually being done – the vast array of projects and struggles that go unnoticed by the media. Yet deep down, we know the question will haunt us: Are we doing enough, and fast enough?

Prioritizing the dynamics of life over form

The model change is inevitable because the planet's resources are reaching their limits, and it becomes increasingly obvious that the Planetary Garden is finite. The project timeline takes precedence over the plan, and temporal work prevails over spatial composition. That's what Putting Life first looks like. We start by placing ourselves within a temporal cycle, both cyclical and linear, whose trends are known: climate disruption, population growth, and resource depletion. With this in mind, we must take immediate action promoting fertility and diversity while adopting a long–term perspective. Change management practices, save energy, then make way for the development of new gardens.

The fragility of a project – the fact of placing this project in jeopardy – would not result from weak analysis, which can always be improved, but from the failure of the dream.
Gilles Clément Le Rêve (The Dream) – ENSP 2009

That's where the landscapist brings shared authorship with non–humans into the realm of possibilities, but also invents mechanisms of collective creation. Collaborative design opens up a range of extremely promising practices, and this book presents a few of them, selected from a large number of initiatives.

For if Life is the Art of encounter, as Vinicius de Moraes sings, the aesthetic of the living world, and for the living world, is above all a relational aesthetic.

We call this linking of a spatial situation with atemporal work plan, used as the basis for co–construction, the Map of the Commons. We came up with this concept in our study "Putting Life First" (« La Préséance du vivant ») in Bordeaux in 2012. Ten years on, it has given its name to the exhibition and then to this book, as it's now shaping all our practice.

This radical reversal of the traditional project management sequence (sketch, project, tender documents, execution documents, etc.) challenges both the engineer's and the gardener's cultures. That's because the tasks assigned to landscapists are still derived from architectural contracts – the ones that are intended for constructing buildings and pouring concrete, but not for the ongoing support of living systems. A regulatory system for this scope of work, together with new frameworks that are more suited to ecology, will be crucial for the future of our profession, and will require the mobilization of more than just landscape professionals.

Putting Life first is also an urgent call to equip ourselves with the means to do things differently in the context of public procurement.

In the world of agriculture, which is largely beyond the reach of various planners, Putting Life first means caring about biotopes, seeds, and farming methods that avoid poisoning our soil, water, and bodies. Moreover, industrial farming is unsustainable energy–wise: the petrol bill for our grains and vegetables is outrageous. In this book, we won't have the chance to explore the many initiatives coming up against this model, however, the agricultural sector offers many alternatives that treat fields and vegetable gardens as ecosystems and guide natural dynamics through a nuanced, experience–based understanding of the living world.

That said, Putting Life first is neither a global adoption of some virtuous model nor copying a practice observed elsewhere. Every place on the planet has its own specific characteristics, and, once we start appreciating the potential diversity offered by a habitat, we will inevitably end up with a variety of landscapes and gardens capable of evolving over time.

Putting Life first means fighting against homogenization. Nurturing life dynamics means allowing context–specific situations to express themselves. It's unrealistic to expect everyone to adopt this principle, but that's how biological reality is. Plus, it offers significant savings through non–spending.

Encouraging the development of new design and management practices

Radical transformation is possible. Take Saint–Nazaire, a port city with its imposing industrial infrastructure. Here, changes in city management resulted in a transformed landscape that creates a sense of abundance and exuberance, making one feel like being immersed in an ecosystem. Let's not forget that, just a few years ago, those arriving at the train station walked out of the main entrance straight onto artificial grass. Today, these grasses are beautiful and alive.

The ecosystem services approach has introduced into the landscape an engineer's perspective, one that is quantitative, measurable, and easily translatable into statistics and probabilities. This scientific tool is invaluable for understanding the proportions of things, the major trends, the dynamics at work and the threats that affect them. It backs up the benefits of "urban forests" and other biodiversity "hotspots" with verified scientific data. It's a tool that we use on a daily basis.

Let's keep in mind, however, that landscapes are not machines, no matter how sophisticated we imagine them to be. Even with all our computing power, no digital model can accurately predict their evolution. Life just doesn't care about our efforts at algorithmic prediction.

On a planetary scale, and especially in human-altered environments, we have to trust emergent ecosystems in order to facilitate dynamic relationships between species and generate newness and diversity. To achieve this, it's important to have areas of unrestricted evolution, the Third landscapes where life would keep innovating.

We should teach strategic principles for dealing with chance, the unexpected and uncertain, and ways to modify these strategies in response to continuing acquisition of new information. We should learn to navigate a sea of uncertainties, sailing in and around islands of certainty.

Edgar Morin
Seven complex lessons in education for the future
UNESCO Publishing, 1999

This perspective embraces Indecision. Living day by day, in tune with the unfolding of life, establishes a relationship with uncertainty and unpredictability as the major condition of becoming. Accepted as inherent to life, indecision doesn't shut the project down but maximizes the possibilities for new combinations to arise. Let's make it our working methodology and adjust our gardening and management methods accordingly. The Manifesto of the Third Landscape states that every area that escaped human management is precious.

Today, accommodating life is a challenge. We have to let ecosystems regenerate, to tend rather than develop... even to un-develop. To make room for life, renunciation and withdrawal are unavoidable, deliberate attitudes.

Giving up dominance and control is not a defeat, it's innovation. We abandon harmful practices and come up with more beneficial methods. This book shows what conscious, engaged citizens, the Planetary gardeners, are doing right now. Here, Putting Life first is not a theory, but a collection of enthusiastic practices and attitudes. In this spirit, we launched the Call to create the Others' Kitchen Garden, an integral part of the exhibition held at the Potager du Roi (the King's Kitchen Garden) in Versailles. A temporary project spanning a year of collective gardening from October 2021 to October 2022, it was the key artistic commission by the exhibition curators and a shared experience for over 200 gardeners. Once again, we thank everyone for their help and commitment.

This project is an important milestone because, set within a historic landmark, it shows that we can still conduct gardening experiments in this place of international research and excellence, while cherishing the past and its aesthetic codes. Ever since its creation, between 1678 and 1683, by Jean-Baptiste de La Quintinie, Louis XIV's other gardener (actually, a lawyer-turned-gardener), the Potager du Roi has been dedicated to gardening and horticultural research, as well as technological innovation in the management of living systems. Proud to have played our part in this program, 340 years after its launch, we honor the generations of gardeners that have tended this one-of-a-kind garden. May it continue its mission as a place of innovation, knowledge, and exchange of best practices.

If you return to Versailles today, you won't find any trace of the Others' Kitchen Garden. As stipulated by the contract, it moved on in October 2022, with its traveling groves spreading to five other gardens across Île-de-France, making room for future experiments. You will find this garden featured, among other projects, in this book, as both a manifesto and a methodology, a record of one of our Calls to Create. At the end of the book, we will share some pointers so you can launch your own call, too.

Because anyone can start a garden – no matter how small, and regardless of their age or skills. Consider this book as an invitation to become the Planetary gardener. We hope it will inspire you.

2. Adopting the viewpoint of the *Planetary gardener*

What is life? Something that sets Earth apart from every other planet in the Universe? That used to be a good answer, but probably it won't stay so for much longer, as Exobiology, the science of life in the Cosmos, is on the brink of revolutionary discoveries.

Or is it something that has the capacity to reproduce thanks to the genetic inheritance driven by a mysterious vital force puzzling both scientists and mystics? That's a good answer too, except that technology is close to creating machines able to not only reproduce identically, but also learn and improve based on their surroundings.

These dizzying yet so close horizons remind us of who we are: early 21st–century *Homo sapiens*, infinitely multiplying questions and endlessly questioning answers. Scientists call this the anthropic principle: among the scenarios of the Universe and our planet's evolution, we have to choose the ones that let us ask today, "Who are we?"

2.1

Everyone is an *ecosystem*

Think of yourself as one living being among many, made up of billions of other organisms evolving in symbiosis. Let's reconsider our place at the top of the genealogical tree of life and accept the responsibility that our species, and each one of us, has for the future of the planet. Living bodies are built from chemical elements originating from stellar explosions. These are the very same elements that, pulled together by gravity, have formed our planet. We view the world based on our cultural history, our scientific perspective and our collective and personal hopes.

The most astonishing recent discoveries reveal that we are not only home to, but also composed of billions of microbes. Not all of them are harmful; in fact, most are essential to our vital functions. Their coexistence is regulated by our immune system, unique to each individual. When we think about these ecosystems, it becomes clear that we are an inseparable part of the living world, contributing to the countless dynamic balances that make our planet a place where life can thrive.

Fig 2.1.2
We are mostly liquid
Chemical composition of the human body

We are mainly made up of oxygen, carbon, and nitrogen. Using a limited variety of atoms, our body can build complex structures that work together and exchange information through extremely sophisticated feedback loops.

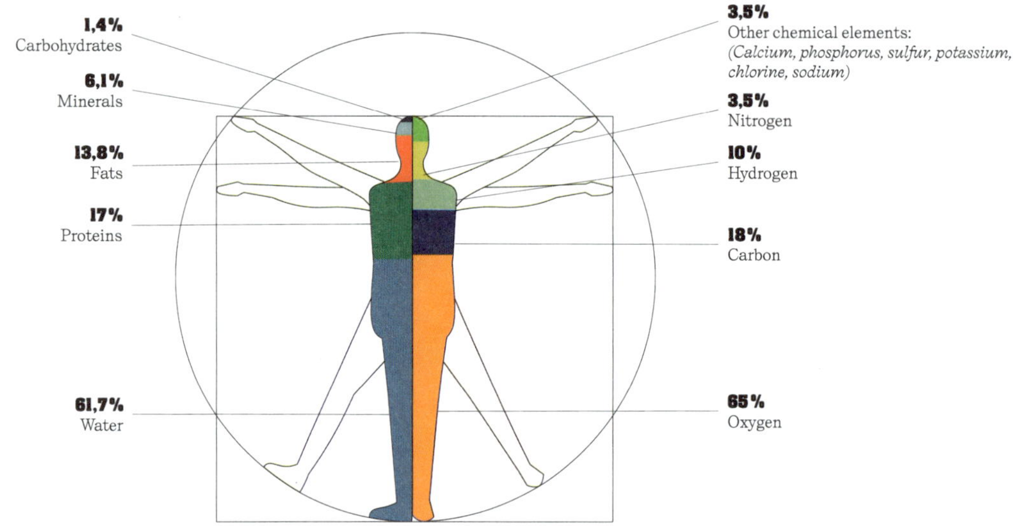

Fig 2.1.3
You and I are stardust
Cosmic origin of the human body (by mass)

After the Big Bang and the nuclear fission and fusion reactions it triggered, stars and galaxies came into being. Extremely high temperatures led to the creation of hydrogen – the simplest chemical element – followed by progressively heavier atoms. This cosmic origin of matter is common to all living and nonliving things in the Universe.

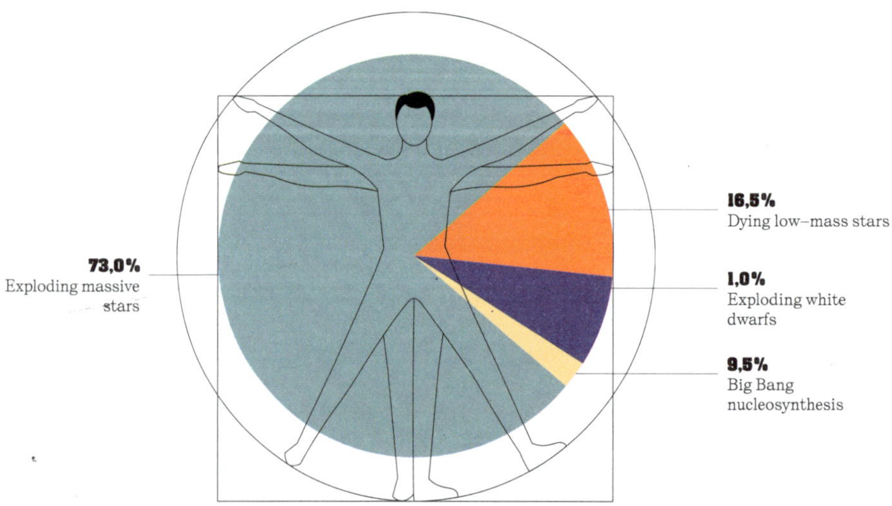

Fig 2.1.1
«I is a collective»
The fauna and flora of the human body

The fauna, flora, mycosphere, and virome on our body's surface help maintain the biotic balance of our skin and its vital functions. This diagram shows that our hair, nostrils, skin, vagina, oral cavity, esophagus, stomach, and colon each host their own ecosystems in a dynamic equilibrium. Coming from both the outside and the inside, these microbial beings are essential for a whole range of functions such as digestion; they contribute to our hormonal balance, and even affect our mood.

We are 90% microbes and only 10% specifically human. Our billions of bacteria are in fact autonomous living beings, working together to form the human body that allows us to live and perceive the world. Humans are holobionts, which means organisms made up of other organisms.

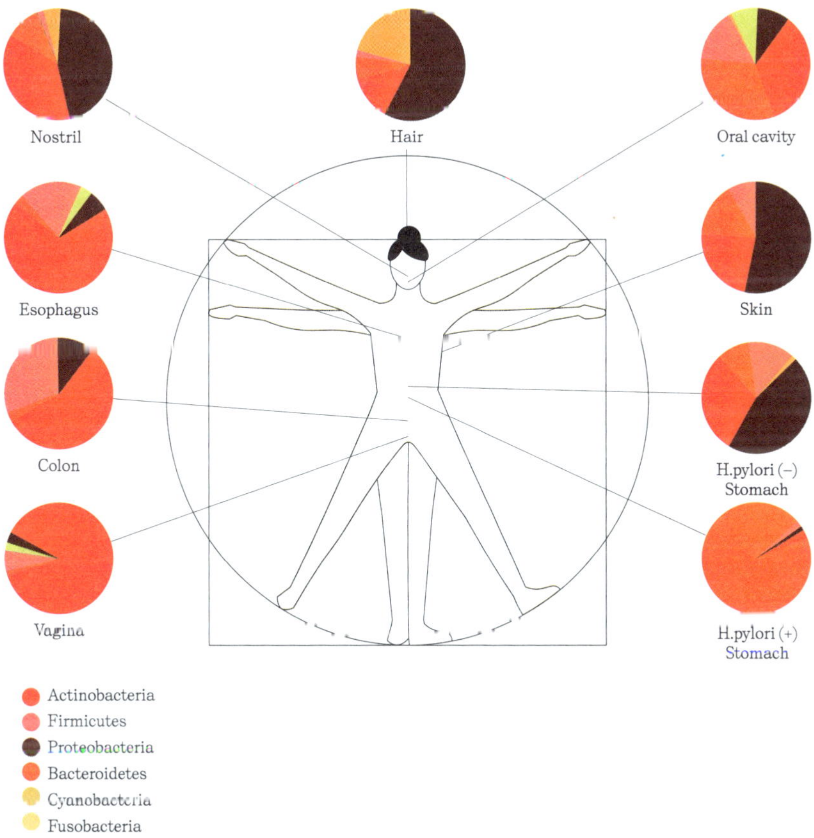

Fig 2.1.1 «What Elements Are Found in the Human Body?», Ask a Biologist, Arizona State University + integral designers ʃ
Fig 2.1.2 Roberto Ragazzoni, INAF–OAPD (Osservatorio astronomico di Padova) + integral designers ʃ
Fig 2.1.3 Coloco + integral designers ʃ

2.2

Life is *speeding up*

Life on Earth is a 3.8 billion–year adventure. On the grand scale of the cosmos and our planet, *Homo sapiens*, with their large brain and technical prowess, have only just arrived. Technological revolutions follow one another, speeding up time. 400 generations have passed since the spread of agriculture 5 to 7 thousand years ago. Today, we are profoundly altering the biosphere itself (genetics, geo–engineering, ecosystem management, biotechnologies). How will we live tomorrow?

Life as we know it today is the outcome of hundreds of millions of years of coevolution. Cyanobacteria, and later plants, learned to make their own food using the energy from solar radiation: they are autotrophs. All animals depend on them for food. Fungi have formed alliances with both animals and plants, and, by feeding on dead organisms, they return fundamental elements to the life cycle. Amazing partnerships have developed among all these beings of vastly different sizes and abilities. They have shaped the world to fit their needs while continuously evolving to adapt to their environments, which created the incredible diversity we see today. In ecosystem dynamics, each of these beings is part of a complex web of interdependent relationships: when one of them disappears, the entire system is thrown off balance.

We humans can now change the genetic code of living organisms, including ourselves. This opens up perspectives that are as fantastic as they are unsettling. Life as a category overflows on all sides.

Fig 2.2.1
Life endlessly explores its forms
Schematic tree of the evolution of life

This phylogenetic tree shows the evolution of life since it first appeared on Earth. Dotted lines indicate major events in the history of life since the Earth was formed. The extinction of the dinosaurs made way for the evolution of mammals, including the present–day human species – *Homo sapiens sapiens*. We are merely a step, just one example of living beings that resulted from evolution.

https://www.evogeneao.com/en/explore/tree-of-life-explorer

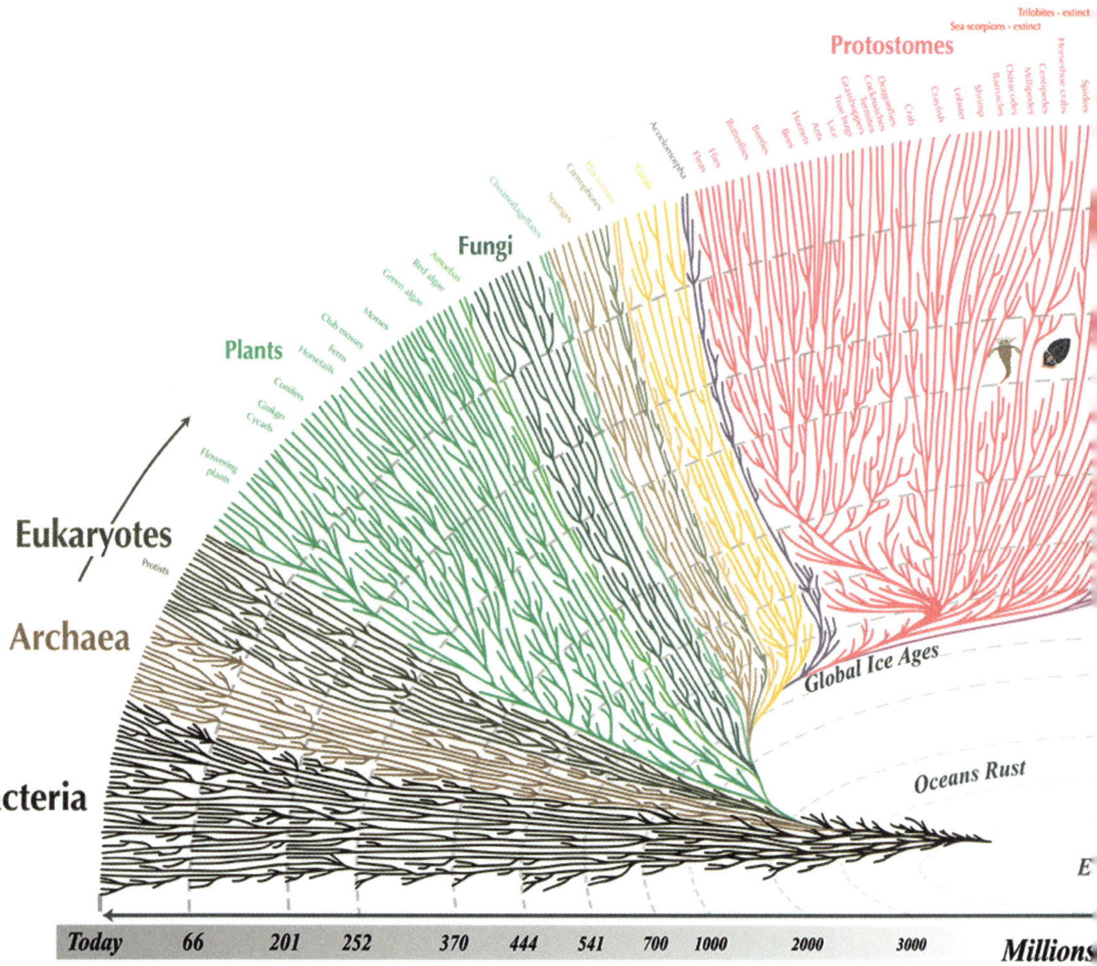

All the major and many of the minor living branches of life are shown on this

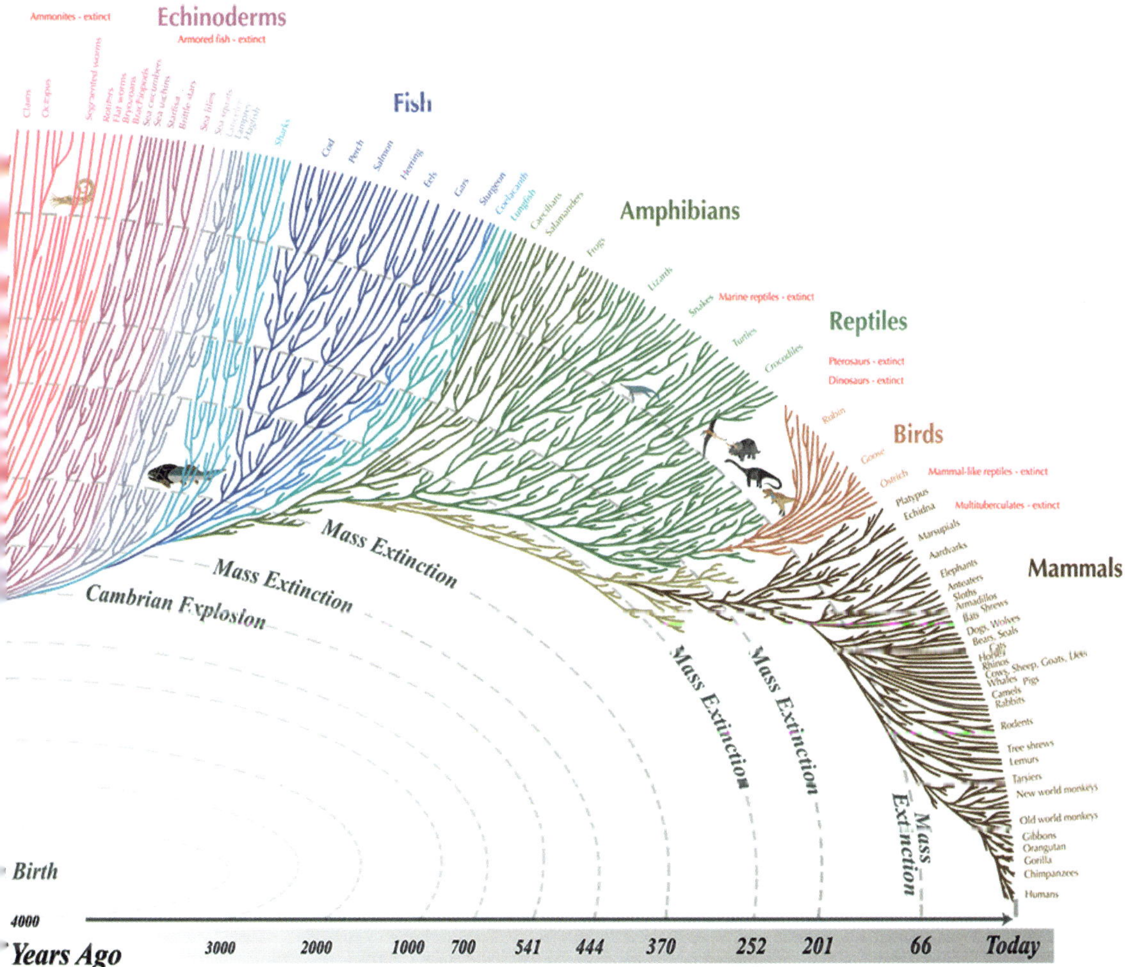

am, but only a few of those that have gone extinct are shown. Example: Dinosaurs - extinct

Fig 2.2.2
We are vertebrates
Phylogenetic tree of vertebrates

This tree shows a selection of fossil vertebrates and their current representatives, with the probable links connecting them from their origins to the present day. Each branch allows us to follow, step by step, the changes over time that have produced the current forms of vertebrates. The connections highlighted here trace the evolutionary journey of more than 500 million years, from the common ancestor of the vertebrates – a tiny jawless fish – to its current and fossil descendants.

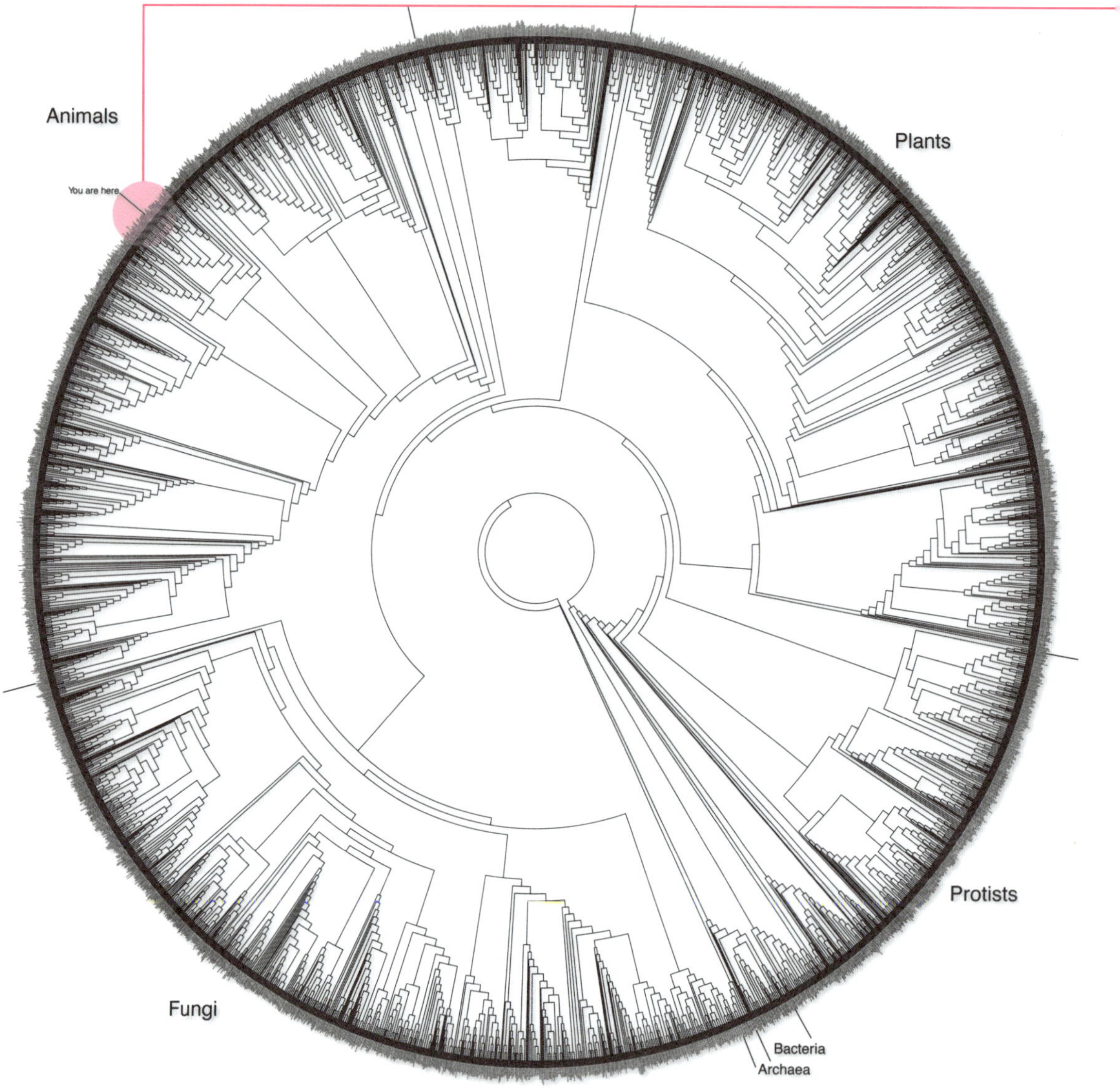

Fig 2.2.2 David M. Hillis, Derrick Zwickl and Robin Gutell, University of Texas, 2003

This image ties back to the previous page, where humans are shown as the peak of evolution, while here, they are just one species among many.

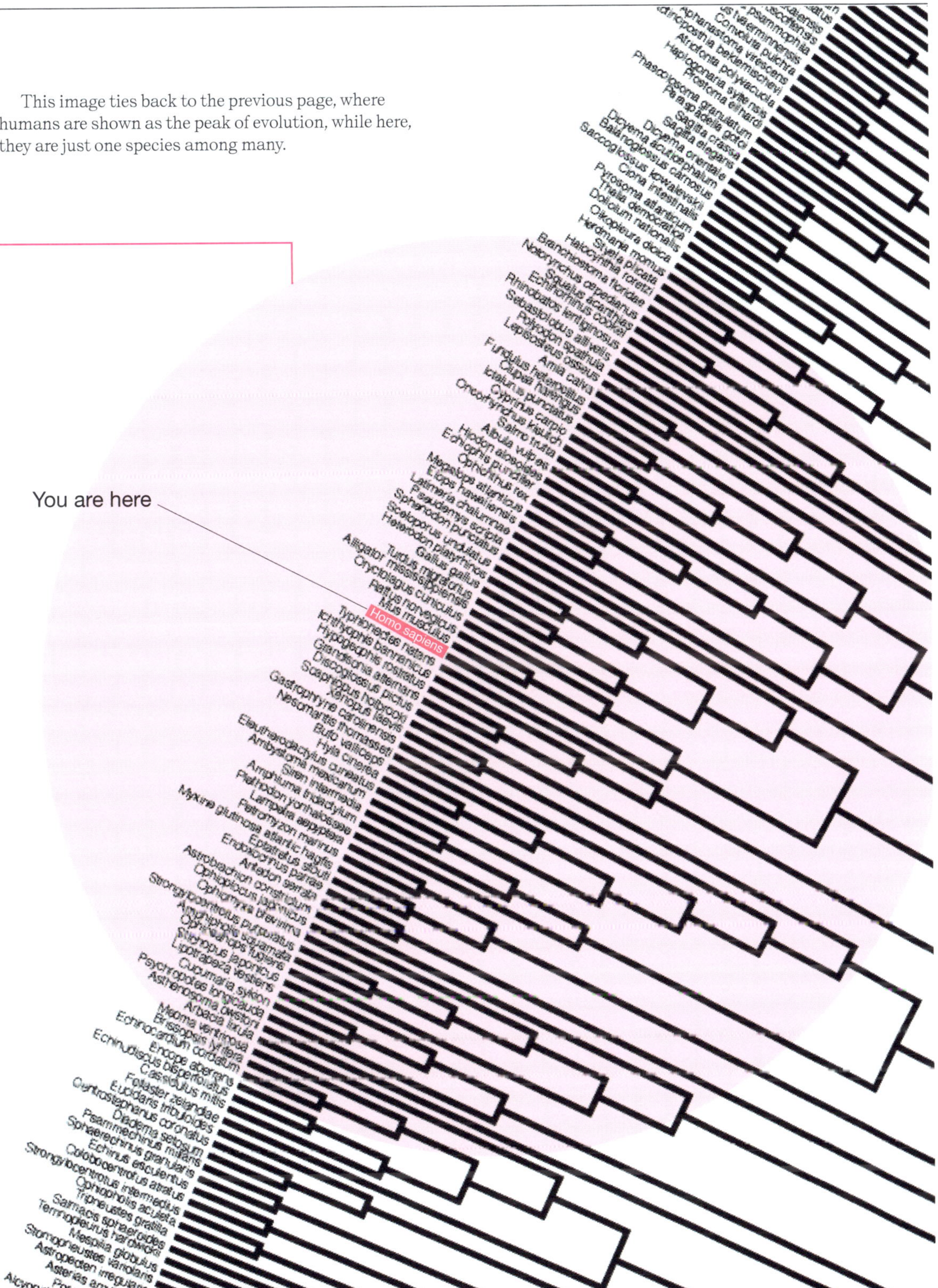

2.3

The depth of *Life*

Life is a continuum; no species or individual can exist in isolation. Eighty percent of the planet's biomass resides in the soil – but, unable to see it, we barely understand its importance. We have to make visible the roots and the underground world, the depths of the oceans, and the atmospheric layers – all of them. We need this depth in order to live.

We are realizing our impact on the planet, as well as the finite nature of this planet's resources: water, oxygen, land, raw materials, biodiversity... Today, wild mammals make up only a small minority.

The mass of human-made structures and objects is said to have exceeded the total mass of living organisms. Some people believe that ecosystems and agriculture can be managed like computer systems. Yet, life resists being modeled outside of laboratories and is not easily programmable. We are getting ready for space travel, for virtual realities, for enhancing our species by genetics and technology. However, we cannot thrive in isolation from the rest of the living world with which we form an interconnected whole, and our duty is to preserve this balance.

Fig 2.3.1
Water and air are finite
Global volume of water and air

The spheres represent the total volume of water on Earth and air in our planet's atmosphere, thus making us realize the limits and boundaries of the biosphere.

Fig 2.3.1 ©www.sciencephoto.com/media/159214/view?registration=success

Fig 2.3.2
The landscape extends beneath the oceans
Map of the ocean floor

Marie Tharp and Heinrich Berann created the first complete map of the ocean floor in 1977. They have shown that the ocean floor is not a flat, muddy plain but has mountains, ridges, and canyons – and thus discovered mid–ocean ridges. Our knowledge of how the planet and its ecosystems work remains young and fragile.

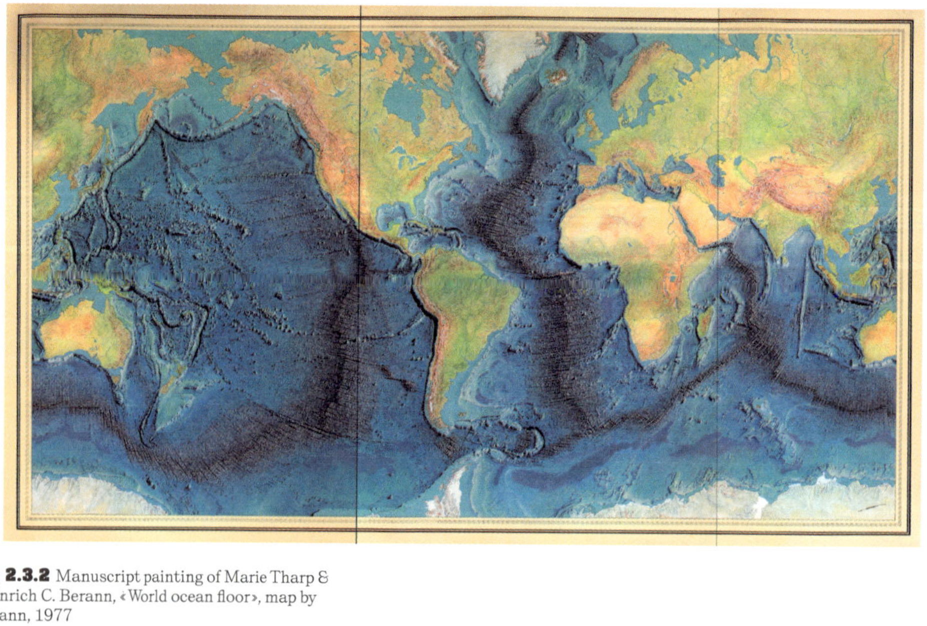

Fig 2.3.2 Manuscript painting of Marie Tharp & Heinrich C. Berann, «World ocean floor», map by Berann, 1977

Fig 2.3.3
Asphalt and concrete are taking over
The global mass of human–made products exceeds all living biomass

The dry mass of everything produced by humans, including metals, asphalt, bricks, aggregates, and concrete, has surpassed that of the biomass. Many scientists see this as a turning point in human history.

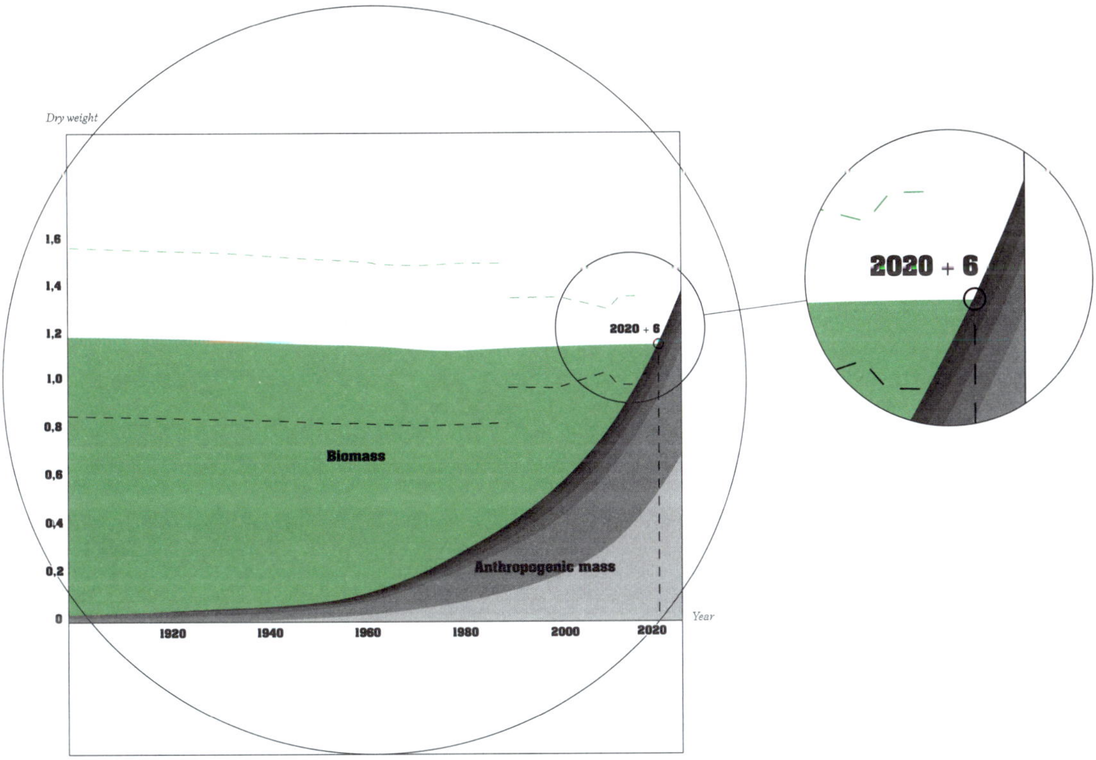

Anthropogenic mass

- Concrete
- Aggrerates (for example, gravel)
- Bricks
- Asphalt
- Metals
- Other (for example, plastic)

Fig 2.3.3 E. Elhacham, L. Ben–Uri, J. Grozovski, Y. Bar On, R. Milo, et al., «Global human–made mass exceeds all living biomass», *Nature* 588, 442–444 (2020). https://doi.org/10.1038/s41586-020-3010-5 + integral designers ⌋

Fig 2.3.4
The weight of life
Distribution of biomass on Earth

The bulk of living biomass is made up of plants, followed by bacteria, and then archaea (microorganisms). In the animal kingdom, arthropods – that is, myriapods, crustaceans, arachnids, insects – make up most of the mass. Of all the Earth's mammals, 60% are livestock, 36% are humans, and 4% are wild animals (by weight, not by count).

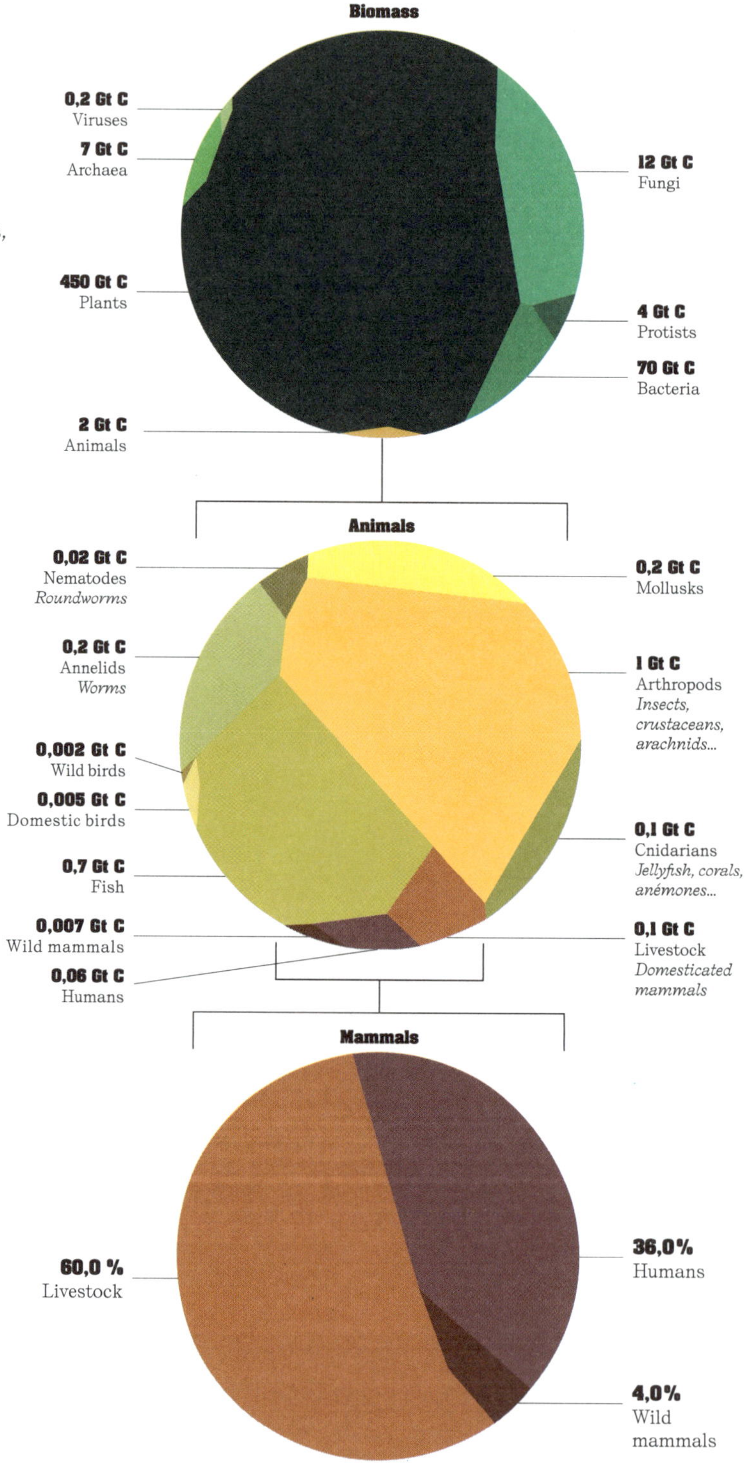

Fig 2.3.4 Yinon M. Bar-On, Rob Phillips, Ron Milo, «The Biomass distribution on Earth», Proceedings of the National Academy of Sciences, June 2018, 115 (25) 6506–6511; DOI: 10.1073/pnas.1711842115 + integral designers]

Fig 2.3.5
Water is a precious resource
Distribution of water on Earth

71% of the Earth's surface is covered by water, with 96.5% of this water contained in the oceans. This diagram shows that nearly all the Earth's water is salty and found in the oceans. Of the small amount of freshwater left, only a tiny fraction is available to support human, plant, and animal life.

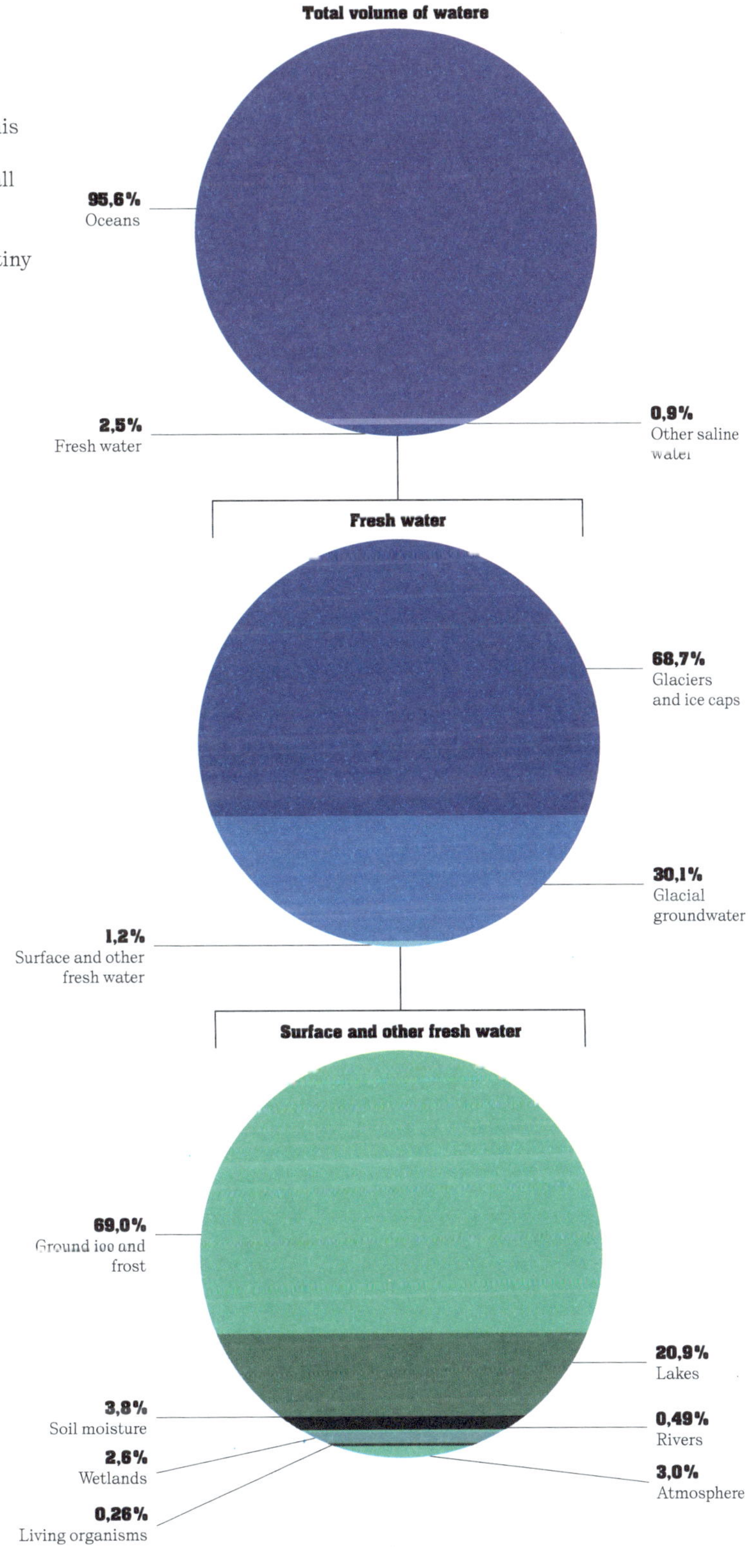

Fig 2.3.5 Igor Shiklomanov's, ‹World Fresh Water Resources›, in Peter H. Gleick (editor), 1993, *Water in Crisis: A Guide to the World's Fresh Water Resources* + integral designers ∫

Fig 2.3.6
Living soil shapes climate and landscapes
Lydia and Claude Bourguignon, Directors of LAMS[1]

Depending on the ecosystem, living soil contains between 1 to 3 tons of microbes per hectare. These microbes have 350 times more biochemical energy than we do, which equals the energy of 1,000 tons of humans per hectare. Here we are speaking of the most powerful living energy on Earth that controls plant growth, the transformation of soil elements into assimilable ones, as well as ocean salinity, and climate.

In addition to that, the soil fauna weighs more than the fauna living on the surface. These microorganisms perform all biochemical reactions necessary for terrestrial matter to become alive. They harness both solar and terrestrial chemical energy to bring minerals and organic matter in the soil to life.

On the other hand, by ceaselessly digging tunnels, the fauna ensures the constant mixing of the soil, allowing water and oxygen to penetrate and minerals to continually rise to the surface. Thanks to this microbial biochemical activity and the physicochemical activity of the fauna, plants can nourish themselves and grow.

Plants, through photosynthesis, capture carbon and enrich the soil with humus, which can then feed more plants. These new plants, in turn, capture more carbon, creating a positive feedback loop.

Evolution has created complex and fundamental relationships that span from soil to microbes, plants, animals, humans, and climates. Such complexity requires humility in managing soil. Overly simplístic methods of chemical and robotic farming fail to respect these relationships, leading to soil and climate degradation and creating bland and lifeless landscapes.

To put an end to climate disruption, it's crucial to restore soil fertility and bring back the balance of farming, forestry, and grazing. Humanity is facing a monumental task: planting trees and hedges to restore soil fertility, balanced climates, and beautiful landscapes.

[1] Laboratoire d'analyses microbiologiques des sols (Laboratory of Soil Microbiological Analysis)

Drawings Erwin Lichtenegger
Scale 1:30
Credits https://images.wur.nl
Wurzelatlas mitteleuropäischer Ackerunkräuter und Kulturpflanzen, Lore Kutschera und Erwin Lichtenegger, DLG-Verlag Frankfurt am Main, 1960
Wurzelatlas mitteleuropäischer Grünlandpflanzen. – Band 1 Monocotyledoneae, Lore Kutschera und Erwin Lichtenegger unter Mitarbeit von Monika Sobotik, Gustav Fischer Verlag Stuttgart/New York, 1982
Wurzelatlas mitteleuropäischer Grünlandpflanzen. – Band 2 Pteridophyta und Dicotyledoneae (Magnoliopsida). Teil 1 Morphologie, Anatomie, Ökologie, Verbreitung, Soziologie, Wirtschaft, Lore Kutschera und Erwin Lichtenegger unter Mitarbeit von Monika Sobotik, Gustav Fischer Verlag Stuttgart/Jena/New York, 1992
Wurzelatlas mitteleuropäischer Grünlandpflanzen. – Band 2 Pteridophyta und Dicotyledoneae (Magnoliopsida). Teil 2 Anatomie, Lore Kutschera und Monika Sobotik unter Mitarbeit von Erwin Lichtenegger, Gustav Fischer Verlag Stuttgart/Jena/New York, 1992
Bewurzelung von Pflanzen in verschiedenen Lebensräumen, Lore Kutschera, Monika Sobotik, Erwin Lichtenegger, Dieter Haas, OÖ. Landesmuseum Linz, 1997
Wurzelatlas mitteleuropäischer Waldbäume und Sträucher, Lore Kutschera und Erwin Lichtenegger, Leopold Stocker Verlag Graz/Stuttgart, 2002
Wurzelatlas der Kulturpflanzen gemäßigter Gebiete mit Arten des Feldgemüsebaues, Lore Kutschera, Erwin Lichtenegger, Monika Sobotik, DLG-Verlag Frankfurt am Main, 2009

wurzelforschung.at

Fig 2.3.6.2
Ribwort plantain
Plantago lanceolata

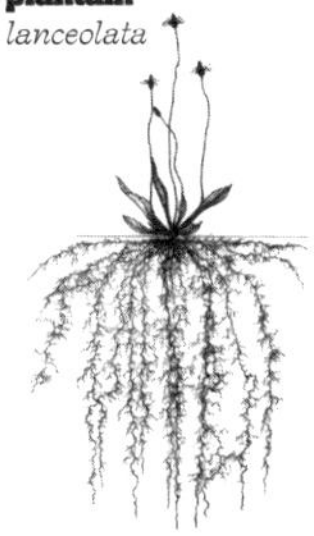

Fig 2.3.6.4
Cultivated alfalfa
Medicago sativa

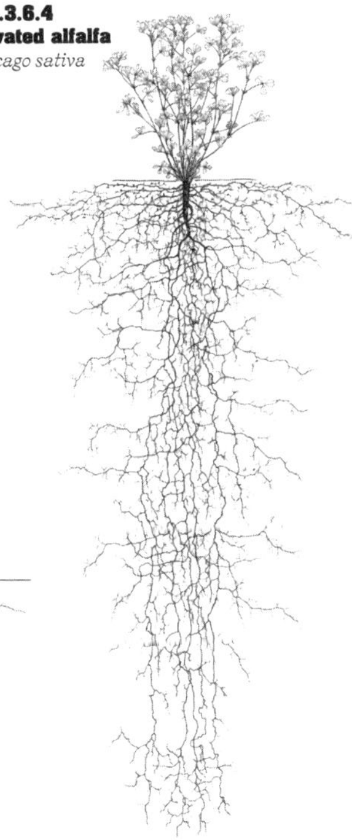

Fig 2.3.6.9
Mountain sainfoin
Onobrychis montana

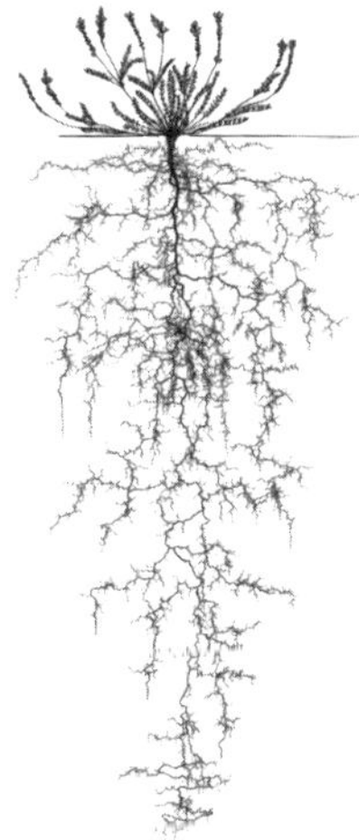

Fig 2.3.6.5
German greenweed
Genista germanica

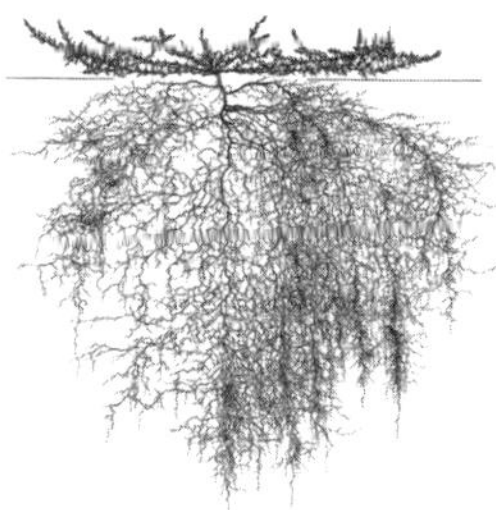

Fig 2.3.6.8
Spear thistle
Aegopodium podagraria

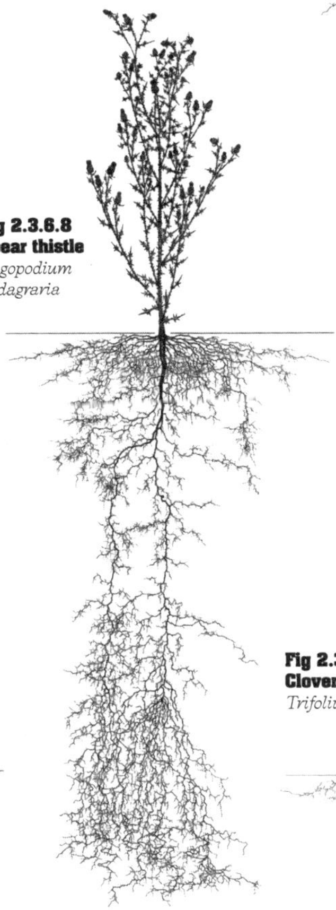

Fig 2.3.6.6
Arrow-jointed broom
Chamaespartium sagittale

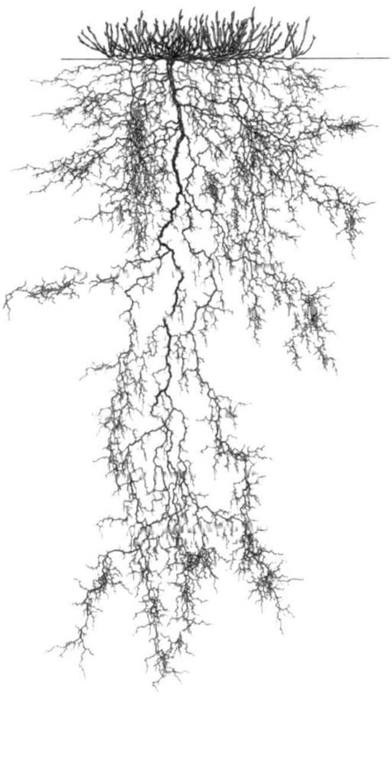

Fig 2.3.6.10
Clover
Trifolium trichocephalum

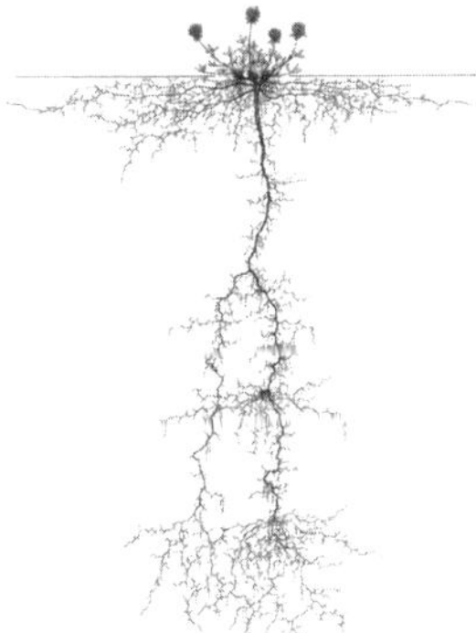

Fig 2.3.6.11
Spotted hawkweed
Hypochoeris maculata

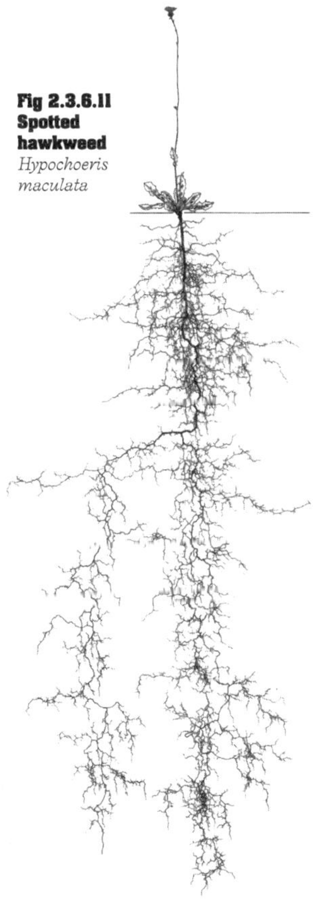

2.4

Temperature: *a key factor*

Temperature is one of the key factors influencing biological spread since the end of the last glaciation: as the climate got warmer, species were able to migrate from southern Europe, progressively reclaiming the tundra and shaping the landscapes we know today.

This happened alongside the development of human activities that required large-scale deforestation. Since the industrial era, the use of natural resources has accelerated exponentially and shows no signs of slowing down. The waste from our activities pollutes water and soil. We encroach on and fragment the habitats of all species, causing many to disappear: this is a sixth mass extinction. To survive, many species, including our own, have to migrate. For example, Mediterranean species, which can migrate relatively quickly northward, are doing so. Others need human assistance.

For the gardens and landscapes of the future that we are creating today, the thorny question of which plants to choose comes up: should we revert to those from before the colonization of the Americas?

Should we look ahead to the future climate to set up ecosystems that can survive it?

Should we draw inspiration from emerging ecosystems that spontaneously occupy available niches, even if they mainly consist of so-called "foreign" and "invasive" species?

These questions not only concern scientific expertise, but also politics: who has the right to live here?

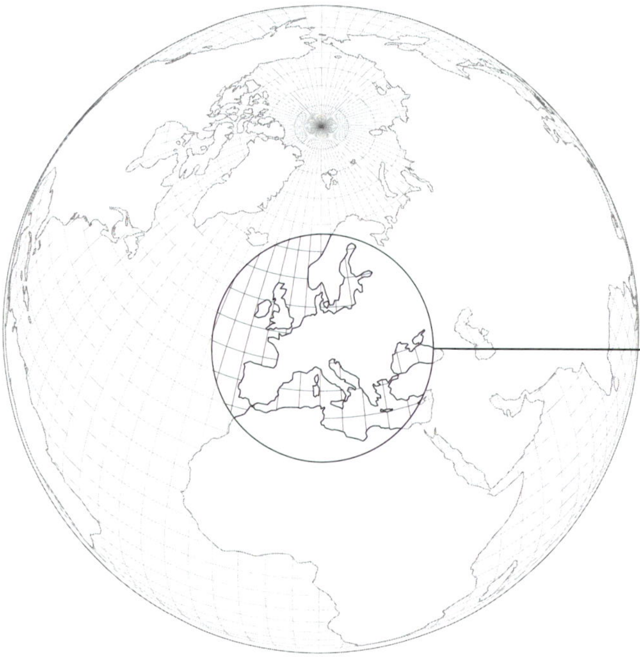

Fig 2.4.1
The last glaciation

12 000 years ago, during the Late Glacial period, the tundra still covered Europe. The trees we know today had retreated to milder areas, presumably in Sicily and the far south of the Iberian Peninsula.

Fig 2.4.5
Mechanization

The "Green Revolution" of the post–World War II era brought about mechanization and increased yields on one hand, and land abandonment with forest regrowth on the other. Land consolidation was accompanied by giving up the least profitable lands. Today, around 30% of France is covered by forests.

Fig 2.4.1—2.4.8 Pablo Georgieff + integral designers ∫, qgis.org

Fig 2.4.2
Forest development

Back in the Boreal period, 7000 to 5000 years ago, birch and pine trees moved north first, followed by the variety of deciduous trees we know today. The Mediterranean Sea was a barrier, so the species from northern Africa were unlikely to cross over.

Fig 2.4.3
Deforestation

Around 5000 to 7000 years ago, Homo sapiens migrated from Mesopotamia with agriculture, progressively clearing large areas of forest. This continued for several millennia during the Iron and Bronze Ages. In less than 400 generations, the face of the Earth was dramatically altered.

Fig 2.4.4
The lowest point

In the 18th century, Europe was largely deforested: France reached its lowest point around 1780 with 12% forest cover. In the colonies, vast plantations were carved out of tropical forests, facilitated by slave labor. Maritime traffic spurred planetary mixing and the globalization of trade.

Fig 2.4.6
Urban expansion

Metropolitan expansion often comes at the cost of high–quality land; it hastens soil sealing, while infrastructure development leads to land fragmentation. Land consumption outpaces population growth, accelerating the artificialization of surfaces.

Fig 2.4.7
Assisted migration

Species distribution maps are changing at an increasingly rapid pace: laboratories use climate data to model their future evolution. Meanwhile, efforts are underway to assist the migration of the least resilient species, and conservatories are gathering seeds and genetic material for the challenging times ahead.

Fig 2.4.8
The warming ramps up

Massive deforestation continues in the tropical belt, driven by globalized markets. Scientists are sounding the alarm about the sixth major extinction event of the Anthropocene. Climate change disrupts the living conditions of species; in Europe, this is pushing them to migrate to the north. But will they manage to move fast enough to survive?

2.5

Resilience at work

Emerging resilience practices are trying to balance short–term profit–seeking: regenerative economy, ecological redirection, renunciation protocols, zero net artificialization are all examples of useful initiatives. These efforts are aiming to bring the living beings back into a system of relationships where humans are just one component. We live in a contradictory time: while extractive fever is spreading worldwide, resistance, awareness, and alternatives are cropping up everywhere.

The issue of planetary boundaries and the need to shift our lifestyles have found their way into public opinion. While major global negotiations often struggle to produce agreements that match the scale of the challenge and are only partially implemented, a diverse array of initiatives is developing at the local level. Many of us have a growing desire to take action, changing our consumption habits and making commitments in both professional and personal spheres. Future scenarios make us feel anxious and hopeful at the same time, wondering if we are able to reduce our impact on the biosphere, preserve biological fertility, and invent new modes of governance and resource sharing. Environmental justice and social justice are becoming increasingly linked in activist demands.

As landscape architects, we stand at the intersection between understanding global issues and translating them into actionable projects. Moreover, our work is site–specific: we collaborate with networks of stakeholders who live in these places and care for them.

Fig 2.5.1
It's time to see ourselves as the Planetary gardeners.
Planetary boundaries

Planetary boundaries are the thresholds that humanity shouldn't cross if we want to maintain the environment fit for sustainable life in a safe ecosystem. These boundaries highlight the urgency of getting interested in the depth of life, the Planetary garden, the critical zone in which we must find solutions to live.

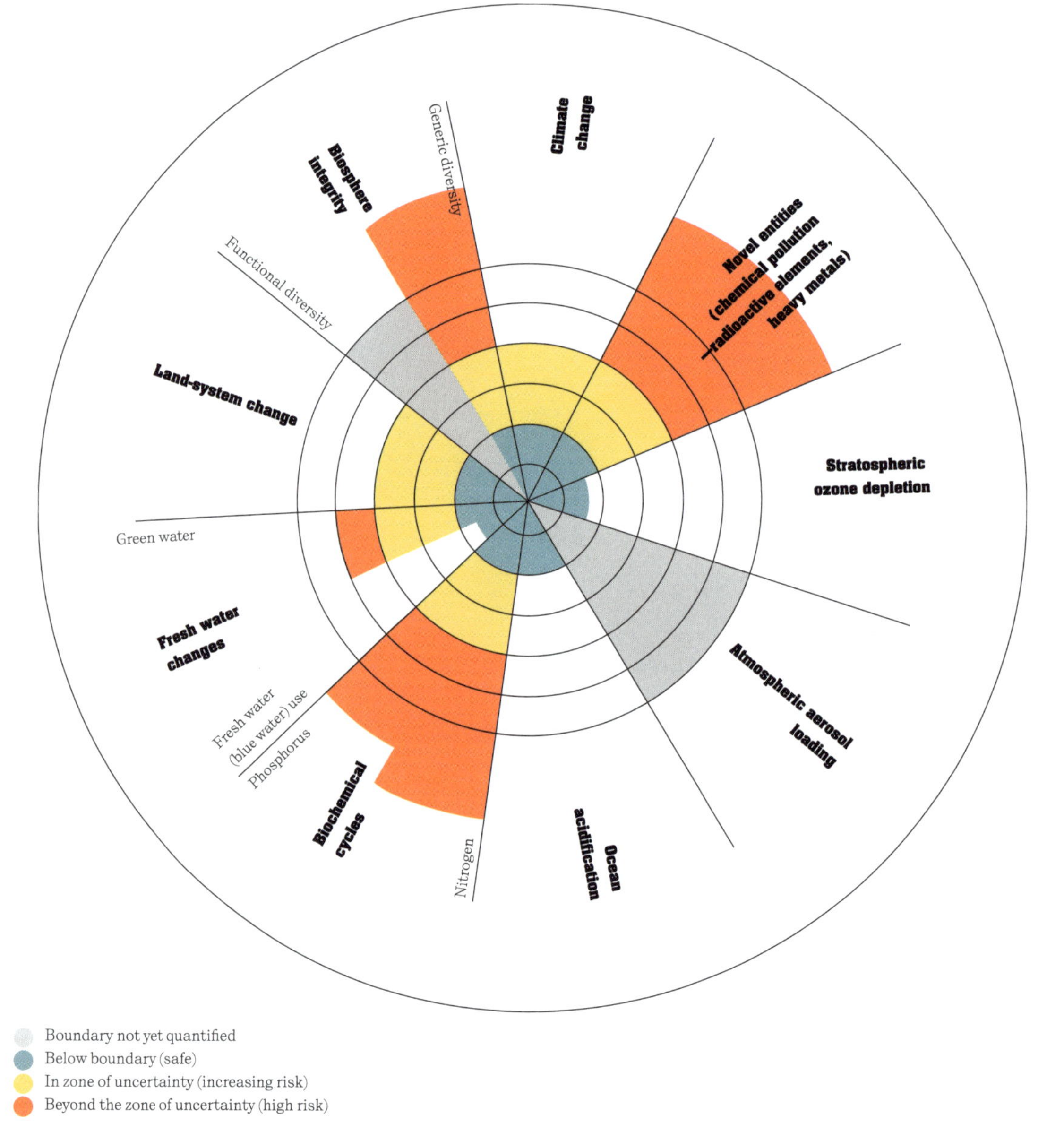

Fig 2.5.1 ‹Planetary Boundaries: Guiding Human Development on a Changing Planet›, Steffen et al., *Science*, 2015

Fig 2.5.2
Can we decide our future?
Four energy prospects

The co–originator of the permaculture concept proposes four major energy scenarios helping us envision the range of culturally imagined and ecologically probable futures for the next century. These scenarios underscore the collective choices we need to make today and how we can organize ourselves to face them.

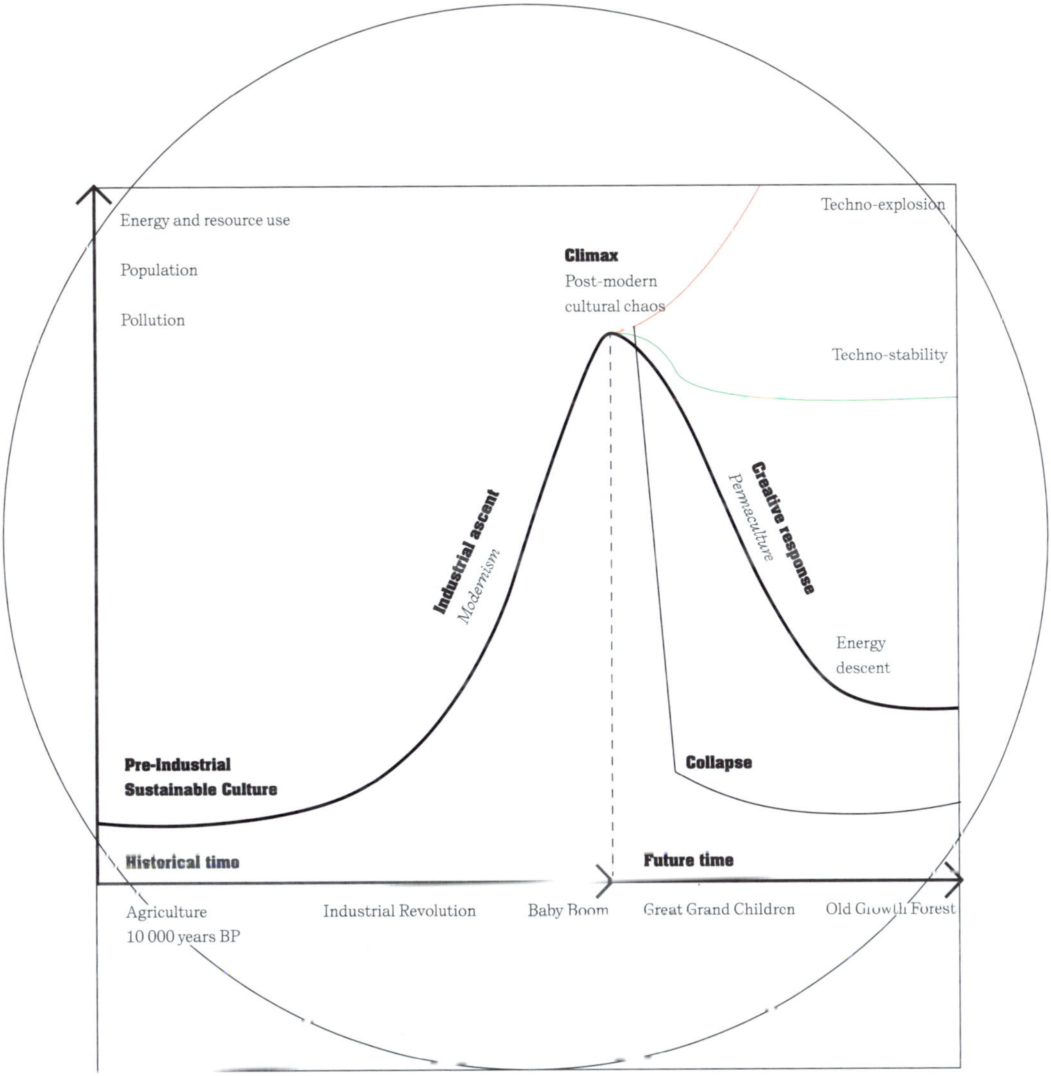

Fig 2.5.2 David Holmgrem, www.futurescenarios.org/2–energy–futures/2–1–four–energy–futures/ + integral designers]

Fig 2.5.3
Who owns the Earth?

Land is at the heart of major social and environmental struggles

Created by an Argentinian collective called the Iconoclasistas, this map flips the conventional representation of the world, highlighting all the indigenous struggles across the globe to protect native seeds, farming soils, and land ownership.

Amérique du Sud : Les femmes des mouvements ruraux de réappropriation territoriale résistent aux tentatives d'expropriation et de privatisation des grandes sociétés agroalimentaires, ainsi qu'aux monocultures de soja et de maïs.

South America: Women of the rural movements for territorial reappropriation resist to the expropriation and privatisation attempts of large agribusiness corporations and to soy and maize monocultures.

À QUI APPARTIENT LA TERRE?
WHO OWNS THE LAND?

Dans un monde où les corps et les territoires créateurs de vie sont considérés comme des objets de conquête, sont pillés par des actes néocoloniaux et capitalistes, et menacés par une violence machiste et patriarcale qui se manifeste à de multiples niveaux, les femmes résistent et organisent leurs communautés autour d'une structure sociale reposant sur la pratique du soin, en protégeant les biens communs et la souveraineté alimentaire.

In a world where bodies that give life and territories are considered objects of conquest, plundered by neocolonial capitalist acts and threatened by multiple forms of sexist male patriarchal violence, women resist and organise their communities through care economies, protecting common goods and food sovereignty.

Monde arabe : Les femmes maintiennent une économie domestique au beau milieu de conflits armés et supervisent l'assistance en matière de santé, d'alimentation, de refuge et d'éducation au sein de leurs communautés.

Arab World: Women maintain a care economy in the middle of massive armed conflicts and supervise health, nutrition, shelter, and educational assistance in their communities.

Méso-Amérique : Les femmes font face aux traités de libre-échange, à l'extension des conflits armés et au maïs transgénique. Elles protègent la diversité des espèces existantes.

Central America: Women stand against free trade agreements, the spread of armed conflicts, and genetically modified maize, and protect the diversity of the living species.

…work

…represent 25% of the world …of the world population. …gathering water and …als, they perform invisible …r their domestic work, …children and the sick, …eparing food–all activities …ligatory) extension of their …ctions.

Exode rural et répression

Fondé sur les monocultures et dominé par des multinationales, le système alimentaire agro-industriel nourrit 30 % de la population mondiale et emploie, dans des conditions déplorables, une infime partie des travailleurs ruraux. Ce système détruit l'environnement, appauvrit les peuples autochtones et les chasse de leurs terres. Il se développe à travers la militarisation et la répression, entraînant ainsi la perte des droits collectifs sur les biens naturels et la transformation de la propriété commune en propriété privée.

Rural exodus and repression

The agro-industrial food system, based on monoculture and dominated by multinational firms, feeds 30% of the world population and employs–in appalling conditions–a minuscule portion of rural workers. It destroys the environment, impoverishes and drives out native populations, and thrives through militarisation and repression–thus causing the loss of collective rights over natural assets and turning public goods into private property.

Souveraineté alimentaire et culturelle

Grâce à des pratiques de défense des biens communs, de protection de la culture populaire et solidaire et du respect de la nature, les femmes des zones rurales préservent l'agrodiversité face à la progression du dépouillement néocolonial. En outre, elles assurent la survie de plus de 6 000 langues vivantes dans le monde entier. Majoritairement méconnues, celles-ci ont évolué au fil des siècles et sont porteuses de traditions et de pratiques inestimables. Les femmes rurales sont ainsi de véritables gardiennes de la mémoire de la terre.

Food and cultural sovereignty

Through practices that defend public goods, protect shared traditional culture, and respect nature, rural women ensure agricultural diversity in the face of neocolonial dispossession. They are also guardians of the over 6000 languages spoken across the world, which developed over the centuries, bear rich traditions, and are mostly unknown. As a result, these women are the keepers of the memories of the Earth.

…psala Conflict Data Program, entre otras. Proyección mapamundi: Peters-Gall

Iconoclasistas.net / Album-Deco.net

3.

Acting now

In recent years, we have seen the rise of new design methods, in which our thinking about landscape expands to include our relationships with the living world as a whole. We look at everything we do through the lens of temporal evolution, making this approach central to our projects and thus enhancing our work. A growing range of disciplines involved in these projects are reorienting their input towards considering natural dynamics.

Elected officials, technicians, engineers, and urban planners get interested in the living world and acknowledge the importance of respecting it. In this book, we present twenty optimistic visions that have sparked new ideas and solutions.

Together with the authors of these projects – whom we thank for their creativity and input – we have examined their practices using the four criteria explained in the pages that follow.

Creating protocols for *life*-focused projects.

Collaborative creativity
The score for a collective performance

Together with her landscape designer husband Lawrence Halprin, contemporary choreographer Anne Halprin developed a notation system that can be applied to all sorts of performances, from dance to the design of public spaces. The system involves rhythms, feedback loops between actions, and the emotional quality of interpretations. A true source of inspiration to be rediscovered for collective action projects.

© Ann Halprin, 1962

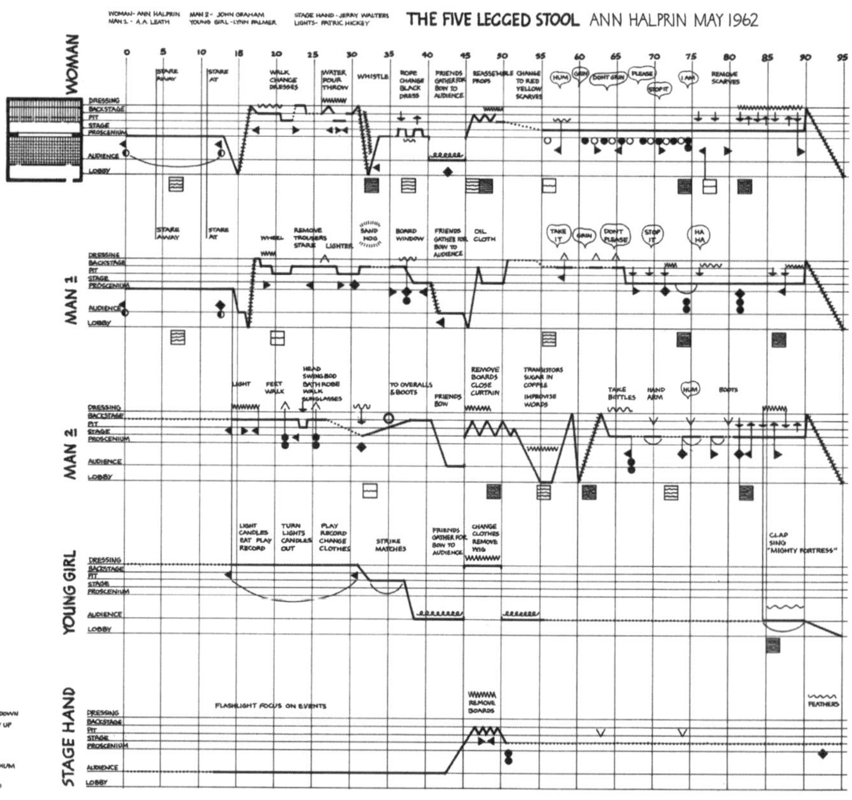

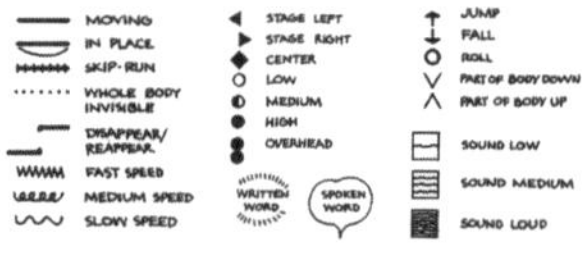

Besides questioning the traditional tools of project representation, landscapers are becoming increasingly interested in what truly allows life to continue: the interaction and connection of various forms of existence in the context of uncertainty. This shift in perspective echoes the urgent demand of many of our planet's inhabitants for a change of status: they, too, want their existence to be finally acknowledged. The assumption that there is only one world and the future only goes in one direction – the one that has guided capitalism, imperialism, and colonialism – is starting to erode. Instead, we come to realize that we are dealing with a polyphony of worlds, futures, and beings that constitute a pluriverse. The projects presented in this book are part of the policy of exposing the potentials that have been previously frozen in the realm of figuration, or left to languish on the margins. Seen this way, the landscape appears as an assembly of layered and multiform rhythms. These rhythms emerge from the movements and relationships of human and non–human origin that together generate this world. Letting go of a one–dimensional narrative of growth means improvising. By tuning into uncertainty, we learn to appreciate it. Here, elements of graphic representation are used not as outlines of shapes, but as tools for organizing data. Instead of reducing the world to a fixed image, they offer representations that need to be activated. In other words, the viewer must continuously engage with them, making connections to possible actions. The performative aspect of these drawings is exactly what turns them into scores.

Christopher Dell

3.1 Considering the project as a neg *platform.*

landscape otiation

The project of transforming a landscape highlights the perspectives of the various stakeholders, whose intentions are determined by their differing, and sometimes even contradictory, mandates. Decision–makers such as elected officials, owners or managers, have different time frames, constraints, and material resources that need to be harmonized in order to make a project happen. A landscape project reveals the dynamics of evolution and highlights human pressure on ecosystems. It presents a vision to share, where each territory is seen as a fragment of the Planetary garden to be cultivated together. This involves taking on new responsibilities, questioning our practices in relation to the living world, and sometimes rethinking our ambitions, or even abandoning certain plans. As landscapers, we act like diplomats between species, trying to balance the interests of some with the needs of others. Experience, a pedagogical approach, and creativity are crucial if we want a vision to be embraced by all stakeholders.

3.2 Building *commu* gardening toge

nity **by** **her.**

Let's think of the participants of a project – that is, all of the living beings involved – as its collective author. Within this larger group develops a human team that needs to be mobilized to build and sustain the garden over time. The issue here is not to delegate these tasks only to specialists – who, by the way, are often under-appreciated – but to create opportunities where a wide variety of people are invited to take part in the work of creating a garden. This way, we can deepen our knowledge of and connection with living things, share the synergies born from different experiences, and learn to resolve conflicts and misunderstandings that can arise around a shared garden. Working together allows us to give more value to the professions that interact with living things, and to re-learn how to coexist with other forms of life. It also promotes, through *Call to Create*, values such as autonomy, generosity, solidarity, and mutual support, often inspired by the living world.

3.3 Creating project that unfold over

frameworks

time.

Many projects establish strategies that facilitate ongoing collaboration between landscapers and garden workers, which is essential to building a deep connection with living systems, one of care and understanding. This challenges our idea of a perfectly completed project and questions the distinctions between the practices of architects, ecologists, landscapers, and so on. In a garden, revisiting and changing, time and again, what has been done before is not a failure but a creative act of renewal and invention. In a garden, construction and management are hard to separate. The conventional distinction between investment and maintenance budgets becomes therefore less straightforward – and so does the role of the gardeners performing a work that evolves along with the seasons. In other words, whether it's the species spreading throughout the garden, or our intentions to somehow guide their growth and interaction, both need time to unfold.

3.4 Demonstratin the living wo

aesthetic resolu

g care for ld through *tion.*

When a landscapist prioritizes the dynamics of life over form, design becomes less visible. Geometry, a symbol of human control over nature, no longer imposes its mark on the gardens. As a result, what distinguishes a garden from free evolution – even something as subtle as a mown strip, or a touch of pruning to add some transparency – becomes of utmost importance. This kind of aesthetic resolution prompts a change in perspective, sharpens attention, and sparks curiosity. Treating the framing, the viewpoints, or the approaches aesthetically can highlight the care given. This ongoing give–and–take between the gardener and their work site creates a continually renewed aesthetic, giving rise to the *Garden in Motion*. The garden becomes a collaborative space between the planned project and the daily interactions in an ever–changing context. We have to learn to recognize this new, wilder, and more spontaneous beauty.

3.A Asfalto mon amour

— Lecce

Guided by indecision

Initiated by a third place called KNOS, this Call to Create is about gardening a 15 000 m^2 parking lot with almost zero resources. There could hardly be a better case for the 'laboratory of Indecision', where gardeners work with nature using the least effort for maximum fertility. Six workshops held between 2012 and 2015 saw more than 200 people work on this garden. Getting into action while trying to find the center of gravity of such a changing team would disrupt any attempt at a vertically organized project. One has to *Navigate the Garden*, taking action with a festive spirit. Spontaneity is about valuing the initial drive to act, the drive from which the platform for negotiation and decision-making will emerge.

The un-design process that follows puts form in second place; it is the dynamics of life that shape the project, and these dynamics may be documented afterwards.

With ten years of hindsight, one thing is clear: by holding water that evaporates less in the summer, asphalt and the layers underneath provide an excellent living environment for Mediterranean plants – as shown by the plants' exceptional growth. Asphalt, I love you, they seem to murmur.

Mission Direct collective action
Location Manifatture KNOS, Lecce, Italy
Geographical coordinates 48°51'45»N, 2°17'15»E
Project duration 2013 – ongoing
Size 15 000 m2
Client Self-production
Grouping Coloco, Labuat, LUA, Scuola del Terzo Paesaggio
Team Coloco Pablo Georgieff, Miguel Georgieff, Danilo Capasso, Giulia Piccione, Leonardo Delogu, Gonzague Lacombe, Pico "il paladino dell'asfalto", Dagmar Dudinsky, Christophe Foubert
Photo credits Danilo Capasso (unless otherwise specified)

Asphalt out, *gardenisw*

— Coloco on arrival to Lecce

Freed from the domina
and geometry, the ga
remarkable place for
relationships with life **– t**
ceases to amaze us.
This garden is a perfe
the journey of collaborati
things. We explore w
only collaboration ca
a competitive approa

in !!!

nce of fences
den turns into a
reating *new*
he life that never

ct place for *continuing*
on **among living**
hole new areas that
reveal, and that
h keeps out of reach.

3.A

Asfalto mon amour: *under the asphalt, the garden!*

Opening up to the unexpected is not improvising, but creating the conditions for welcoming the unforeseen. This is why a good project relies on what eludes it. Luckily, there is always something that eludes us... like a spontaneous swing of a pickaxe on an asphalt esplanade. In this way, human planning can give rise to a place that welcomes the diversity of life, humans included. A place that may look like a garden grown all by itself in a space abandoned for decades, but that is actually the result of human effort. An effort that doesn't try to put everything in its place but knows when to let go of planning. An effort that knows how to let it be.

Michele Bee

← ©P. Georgieff, Coloco

3.1
Considering the landscape project as a negotiation platform

We started negotiations with the government of the Apulia Region, with which we had worked on a program document for the interventions on the site. Our initial goal was to carry out a project, so the very first discussions took place within the participant group.

From the first strike of the pickaxe, this sparked a whole chain of reactions. The idea of doing something with this abandoned space gained traction. The unused parking lot became a subject of controversy, leading to a series of negotiations – sometimes latent – with local residents, with the university housing, and also with the Region as the owners of the space. Years ago, the Region had initiated its transfer to the Province to turn it into a sports field, but halted the process to give the lot back to the community.

The plants, too, joined the negotiations, debating the space between each other, then asserting themselves in the landscape. So present on the site today, the vegetation has all stemmed from the initial momentum created by the first pickaxe strikes.

We began by letting this momentum lead so we could discuss how the project should be carried out. Negotiations came as the next step. Very organic, the resulting design looks almost spontaneous – a visible reflection of all invisible negotiations. Had we started with some predetermined design, put in place and implemented, the outcome would have never been the same.

3.2
Building community by gardening together

The project began as a traditional architecture workshop. Everyone wanted to leave their mark, come up with a project, a design, an idea. Our first response was to slow down these attempts at immediate action and find a way to move forward together, without favoring one person's idea over another's. However, it's never easy to make your first mark on a blank canvas. It was an individual and somewhat anarchic act of someone who, without saying a word, started breaking the asphalt that got us going. Years later, this person, nicknamed The Asphalt Paladin, would win the Golden Pickaxe prize - a pickaxe broken in action and sprayed with gold paint.

The initial community, mainly formed by the workshop participants, evolved as the project went on together with its challenges. At certain times, we had to abandon the space because we couldn't maintain it. Then the community of enthusiasts stepped in, made up of people who, whenever they can, try to clean up a bit and keep an eye on things. This 'caring abandonment' gave rise to a 'biopolitical' community; it includes the humans forming connections with the pioneer plants that have always been there, and with those we brought in, but also the plants forming connections between themselves, and all of them connecting with each other.

Today, the garden is proliferating, and the individuals that have been successively involved in the project are using this approach in their own work. A community of thought and practice is spreading out. Beyond the Knos garden, the Scuola del Terzo Luogo, a 'third place school' that does not define itself and has none of the conventional attributes – no teachers, no programs, no location – continues to exist and brings people together to pursue other projects around the world.

3.3
Turning the project into a score that unfolds over time

We have gathered, here and now, to create a garden. We invite you for a technological streap-tease: put aside your smartphones and be fully present to the life that we'll be unleashing together.

Spontaneity and indecision are demanding: they require your full commitment to the relationships with the others in order to do things together – even before you know exactly what you are going to do, and how. We have to take time to share ideas and dreams, match them with logistical realities, and agree, in good spirits, on what to do today. All of that, without forgetting to plan for tomorrow and to think about the long-term future of our daily efforts.

Along the way, we find ourselves defining our methods of action and drawing diagrams – both to explain them to the newcomers and to deepen our own understanding of what we are doing. This is how the Dramatic Arc of Indecision (shown further on) has been sketched out.

A score is not a sacred text meant to be, pardon the word, executed. You can doodle it on a lunch napkin stained with tomato sauce. It's both a record of what has been collectively improvised and a temporal work plan for what's coming next.

This is where it becomes a useful working tool, allowing us to track, as well as to prepare for the moments of intensity that make collective creation such an exhilarating work.

Every time, we can't wait to return to the garden and rediscover what life has accomplished while we were away. This mindful stroll initiates and inspires each new round of actions.

3.4
Expressing care for the living world through aesthetic resolution

The point we want to make here is that we intentionally left the project somewhat alone without ever abandoning it. This created a unique aesthetic, where the design disappears behind the vegetation. Occasionally, we tidy up the edges, which is seen as an aesthetic act – human intervention is visible but kept minimal.

There was no predefined notion of composition. The composition emerged from a series of dynamics and negotiations, whether it's deciding where to plant trees or how to cut the asphalt strips. Everything was done step by step, using the resources and the manpower available at the time. It's a complex equation where various factors come together to materialize into what we get done. It's a constant adjustment between intention and form. This process was crucial for learning. We engaged with materials, asphalt, living organisms, plants. A whole set of spatial arrangements generating this particular aesthetic resulted from our physical encounter with the materials. One can see that the project wasn't drawn out on paper before being implemented. Imperfections in the layout, things that appear a bit off, were all worked out directly on the ground, using the body and its movements as a measuring tool. It was the dancers who led the initial work of making sense of this oversized space. This, by the way, made us question the outcomes of using precise digital and geometric tools in our projects.

The garden's aesthetic is not a preconceived decision, but the result of a process, a dialogue with life itself.

↑ ©P. Georgieff, Coloco

Let's raise *indecision* **t**
of decision-making.

— **Gilles Clément** *Manifesto of the Third Landscape*

It's when we *liberate t*
outcome **that the expe**
and things start takin
Letting indecision guid
the logic of cycles a
it's a never-ending
up a terminology is
we persuade others
indecision?

the political level

e process from the
ence can happen
shape.
e us **and following**
nd recycling:
rocess. This brings
ue: how can
when talking about

The Manifatture Knos

This project took place in the Italian city of Lecce, located in the Salento region in the southern part of the country. It's a landscape of a particular beauty, a vast rurban area dominated by olive groves and vineyards, with a diffuse network of small towns scattered across. The Manifatture Knos is an independent cultural center occupying a former technical school for metallurgists that was abandoned in 1994. The public space, owned by the provincial administration, was made available, free of charge, to a non-profit association called Sud Est in December 2006.

In 2012, a group of fellow citizens met at the Manifatture Knos for the first session of a periodic workshop called "Incontri del Terzo Luogo" (The Third Place Meetings). The workshop was initiated by Michele Bee. Researcher and activist inspired by Gilles Clément's "Manifesto of the Third Landscape," Bee decided to reach out to Clément to organize a workshop in Lecce where Clément's theories could be tested in a real-life setting.

Just like in previous sessions, during this workshop the participants were divided into project groups that competed to develop the best idea and persuade the others that theirs was the one to implement. After two such sessions, Gilles Clément suggested bringing in Coloco to help get things moving.

Asphalt out, gardening in! proclaim Coloco with a raised fist, facing the quixotic task ahead. The asphalt field looks unconquerable in its sheer vastness. It's like the crystallized rage felt by many at the sight of life being destroyed through the blind pursuit of immediate profit.

The initial proposal – using explosives and machines to tear up the entire asphalt layer – turned into "Asfalto mon amour" during a now-famous lunch. The idea of treating the sterile parking lot with tenderness opened the way for modesty and patience: let's work with what we've got and with good cheer. Let's simply help l ife to take root and flourish.

Asfalto mon amour

Feeling the freedom offered by the vast expanse of asphalt is exhilarating. The intense blue sky of Puglia creates a striking contrast. The urge to run is irresistible. I sprint in a wide diagonal and return in a sweeping curve, leaning with arms outstretched like a bird's wings. The others, dazzled, tread the asphalt cautiously and do not venture far from the edge.

The dancers take the lead; they invite everyone to take off their shoes and feel the texture of the asphalt. They encourage us to try different ways of moving and occupying the space, to gauge it with our bodies and movements. Agronomists and botanists help us identify water paths and track the sun's trajectory; they talk about the strength of winter winds.

Architects and urban planners help us situate ourselves within the city and its history; they take us on a walk along the ramparts to explore the surroundings.

The team at the Manifatture Knos recounts the adventures that have led to the current situation. Nothing is guaranteed; practicing indecision means negotiating all the time.

With all this information, we can now decide where to start the work. The thrill of grabbing the pickaxe. For many, it will be their first time, but not for me. I show the move to avoid injuries and optimize the efficiency of each strike. Nothing else matters now; it's me versus the asphalt. David and Goliath. My firstimpact will inevitably be minimal: a few square millimeters against the 150 million of the parking lot. It will take countless pickaxe strikes. But that's not what I'm thinking about as I swing my tool. I'm curious. I want to see what this ground is made of, how thick the asphalt is, and what's underneath.

Everyone takes their turn with the pickaxe, and soon a young woman shouts "Land ahoy!" – like sailors crossing the open sea. Sharing this epic journey brings us together, 'I' become 'we'.

The art of gardening on asphalt requires specific skills. We master grinders and jackhammers; at some point, we even get help from a mini excavator. Demolition quickly produces plenty of rubble. What do we do with it?

↗ ©Christophe Foubert and Danilo Capasso

← ©P. Georgieff, Coloco

Gardening is a performance

Demolishing the asphalt layer allows us to plant while leaving some substrate for spontaneous growth. Ideas, desires, dreams start taking shape as we go. We try different techniques and work methods, letting everyone experiment if they feel like it. There's no client to please, no public money to justify the use of, no gallery to impress. It's simply an experimental playground that has opened up because everyone wanted so, and where we enjoy getting together from time to time.

It's a fact: the situation is highly inspiring. We realize that our collective physical effort, seemingly modest, has an incredible power of transformation. Soon, a botanical survey confirms the presence of over 80 species, nearly two-thirds of which are spontaneous. Pennisetums are particularly effective at quickly spreading across the entire area and filling in the smallest cracks in the asphalt. The parking lot is also becoming a garden. Who said the two uses can't coexist? Once the initial panic among the few parking users subsides, sharing the space becomes natural. Neighbors now come here to walk their dogs, groups of teenagers smoke quietly, and the Pakistani community plays cricket. The walls surrounding the garden-parking lot turn into an open-air graffiti gallery.

In May 2015, the annual meeting of Trans Europe Halles, the European network of independent cultural centers, was held at the Manifatture Knos with over 350 attendees. For the occasion, a nighttime performance was conducted, playfully mixing the codes of gardening, dance, and opera. CarMen was a tribute to Ant Farm, an iconic collective of the Californian counterculture of the 1970s. Despite several timing issues due to short rehearsal time, everyone found the performance, with its crossbreeding of disciplines and languages, extremely refreshing.

"Cent plants-sans plans" ("One hundred plants and no plan") invited the participants to collectively create a part of the garden following this homophonic protocol (in French, 'cent plants' and 'sans plans' are pronounced almost similarly – t/n). It turned into chaos, as expected. But, interestingly enough, the dialogue brought out a number of priorities: first of all, no trampling, but also considering the way the plants will grow, as well as the phytosociological and aesthetic aspects of placing one species next to the other. Today, the whole thing has evolved into a small grove of pines with varied undergrowth, and with euphorbias and bulbines dominating the edges. It's cooler here during the intense summer heat, which sometimes reaches fifty degrees.

«Botanical Dub», a series of sound creations, also came to life under the scorching sun of the garden-parking lot. Dr. Capasso, equally comfortable with cutting-edge urban theories and digital controllers, unleashed the deepest bass lines in the purest Jamaican style. Switching between Latin, French, and Salentino, the garden's plants were presented to the audience who swayed to the beat. A botany lesson has never been so syncopated.

Known far beyond Apulia, "Asfalto mon amour" has inspired many sister projects. The Depave collective in Oregon has even published a manual on de-asphalting, complete with cheat sheets to help implement your de-paving project. In Rio de Janeiro, indigenous people from several tribes gathered to assert their rights by planting a food forest on the asphalt. Looking back in time, there's an image of Californian hippies armed with crowbars to attack the asphalt. In the art world, Lois Weinberger has created several installations that welcomed ruderal plants on demolished surfaces so they could access the earth.

What really matters here are the things we have learned about ourselves, about the collective, and about the shared authorship with non-human beings. Written in a series of brief morning sessions before getting to work, the book called *Naviguer dans un jardin* (*Navigate the Garden*) records the dynamics of this non-hierarchical experience. We invite you to check them out.

↑ A sketch from *Poetica della zappa*, published by DeriveApprodi, 2018 © Drawing — P. Georgieff, Coloco

INDECISION
=
DECISION RENOUVELLÉE EN PERMANENCE DE MAINTENIR LE MAXIMUM DE POSSIBILITÉS OUVERTES
CHOSE FAITE
NOUVEAU PALIMPSESTE DES POSSIBLEI
UN PAS EN AVANT
ENVIE DE CONTINUER
JOIE
ESPEARIEN
AUTRES PICS
NOUVEL ELAN
DOUTE
t

The third landscape school

As the workshops went on, the idea of creating a school gradually took shape. What would 'creating a school' mean in this context? Defining a 'model' to develop and implement a knowledge transfer project? When the workshop kicked off, it was clear that the school had already started forming, that it was growing and getting stronger, and that now we had to consider how it could last over time. How can we continue to welcome everyone for free, with minimal resources to meet the needs of this kind of social project – so that it could, in turn, enhance the city's territorial project through the quality of its experiments?

The emerging School of the Third Landscape got involved in creating a municipal planning document, the Documento Programmatico, which the local administration is in charge of. This document formalizes the wish to create new configurations for collaborative action and territorial management.

Developing new projects for territorial governance in Europe is a key issue. Given limited public resources, the search for new models of intervention and management is a major project for the next fifteen years. What is being created in Lecce is very useful in this context: here, public interest, the commons, as well as collective and shared management are being explored both conceptually and physically.

This research can definitely contribute to the "New Deal" for territorial action that we so desperately need, and become a milestone in the political recognition of a new way of managing urban areas. 'Indecision' means continually choosing to keep as many open avenues for the future as possible. This approach should be clearly distinguished from neglect and abandonment, and receive the political respect it deserves.

↑ ©Francesca Borrelli
→ ↓ ©P. Georgieff, Coloco

3.B The Cloître workshops

– Le Cloître–Saint–Thégonnec

Make do, and you'll do better

Tasked to transform the public spaces of the village of Le Cloître–Saint–Thégonnec, atelier Bivouac chose to do it together with the villagers, which helped drive the project towards local energies and how they could be mobilized. The success of this project was due to the simple arrangements, as the team sought to make the most of the resources at hand.

Exchanges between local residents and technical services backed up by the work of thc landscapcrs madc it possible to develop, collectively, a new framework for project participants. Here, Putting Life first meant replacing continuous asphalt surfaces with green areas.

The choice of techniques and materials, as well as the resulting aesthetic resolution, are indicative of fair, up–to–date, tailored solutions that were found by managers and users addressing the project's challenges together.

Mission Collaborative study on public spaces and research for transforming the church square, with Project Management Assistance (PMA) to oversee the work.
Location Le Cloître–Saint–Thégonnec
Geographical coordinates 48°28'50.2"N, 3°47'41.6"W
Size 1000 m²
Status Public space
Budget 31 450€ (fees + production)

— Team Atelier Bivouac
Client The Town Hall of Le Cloître–Saint–Thégonnec
Landscape designer Atelier Bivouac
Réalisation In–house (the Town Hall'sTechnical Department, PMA by atelier Bivouac)
Gardeners Maintenance by the Technical Department

— Phasing
Design study March 2017
Production October 2017

Photo credits Atelier Bivouac

A residency in Le Clo
gave us the opportun
We thought it would
reopen Capsell, the l
been shut down, for t
residency. Reopened
d'aménagement publ
Counter), it served pr
of discussion **with res**
allowing everyone to
progress from beginn

tre-Saint-Thégonnec
ty to *take our time.*
e a good idea to
st local bar to have
ne period of this
as CAP (Comptoir
c, or Public Amenity
marily as *a space*
dents and officials,
follow the project's
ing to end.

3.B

The Cloître workshops: *collaborative construction of a village square*

After a preliminary study with CAUE 29 (the regional Council for Architecture, Urban Planning and the Environment), the municipal team of Cloître–Saint–Thégonnec asked us to join them in thinking about the future of the village's public spaces, and to get the residents involved as well. Our approach has been based on the premise that the village already had the resources needed to reshape its public spaces. So the whole story began with an inventory, a kind of treasure hunt: identifying and quantifying the available material resources and local skills. Our point was to "work with what we've got", seeing the economy of means as a leverage for creativity and solidarity in developing new uses.

Atelier Bivouac

3.1
Considering the landscape project as a negotiation platform

Week one: we reopen the former bar on the Church Square, known as the Capsell, renaming it for the occasion as the CAP (short for Comptoir d'aménagement public, or Public Amenity Counter). Frameworks for meetings and debates are established: public workshops, individual interviews, and open hours around a model will bring together residents, elected officials, associations, and municipal employees. Combining local expertise and our insights as landscapers, project intentions start to take shape.

On Saturday, some thirty people gather in the square to map out, with the help of stakes, two development scenarios on a scale of 1:1. One person moves a chair to find a spot where they can picture themselves sitting, another starts their car and drives across the square to test the trajectory of a new driving path, while someone else moves a stake to make a planting pit bigger and create more space between the road and their house. Experiencing the layout at full scale lets participants and designers directly interact with the site and understand the impact of different changes.

Project completed. A few months later, a phone call. A driver misjudged a turn at night and scratched their car on a rock. Before, the asphalt offered plenty of space. Now, they need to learn to negotiate their way through a living environment: rocks, children, ferns, bikes, and benches. Sometimes, adaptation takes a bit of time.

3.2
Building community by gardening together

As we host the elders at the Public Amenity Counter, they fondly recall the shops, the village rituals, and the religious ceremonies that used to liven up the Church Square and marked the daily life of the village. The Capsell was the last bar to close, four years before we came. The municipality bought the place with an idea to turn it into a community café, but their current priority is to deal with the threat of school closure. Here, building community is an everyday battle. We realize how much the reopening of the bar during our residency rekindles the demand for a meeting place. People stop by, curious, enter to order drinks, then find themselves talking to the landscapers about the redesign of the Church Square. "So, when's the bar reopening?" they ask. "The town hall is still looking for new owners. If you're around on Saturday, we're planning a rock brushing contest in the Church Square. Interested?" Once the rocks are in place on the square, we give them a little welcome ceremony that ends with us all having fun at the bar.

3.3
Turning the project into a score that unfolds over time

Unlike some of our other projects that span several seasons, our work at Le Cloître was completed in a very short time without setting up a framework for potential follow–up management. As the implementation was done in–house, we made sure to plan ahead with the municipal workers, taking into consideration their skills and management resources so they could be as autonomous as possible.

This project, the first one we carried out in Finistère, caught the attention of CAUE 29 and the BRUDED network (which shares between local authorities the experiences in all areas of sustainable development). We had several visits from elected officials to show them a real–life example of how rural municipalities with limited financial resources can transform their public spaces. How do you carry out work in–house, leveraging the skills of your municipal employees? How can you be creative on a tight budget, taking stock of the resources available within the project site? How to engage local residents in the conversation about the future of public spaces? Thanks to the exposure from these two advisory bodies, the project has spread over time and throughout Brittany, leading to new commissions inspired by this methodology.

3.4
Expressing care for the living world through aesthetic resolution

The landscapes of Le Cloître–Saint–Thégonnec are defined by the presence of stones. There are the stones of the old houses with their granite walls and slate roofs, and then there are multiple granite outcrops in the area. They appear sporadically in the middle of agricultural plots, in gardens, at the corners of houses, in the heathland, and along the roads. These mineral features punctuate the village and shape its identity. Throughout history, the subsoil pushed up and broke through the surface, forcing people to negotiate with it. In the fields, crops are moved aside in front of the rocks, and in gardens, flower beds are arranged around them. For children, the rocks become playgrounds, perches, islands, and whales.

The stone blocks we placed in the square had been discarded during the construction of a housing estate and a new road. Our project aims to bring back the geological history and reinstall this lost landscape at the center of the public square. Custom pits are cut to match the dimensions of the granite blocks, street furniture is designed to fit the unique shapes of the rocks, and perennials take over, creating a seamless transition between the granite and the pavement. This intervention revisits the image of the rocky chaos to create the impression that the roadway, parking spaces, pathways, and furniture are all interacting and negotiating with this geology.

The approach & the team

A residency in Le Cloître–Saint–Thégonnec gave us the opportunity to take our time. To take the time to understand the aspirations and needs of the residents and officials concerning the public spaces in their village. To take the time to make an inventory of the local resources, both in terms of materials and skills. To take the time to dream up together a unique public space that represents the territory and its residents.

Working and living in the village for two weeks has let us engage in an open reflection process with the residents, technical services, and elected officials. This residency allowed us to exchange ideas, testing and tweaking development choices together. It created time for citizen debate to agree on a project shared by the majority and based on a common vision for the future of public spaces.

Walk-through diagnostics

To kick off this residency, we thought it would be a good idea to assess the village's public spaces with the residents during a morning walk on Saturday, March 11th. What are everyone's needs, aspirations, and suggestions?

This walk-through diagnosis brings to light a series of issues commonly found in many villages: occasionally dangerous car traffic; the need for a better distribution of parking spaces; the wish to make some areas pedestrian-only; considerations for the management of planted areas and the beautification of public spaces that would feel more comfortable if furniture and shelters for outdoor gatherings were added, and so forth. Other questions are more specific to Le Cloître. For example, there is the Wolf Museum that attracts a lot of visitors. So, how can we encourage people to explore the charming alleys of the village instead of just staying inside the museum? And also, how to enhance the friendliness and conviviality of public spaces?

After discussions with the residents and elected officials, we feel that Church Square could be representative of the issues to be resolved concerning the village's public spaces. Together, we decided to make it a priority site for experimentation and to focus the next two weeks' work on figuring out how to redesign it.

CAP, the Public Amenity Counter!

When the older folks talk about the Church Square, they mention the shops that used to be in the houses surrounding it. A smithy, a tobacco shop, a dance hall, and of course, several bars. The Capsell was the last one to close, almost four years ago now. The town hall bought it, but the project for its reopening is still being worked out.

We thought it would be a good idea to reopen this place during the residency because, as a natural meeting place, it would raise questions about community life on and around the square. Residents seemed surprised to see the light shining through the shop window. Some stopped, walked in, ordered drinks, and then realized they weren't in a bar but at the Public Amenity Counter, a place open to all, where we could discuss the future transformation of the Church Square.

Working in residency allows us to be visibly present in the village. We communicate about the project through posters and workshop invitations, but reopening the Capsell allows us to spread the word about our two-week experiment even further. It's an opportunity to create a communication platform for the villagers, a showcase where we display summaries of workshops and meetings. The CAP sessions are first of all about creating, together with residents and officials, a space of debate, and also offering everyone a possibility to follow the project's progress from start to finish.

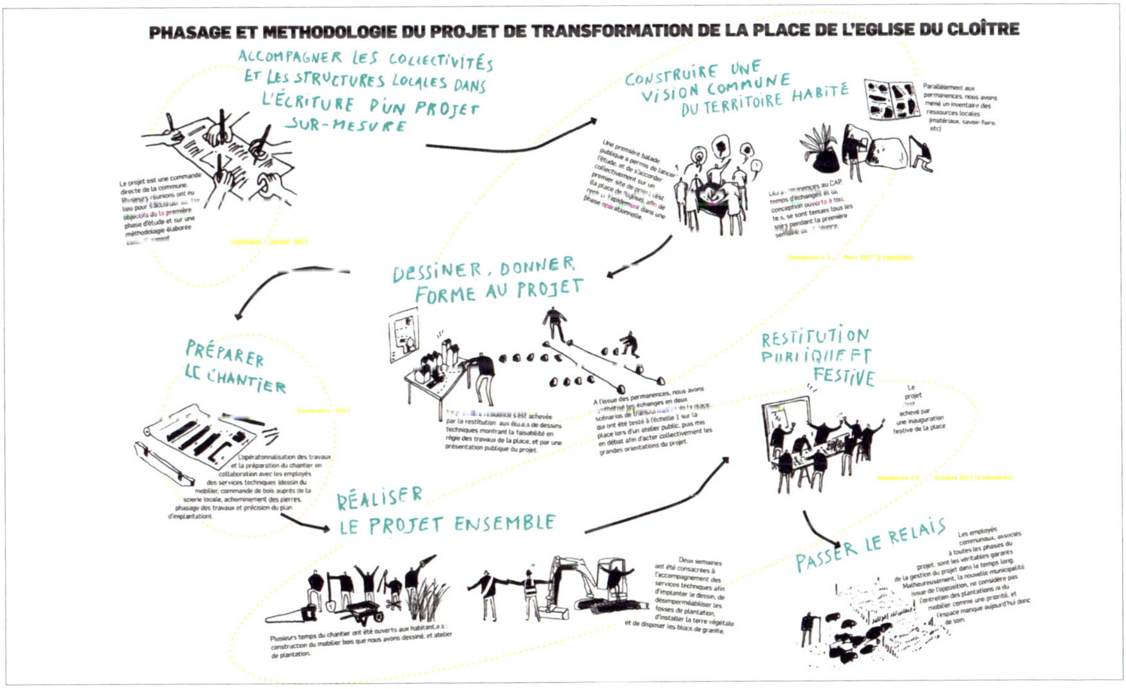

The model of collective research

It's not always easy to imagine the transformation of a public space you visit every day. Daily life unfolds spontaneously in the present. But has this Church Square always been like this?

The history of the square unfolds at the CAP counter, in conversations with the elderly residents over recovered vintage postcards. There used to be many shops and meeting places. "It's the car that killed off the village's small businesses!" one lady admits. Other residents say, "We've always known the square like this, as a parking lot." A large expanse of asphalt, where cars take their ease. You think we could do something different? To facilitate the residents' reclaiming of the square, imagine other uses and open up possibilities, we are going to produce a collective research model.

Colored paper cutouts are provided to residents during open hours to try out different scenarios for sharing space between pedestrians and cars.

Using the model allows them to step back and change the perception of the square to unlock imagination. We're talking more, and ideas sprout throughout the week. The space, once thought irreversible and rigid, is starting to feel more dynamic and flexible. Constraints turn into levers for collective creativity and encourage going beyond standard urban planning solutions.

Making the markers

In preparation for the test setups on the Church square, on Wednesday, March 15th, about fifteen parents, children, and teenagers gather at the Community House to create markers. The workshop space turns into a makeshift carpentry and painting studio, but also a hub for socializing. Using reclaimed Douglas fir wood from the Adrast sawmill, the group crafts the markers together. Each participant quickly takes on a task: sorting, cutting, assembling, painting... By the end of the afternoon, some forty markers of various sizes are produced. These will be used as handy, easily movable visual cues to test potential changes as proposed on the model, making adjustments if necessary.

The workshop ends with everyone enjoying a snack of crepes topped with delicious homemade salt caramel butter cream.

Discovering Le Cloître landscapes

On the Church square, the uniform asphalt surface seems to have erased a piece of the landscape. Nothing reminds us of the town's identity anymore; no rough spots to anchor stories. In the first workshops, people told us that the square looked too smooth and that some vertical elements were missing between the ground, the facades and the cars. We imagined bringing back the rocks as reminders of the surrounding landscape, the elements that would add rhythm and provide places to sit against.

As we toured the village, we took stock of the available resources that could be used to redesign the square in a cost-effective manner, recognizing that the components for the future project were already on local turf.

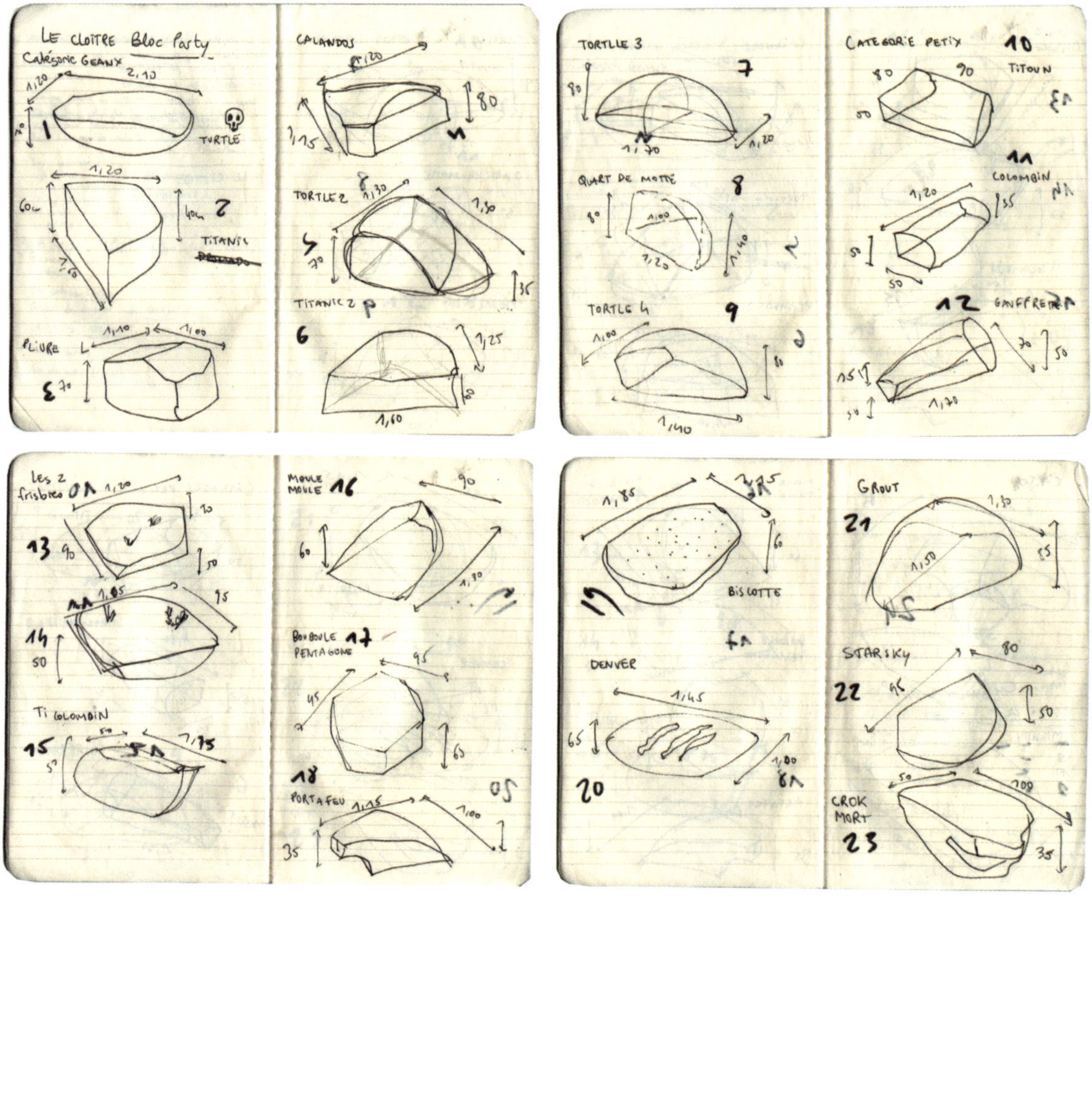
LE CLOITRE Bloc Party
Catégorie GEANX
TORTLE
TITANIC
PLIURE
CALANDOS
TORTLE 2
TITANIC 2
TORTLE 3
QUART DE MOTTE
TORTLE 4
CATEGORIE PETIX
TITOUN
COLOMBIN
GAUFFRETTE
Les 2 frisbees
Ti COLOMBIN
MOULE MOULE
BOUBOULE PENTAGONE
PORTAFEU
BISCOTTE
DENVER
GROUT
STARSKY
CROK MORT

Designing chaos

While doing the inventory, we come across piles of granite blocks of various sizes that have been moved and discarded. It's a rocky chaos made up of individual pieces. We need to figure out how to capture their shapes so we could think, using drawings and models, how to arrange them in the square. How do we convey their organic geometry? Measuring is tricky; it's more about sketching their volume and standout features in our notebooks. We name each rock to give them an identity, to adopt them in a sense. Then comes the time to make models. Using pool noodles from Decathlon as source material, each rock is sculpted in foam at a 1/20 scale. On a large plan spread out on the old bar's floor, we seek the right composition, the right rhythm in their arrangement. The final step is creating templates; we cut them out from the linoleum found upstairs in the Capsell that awaits renovation. Each template corresponds to a rock that will not be just placed in the middle of a planting pit, but requires a custom cut in the asphalt. Three steps of representation and translation to create this rocky chaos, making it look as if other elements of the square are negotiating with the rocks.

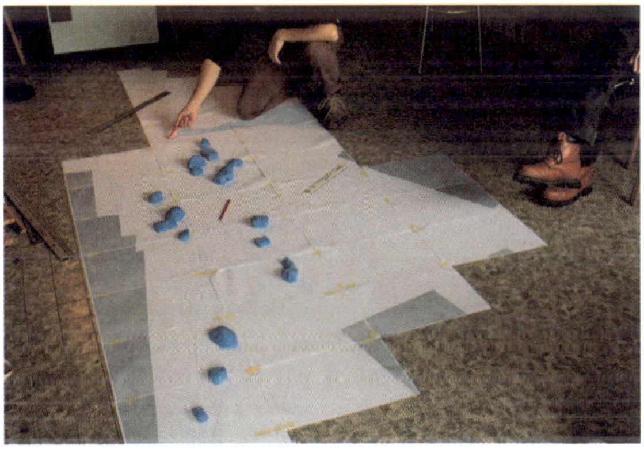

The planting plan

The model of the rock arrangement helps us imagine how life will unfold on the square. Photographing it from above, with a desk lamp mimicking the sun's path, we can see the shadow and light areas, as well as the spots sheltered from or exposed to the wind. What plants would want to grow on the north side of the rock named "Calandos"? How will the Finistère purple moor grass get along with the North American gaura? And what if the European gorse just popped up here and there? Our temporary office in the Capsell overlooks the square, so we can easily move back and forth between the model and the actual site. Plan in hand, we walk through the newly mulched planting pits. Using a plant palette created with a local nurseryman, we note down the planting plan on–site and look from different viewpoints on the square, imagining how the plant masses will grow.

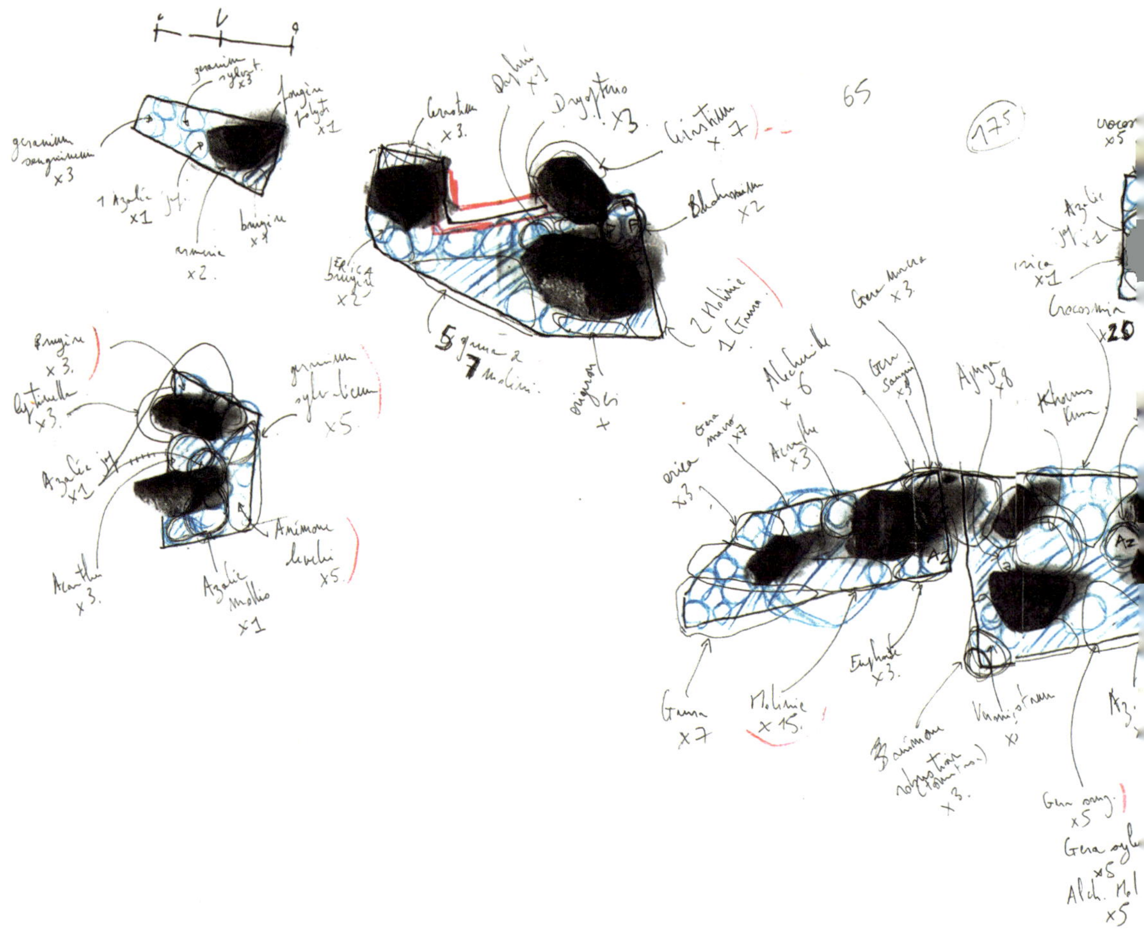

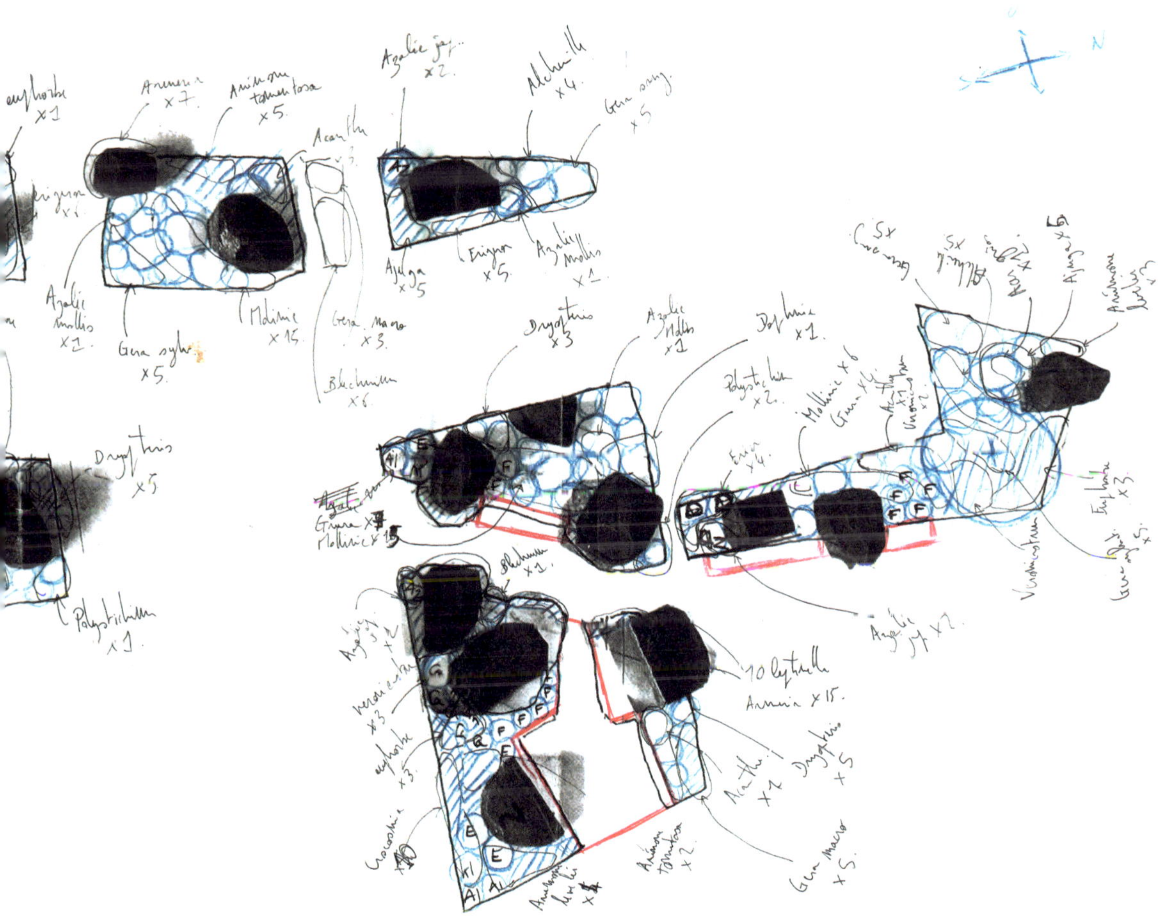

The Granite and the Asphalt

The project aims to bring back the area's geological history and reintroduce the lost landscape, giving it a central place in the public square. Custom pits are dug to fit the dimensions of the granite blocks; the furniture fits the unique shapes of the rocks, and the perennial plants blend it all together, creating a connection between the granite and the asphalt.

The Grand Rock-Brushing Contest

The first two weeks of the construction phase were dedicated to major tasks (implementing the design; cutting the asphalt and making the area permeable again; preparing the pits and installing the rocks). These phases were hard to involve the residents in, so we marked their completion by a public event to celebrate the rocks' installation in the square and the return of the lost landscape. During a pagan ceremony in front of the church, each participant brought their brush and bucket to clean the dirt off the rocks. This celebration was a way to invite the residents back into the project and announce the upcoming public work phase: building furniture and planting.

The Golden Shovel

The success of this project owes a lot to the help we received from two municipal employees, René and Philippe. Their detailed knowledge of the area and the different stages of the village's development; their role as mediators, reassuring the residents who were hesitant about the changes to the Church square, but also their technical skills, patience, and kindness made them key players in the project. The methodology we developed with the municipal council made it possible to involve René and Philippe very early in the process. One of them attended all public co-design sessions, even if they were outside their working hours, thus ensuring that the group always included residents, officials, and a technical services employee. At the inauguration of the square, we honored them with the "Golden Shovel" trophy – a miniature, gold-sprayed excavator on a solid oak base.

PLACE

3.C Happy Garden

– Aubervilliers

Asphalt, immense collective energy, and some time...

This direct intervention method puts into practice the idea of a time–based project. Taking place right under the residents' windows, the ongoing transformation of this former parking lot offers an everyday opportunity to engage with the living world. The gardening style used here supports rather than dictates, allowing for a free evolution through a mix of carefully chosen pioneer species and spontaneous growth.

The gentle yet consistent presence of the gardeners helps create fertile connections between the diversity of species and the garden's aesthetics. Every season brings new charms, and the Garden in Motion principle guides future plant successions. Here, the gardener is also an artist, arranging and playing with the variations of living assemblies.

Mission Recycling of a parking lot into a rock garden
Location Aubervilliers, France
Geographical coordinates 48°54'50.2"N, 2°23'52.7"E
Parking surface 1700 m²
Client OPH (Public Housing Agency) Aubervilliers

Duration of the works 5 days x 7 persons
Budget 30000€ (planning and implementation)
Design Wagon Landscaping
Photo credits Yann Monel, Wagon Landscaping and Gabrielle Voinot

An asphalt surface
blackboard. Just gr
you can *draw your*
ground.

The *flexibility of har*
impermeable grour
transformed **and rec**
a new dynamic of l

is like a giant
ab some chalk, and
arden **right on the**

d surfaces. **These**
ds can't wait to be
ycled to welcome
fe.

3.C

Happy garden, *recycling a parking lot into a rockery*

This project opens up a discussion about reusing the soil directly on–site. With landlords, residents, associations, and schools involved, our aim was to implement a frugal project in which, through a mix of pioneer and alpine plants, we could showcase the richness of our cities' poor soils.

Over time, through workshops, conversations, and gardening sessions spanning several years, through meetings and observations, the garden has evolved. Nothing is fixed, and there are no preconceived notions... In this parking lot turned into an experimental garden, curiosity around plant–related human / non–human encounters has become part of life.

Wagon Landscaping

3.1
Considering the landscape project as a negotiation platform

The Happy Garden came about from tearing down a disused parking lot that had become a source of tension in the neighborhood. Nighttime rodeos peaked in the summer of 2015, leading to a radical decision to take the parking lot apart.

Transforming this mass of asphalt into a garden provided an opportunity to rekindle the dialogue between the residents, the municipal authorities, and the social landlord. Over the years, this area has evolved into a place for sharing ideas about plants, seasons, time, animals, gardening, and so on.

The garden, settled in since 2016, was at risk of being partially removed to accommodate drilling for the metro extension project. The residents have successfully negotiated to keep the garden and have the drills set up in another location.

3.2
Building community by gardening together

When we completed the garden in October 2016, we closed the protective barrier around the site. As we were looking at our finished work, two women came up and asked, "Are they finally going to do something with this parking lot? It's been forever..."

After a good laugh, we explained to them that the garden was already there. We had added to this parking lot several cubic meters of soil and gravel, a thousand perennial plants, and a few hundred thousand seeds of annuals and biennials... not to mention the Sedum. It just needed some time, light, and water to sprout.

One could say it all started there... and then carried on in our gardening sessions, workshops with children, and resident visits, where we chatted, pruners in hand. Although the garden hasn't solved all of the neighborhood's problems, it has definitely turned a former epicenter of tension into a peaceful spot.

3.3
Turning the project into a score that unfolds over time

The commission from the Public Housing Agency (OPH) of Aubervilliers included our team monitoring the project's first year. Since then, the contract has been renewed for five half-day visits a year.

The Happy Garden has turned into a genuine laboratory for studying how plants adapt to this very specific environment, halfway between a rockery and a wasteland. It has also become a test field for applying Gilles Clément's concept of "gardening by subtraction," which involves observing and supporting the natural processes that develop in the garden instead of systematically removing everything that wasn't intentionally planted.

For us, this garden is an example of experimenting and observing how time and various factors like wind, birds, and weather shape its evolution.

Gentle and careful gardening with a long-term perspective is what makes this garden thrive, growing more abundant and lush with each passing year.

3.4
Expressing care for the living world through aesthetic resolution

Rawness! In the Happy Garden, our own intention and the very frugal budget have led us to capturing the raw vibe of a newly emerging garden.

The chosen aesthetic is that of a rock garden and a wasteland. The asphalt blocks remain in place, creating a base for a garden that celebrates the rough side of urban deconstruction and de-waterproofing of the soil.

Here, the vocabulary of ruins and plant colonization is used to display a collection of wasteland and rock garden plants that settle and evolve over time. This garden shows just how fast and powerful nature's comeback can be in a rocky, barren area.

The certainty about uncertainty: a reason to embrace diversity and randomness

Setting ourselves a goal to reclaim the space, we have to figure out the right substrate to add, and devise an appropriate planting strategy. The substrate will mimic the characteristics of poor, well–draining soils found in rooftop gardens and rockeries. As for the planting strategy, the only thing we know for sure is that we don't know. Diversity will be our ally. The initial plant palette is chosen from alpine plants and the plants that thrive in shallow soils.

We decided to maximize our chances of success with this diversity. We are working with a natural dynamic where some plants will take over in the first year, gradually being replaced by others. Often, the plants will need to spread, through seeding, away from their original spot to find a more suitable environment. Over 150 species of perennial or annual plants, including herbaceous, shrubby, or woody types, are planted or sown. The project design is done directly on–site based on the soil depths found. We decided to divide the parking lot into strips. They run parallel to a gutter that used to ensure the drainage and is still functional:

— a strip along the big apartment block, planted with trees, creates a border between the parking lot and the building;
— a bare strip on either side of the gutter serves as water drainage. It also creates a gap that lets you see, once the plants have grown, the extent of the parking lot, and eventually provides a path through the garden;
— a strip of actual rock garden;
— a gravel strip planted with Sedum: the succulent garden that surrounds the entire area.

This joyful variety of layers, species, and types of plants has shaped the garden after a week's work done by seven people. It now defines the main structures of the garden. After five years of monitoring, we have seen the evolution and mingling of plants within the garden. The annual seedlings have disappeared quickly; plants compete with each other as they grow. On the other hand, some new species show up and are welcomed.

VRAC VERT
DISTRISOL

The promise of the asphalt: reversing urban soil functions.

In the city, where the soil is becoming increasingly impermeable, how can we promote reversibility and reclamation through nature? At Wagon Landscaping, since 2009, we've embraced "gardening the asphalt" that turns these black canvases into wonderful project boards. Asphalt is an epitome of urban sprawl that devours the living soil. It seals out water, channeling it into the city's pipe networks. A sterile, hard–packed ground, the "red carpet" for cars, the radiator of our sweltering nights. Yet, it holds a hidden beauty, and its dark surface shines under rainy skies. It is accessible year–round and supports all sorts of uses. Lastly, it keeps the urban ground smooth and integrates drainage management. Beneath the urban floor lies a sub–layer of "supporting" materials, typically draining and inert. Once properly managed, they are ripe to host a whole community of pioneering and wandering plants.

We like to say that there are no "good" or "bad" soils, just different soil types to establish a vegetal dynamic (or encourage spontaneous growth) by selecting the right plant communities. The experience gained from our asphalt gardens has shown that "road soils" can actually become fertile ground for the vegetation to reclaim urban space.

In our asphalt gardens, we opt not to (or rarely) remove materials from the site, but instead cut, crush, and sort materials to create a porous, fertile "neo–soil". On port slabs, parking lots, and densely built residential areas we have experimented with de–waterproofing techniques to restore the fertility of the soil, so it could accommodate some form of nature.

By minimizing material export and thus reducing costly waste production, and by treating urban soil as a resource, we create spaces that welcome small wildlife at a competition–beating cost per square meter. The costs depend on the materials in place, the scale of the project,and its intended uses. In its most "basic" forms, this approach can be ten times cheaper than traditional landscaping.

Just so you know: we are not here to sell something "cheap," but rather to question the amount of energy and funds a project needs. It's better to put money into thinking and expertise than into expensive solutions driven by the logic of percentage–based fee that ties the designer's compensation to the total cost of construction.

Being able to reuse our waste and recycle the materials that already existed on–site lets us save on materials and resources and thus develop a sustainable economy for the project. This adds value by incorporating some very real resilience right into the production process. The site itself generates and shapes the project. However, this doesn't stop us from seeking "luxury," as we invest in materials or design in certain key areas, and overall, create quality spaces for users.

Under the asphalt... life

We use asphalt as a project material: it has served as a foundation for several of our projects, for example here in Aubervilliers.

The Happy Garden was primarily about soil. The project started on the site, shovel in hand. One morning, together with the OPH (the Public Housing Agency of Aubervilliers), we lifted a few slabs and tried to dig below the asphalt layer. There was no underground parking or cellars underneath, but the structure of the parking lot was quite impressive. Under the asphalt, we found an almost 15-centimeter thick concrete slab – luckily, deeply fractured – and then several layers of compacted gravel. Digging painfully to a depth of 40 cm, we barely reached the backfills, also cemented. We poured in a bottle of water; half an hour later, the water was still there. The parking lot was practically isolated from fertile, porous soil.

The parking lot has been demolished, but we kept intact the rainwater drainage gutter that ran through the site, from one end to the other.

The ground has developed an interesting crust. Randomly lifted, the chunks of asphalt and concrete slabs have formed a labyrinth of cavities of different shapes and depths. These fragments of slabs were oriented in all directions, facing south, shade-wards, east, and west. From this chaos, a fertile porosity emerged, capable of supporting new growth.

The idea of a rustic rockery, an alpine garden for the city, quickly came to mind. Why not create here in Aubervilliers an alpine garden worthy of the 19th-century botanical parks and gardens? A visit to the rock garden in Paris's Jardin des Plantes has sealed the deal. The ambition is high; this parking lot transformed into a rockery must become exemplary in terms of floral richness and scale. There was no plan to export materials or bring in soil – this would have required too much money (at least €100/ton) and energy, eating up most of the design and construction budget. The solution was simple: add fertility between the tangled slabs and put together a plant palette suited to this unique environment and matching in richness and diversity the passionate creations of the botanists of the past.

Time and observation: the project's allies

After the design and implementation phases were over, we agreed with the OPH on including in our contract a year–long monitoring and maintenance assignment. In this way, we could keep discussing the garden's evolution with the client and also during our regular encounters with the residents. Completed in October, the site didn't look particularly impressive upon delivery. Only we could appreciate the 40 m^3 of soil scattered in the cracks and the small G9 pots packed in at over 5 per square meter... and don't even ask about the seeding! Delivering the project during the winter season was crucial as the site needed to soak up rainwater. Watered only once during planting, the garden has been left to fend for itself afterward.

In the first spring, the annual seeds did their job: it was an explosion that we had to manage to help the perennials grow. So our initial interventions consisted in creating space around the plantings. Whatever we pulled out was instantly reused as mulch around the planted pots.

The first–year monitoring contract initiated by ourselves has convinced the OPH that this experimental space required careful attention of the gardeners. Our initial efforts helped the garden develop in its first year, but also gave us the chance to talk with passersby about the ongoing experiment taking place at this site.

A few years later, the residents managed to save the garden from being partly demolished to accommodate drilling for the Grand Paris Express.

On our end, after a successful first year, we set up a maintenance contract with the OPH, which has been renewed every year for the past five years. Six visits per year let us continue gardening based on observing the natural dynamics.

Alongside these interventions, we regularly collect soil samples to understand how the plants transform and enrich the soil. This project is part of a research/action initiative funded by ADEME, where we are looking at the evolution of the soils that we have created and the plants. From these observations, we plan to collect a wide range of objective data on the benefits of transforming, without exporting, the initially inert urban soils. Based on long-term observations, these analyses will be used to create a best practices guide for municipalities and urban management services.

Climate change and the implementation of the ZNA (zero net artificialization) policy make the ability to recycle impermeable soils for urban renaturing and greening a crucial issue. Wagon's ten-years worth of experiments in creating fertile soils and designing public spaces on existing urban land has proven the effectiveness of this approach.

3.D The Punk Garden

— Montholon

Discover the thirst for freedom that motivates gardeners!

The sense of wonder drives creativity. No need to consider oneself a sage or to discover the secret to saving the planet – just get to work! From now on, taking the care to settle in with humility becomes the sign of a major project... Éric Lenoir's take on Putting Life first is a tangible utopia tied to a specific place and born from the close connections developed over time with the Others.

This example sparks the freedom to create and make do, stimulating a healthy drive to take action and embody the Planetary gardener within us. Punk gardens are an invitation to explore and play other scores, the ones that place life at the heart of the gardener's work. So why don't we start our own experiments as soon as tomorrow – provided they are as productive as they are nonconformist!

Mission Experimentation, education, showcasing, protection
Location Yonne, Northern Burgundy, France
Geographical coordinates 47°54'59"N, 3°18'30"E
Size Le Flérial – 1,4 ha + 3000 m² for the commercial nursery, La Haie de Morgon – 1,7 ha, La Louptière – 1 ha
Status Private property open to the public by appointment (except for La Louptière, which is a natural sanctuary)
Budget Under 25 000 €, excluding nursery development and land purchase
Project concept Éric Lenoir

Photo credits Éric Lenoir (unless otherwise specified)

— Phasing
2011 Acquisition of the first two agricultural parcels, which had been lying fallow for 3 years. One-year observation period
2012 Fencing of Le Flérial and La Haie de Morgon and start of development work (earthworks, access, structural planting, creation of ditches and ponds).
2014 Acquisition of La Louptière. The parcel will be designated as a protected area, serving as a test case and wooded ecological sanctuary.
2018 Le Flérial has become the benchmark punk garden hosting educational, tourist and professional visits, meetings and various events focused on ecology, landscape, agriculture, and social imperatives of our time.
2020 La Haie de Morgon has become an experimental garden dedicated to food production in the conditions of collapse (of resources and biodiversity). Creation of 7 experimental plots for food production.

Even in the worst *ha*
finds a way to make
gradually transformi
to make it even more

itats, **Life always**
lasting **appearance,**
g the environment
hospitable **to Life.**

3.D

The punk gardens, *experimental and vibrant with life*

Experimenting with the gardens where human intervention is kept to a bare minimum, only to make sure they serve their intended purposes.

Reimagining one's role within ecosystems and landscapes by breaking free from traditional gardening practices to make the most of existing natural balances, boost biodiversity, and develop cooperative approaches to design and maintenance. Proving that you can create and take care of productive gardens with minimal resources, respectful of life, even in the Capitalocene era.

Exploring ways to solve problems associated with limited resources, urban overdevelopment, food resilience, biodiversity loss, and resource depletion.

Eric Lenoir

3.1
Considering the landscape project as a negotiation platform

The project came together after a thoughtful analysis of environmental conditions, human needs to be met, and the ability to meet them. To act without causing harm and within our capabilities; to save energy and resources; to balance technical possibilities, necessities, and the preservation or enhancement of native biodiversity were the cornerstones of this project, which has grown over time.

In view of the global threat to the living world – the erosion of biodiversity is reaching new heights, particularly in arable farming areas such as northern Burgundy – we made a fast decision to reverse the usual approach of transforming a site based on what we thought it would give us. Instead, we started by making a list of everything we could do without.

At the same time, the whole setup was designed to ensure that everything within the gardens is protected from potential external threats, most of all from conventional farming and hunting. The main non-road works aimed to create spaces that would enhance biodiversity (elevated dry areas, different types of ponds, meadows, and hedgerows), and to help plants take root by creating a variety of nano-climates and habitats that the sites were missing.

In La Haie de Morgon, negotiation also concerns the people talking terms with each other. For instance, the individuals or collectives experimenting with the seven plots have to share common spaces and water resources.

3.2
Building community by gardening together

The conceptual phase of the project involved balancing human needs with those of the rest of the living world – which made it both necessary and natural to observe existing balances and set up cooperation and facilitation tools. The necessity to plant hedgerows in this extremely windy area was also an opportunity to create a very useful biotope for crop auxiliaries needed in the nursery and throughout the gardens.

With very limited financial resources available for the project, after the earthworks were completed, we used the species available nearby, those that could be salvaged, and those we could plant directly as cuttings (mainly willow). Even though willow may not be the best choice in terms of biodiversity, it helped protect the site from external threats early on, created nesting spots for arboreal birds, provided shade, and established useful ecological corridors.

These imperfect hedges have also accelerated the formation of a soil richer in organic matter and humus – something the site badly needed after years of conventional farming.

To balance the overabundance of willows, trees and shrubs from local hedgerow species were randomly added, breaking up the uniformity. And so it was with all developments on the project sites.

↑ ©Pierre-Emmanuel De Leusse

3.3
Turning the project into a score that unfolds over time

The three-garden project began with Le Flérial, which was the only one initially planned (and half the size of what we have actually got). The grazing of La Haie de Morgon and the preservation of La Louptière gave us the time needed to analyze the ecological phenomena observed at Le Flérial, where maintenance is limited to the bare essentials. Here, only the paths and a small lawn of about 500 m² (out of 14,000 m²) are mowed, and none of the plants are watered except by rain and dew. The decision to allow access to most species had both advantages and limitations. Domestic animals, wild boars, and deer are kept out of Le Flérial and La Haie de Morgon, while La Louptière has no fencing. Over time, we have come to understand the local ecosystem – which obviously includes humans – far beyond the physical boundaries of the gardens, helping us fine-tune our goals. Meanwhile, the features we have put in place are gradually reaching maturity, yielding results and giving us time to develop the next steps of our projects… or simply enjoy them.

The only thing we can be sure of is that we are merely tenants of a territory whose future after we are gone is not ours to control. Rooted in a constantly unfolding present, we can only acknowledge how much the garden embodies the "No Future" concept, because we don't know what will happen to it after us, no matter what we are hoping for.

3.4
Expressing care for the living world through aesthetic resolution

When you adopt a strategy aimed at removing all avoidable nuisances, you start making use of both the existing and the unexpected. The plans you have drafted are tested by the real conditions on the ground. No, we won't plant where we know the hare passes every day, and no, we won't dig a hole too close to that burrow which might house a weasel or a polecat. As for cutting down this pioneer tree on the pretext that it's not the ideal species, we'll think twice, especially since it provides the best source of shade in the garden.

In La Haie de Morgon, we'll need biomass to support the crops without having to bring it in from outside sources. Therefore, many of the non-fruit trees will be pruned as pollards, letting us use their wood and leaves without ever having to cut them down. These pollards live exceptionally long and are extremely valuable in providing habitat for the wildlife that is looking for cavities or large trunks – not to mention these trees' remarkable aesthetic. In the two gardens that have not been turned into sanctuaries, the ditches, hedges, ponds, as well as raised areas that support a wide range of biodiversity and demanding plant species, all structure the space by making it clear these are gardens. At the same time, they create an odd sense of "wilderness" coming from the great freedom allowed to the plants despite our minimally assessed needs.

Pictured: experimental parcels at La Haie de Morgon. In the foreground, a plot developed by Nadia Aouès.

I don't like slogans. T
the *time* **needed to bu**
and give us the impre
is an easy general sol
– when in fact everyth
of specific cases, eacl
complexity **and** *wonder*

ey cut short
d thoughtful ideas,
sion that there
tion to everything
ng is a multitude
with its own *sublime*
ful imperfection.

The greater the *diversity*, the better the *chances* for Life to sustain itself in this area for a long time.

Le Flérial

At the beginning, there was just one project: to find a 5,000 m^2 plot to relocate my small nursery that uses no chemical treatments, and set up a demo–garden where a few mother plants would grow amidst some joyful local flora, singing birds, and whimsical frogs.

After more than three years of fruitless searching, an opportunity finally presented itself, and it was massive: two agricultural plots of 1.7 hectares each, left fallow on poor waterlogged soil at the top of a windy hill nicknamed "little Siberia", fell into my lap for a pittance (the soil was too bad to attract farmers). The entire project, which naturally had a strong ecological focus, had to be managed by me alone and on a tight budget, with objectives adapted to its unexpected dimensions. What could have been a burden turned out to be a boon: instead of a small garden that wouldn't have let me do much beyond the usual, I now had the chance to prove that giving plenty of space to non–human life was not only possible but would make the Garden thrive in every way.

In ten years, Le Flérial has transformed significantly, looking like a garden in the more designed parts and retaining its wild side in the areas that are not meant to be accessible. Maintenance involves mowing paths and selectively – but never exhaustively – cutting pioneer plants and other unwanted species where they aren't welcome. Field species have been joined by hedgerow, meadow, wetland species, and some transient forest species. With the scythe replacing the brush cutter, you can hear the viper warning of its presence – prompting you to work elsewhere – and avoid slicing fragile amphibians or ground-nesting birds.

The various configurations formed on the site during the initial earthworks created the conditions suitable for new species, which could not tolerate the waterlogged soil in winter that turned into concrete in summer. And, because the original conditions – the fallow land that wasn't especially diverse but still alive – were not completely destroyed to make way for a new picture perfect space, the forms of life multiplied, benefiting from existing balances and interactions. As a result, ornamental and horticultural varieties found a suitable place within the local population of plants, microbes, and animals, their association helping mitigate on-site problems.

“Sooner or later, ever to be *broken*. Sometin sometimes out of des important to take pre against the grain to c new, more *stimulatin* mind, or for biodivers

— **Eric Lenoir** *Le grand traité du jardin punk (The comprehens*

y rule **deserves**
es out of necessity,
re, it becomes
efined ideas and go
eate something
for the eye, for the
ty."

guide to punk gardens), © Terre Vivante, 2021

Put away your *mower,* **come watch the grass grow and count the** *butterflies***!**

↓ A rainwater catchment basin and two experimental plots in La Haie de Morgon

La Haie de Morgon

The living world that integrates humans, the gardens that fit into a human-altered ecosystem whether we like it or not – one of our parcels is dedicated to addressing some of the contemporary social issues.

In La Haie de Morgon, the goal is clear: make this plot a new experimental ground to learn how to grow food with deep respect for Life and resources. The site is designed with trees for biomass and building materials, certain plants for healing, others for food or fertilization – and a significant portion of the land necessarily dedicated to other species, neither human nor exploitable, but whose presence is essential, desired, and beneficial. In this transitory place where one comes to cultivate small vegetable plots for free during a growing season, or to attend trainings and visits, humans are encouraged to adopt the most humble posture possible, finding ways to satisfy their needs with minimal impact on other living beings. Moreover, they have to share rainwater, as there is no drilling or piping to ensure unlimited use of this critical resource.

↗ Experimental plot designed by Nadia Aouès, at La Haie de Morgon

The Garden of La Louptière

Finally, there is one more Garden that completes the trio, even though there is no actual reason to classify it as such. In La Louptière that spreads across one hectare, human intervention is limited to maintaining a path to explore and observe how this place evolves. In less than 10 years, this old meadow has quickly turned into a thick forest covered by a variety of willows, birches, and poplars now over 6 meters tall, forming a thicket that was once impenetrable. Despite being turned into a wildlife sanctuary, La Louptière Garden is not richer in biodiversity than the other two. It hosts different species typical of forests and wooded wastelands, but not those found in meadows, for example. Nevertheless, it remarkably complements Le Flérial and La Haie de Morgon, serving as a benchmark site to demonstrate what a garden looks like when left largely unattended.

Act **minimally to cause minimal** *harm.*

Step back **and let the rest of the** *living world* **express itself.**

3.E
Lago Bullicante

— Rome

A productive fight for a life community project

The Lago Bullicante initiative is backed by several Roman collectives, including the group behind the Ex SNIA environmental project, in which the Bullicante lake plays a key role. Born from a controversial real estate development that has breached the groundwater table, this new lake became a symbol of the community's fight to preserve the ecological value resulting from years of abandonment.

The value given by the community's claims to this *Third Landscape* has led to the expropriation of a part of the site and its declaration as a Natural Monument. Many experts, naturalists, lawyers, and artists have joined the cause of Lago Bullicante. We are happy to invite the lake to speak through its human representatives.

Mission Transforming an urban lake into a communal space
Location Rome, Italy
Geographical coordinates 41°53'42"N, 12°32'23"E
Size A 1–hectare lake and a 3–hectare urban park expropriated in 2014 from a former factory and managed by the Parco delle Energie forum. The entire surface area of the former factory is 14 hectares (partly public, partly private); 7 hectares are still privately owned.
Management Forum territoriale Parco delle Energie

— Status
Before 2014 Private property
Since 2014 Self–managed public property, available for public access
Since 2020 Declared a natural monument

← ©Morteza Khaleghi

↓ ©Mohammad Khavari

BEAC

The Lago Bullicant
idea; it's a *conflict*
Relationships and l
building blocks and
This is a story abou
social creativity and
as project authors.

is not a design
urned into a project.
egalities are its
tools for creation.
t recognizing
natural spontaneity

3.E

Lago Bullicante, *turning an urban lake into a communal space*

In the 1990s, a few kilometers east of the Colosseum, construction started on the site of the former SNIA textile factory to make way for an underground parking lot as part of a large shopping center project. Members of the local community challenged the project's legality and filed a lawsuit. However work continued until, due to forged maps, the excavation team struck an underground water reserve. The site flooded, as did nearby streets, and efforts to pump out the water have failed. The construction project was ultimately abandoned, leaving the "Lago Bullicante" to form around the techno-ruin of the shopping center.

Stalker — Giulia Fiocca and Lorenzo Romito

← ©Fulvia Bernacca

3.1
Considering the landscape project as a negotiation platform

The case of Lago Bullicante exemplifies a shift from a spontaneous event to a negotiation platform; bridging the formal and informal sides, it culminated in the establishment of a legal status for living things. The power of a conflict that started locally and saw intense spikes of tension has been structured through legal and legislative avenues.

This project is a case study in unpredictability, the one where a human error created the potential for nature–driven innovation. The outcome of a conflict over a construction project and subsequent technical failure, this abandoned site became a refuge of various life forms, with humans keeping their distance. The remnants of human activity, as well as the site's pollution, have facilitated the novel and innovative relationships developed by the plants and animals settled in this ecosystem. The Lago Bullicante has formed an environment that was able to survive human violence and even provide benefits to the local community: the diverse life forms attracted and transformed by the lake include the people living nearby.

The dynamic continues to this day. With the lake becoming the subject of national and international research projects, the developer realized that the site, turned "natural" over time, had speculative interest but faced the risk of expropriation. In March 2021, they began to remove the vegetation that had grown there. This sparked a new conflict, first on–site and then at the legislative level, notably at the Capitol where the issue has been addressed from a symbolic perspective, with a focus on the legal status of life.

3.2
Building community by gardening together

The story of this spontaneous, wild place has brought together a very strong community. This neighborhood on the eastern side of Rome has already had a long tradition of self–organization, political struggles, and numerous social centers and associations. Many of these groups have gathered around the lake, acknowledging its significance, learning to take care of it, and questioning its future.

Over the years, local movements have shifted to the site proper. Thus, in 1997, its upper part where pine trees had been planted by the original factory owners became a public park. In 2013, the annual festival of the local social center was set up near the lake and temporarily occupied the skeleton of the shopping mall that still sat in the middle of the lake. It was at this time that the idea of making this place public began to take shape.

In 2014, one week before the expiration of the ten–year deadline allowing the City of Rome to carry out the expropriation of this land for public use, the residents' mobilization pushed the municipality to buy several hectares. These lands became public and were integrated into the Parco delle Energie. Managed through an annual associative assembly, the park has spawned a new discussion about the lake's function, and how it could be used by the residents. The assembly decided to fight to make all the land public. It is currently in a delicate position: the park's management is institutional, but the area left under undefined management is still largely owned by the former developer.

↑ ©Giordano Pennisi — scattomancino.com

↑ ©Giordano Pennisi — scattomancino.com

3.3
Turning the project into a score that unfolds over time

When the construction site around the lake was abandoned in 1992, nature took over and, since then, has been freely occupying the area for nearly 30 years. Located in a very dense and heavily polluted neighborhood, the place has been reclaimed by nature, trees, and non-human living beings. Over 200 bird species have been identified here. Moreover, it's an important migration spot as it is located at the center of a larger green corridor that runs from north to south and from the center to the east of the city.

The spread of life disrupts the idea that projects, planning, legislation, and the status of things alone define a space. This place is self-determined; humans can only care for it and manage the conflicts between the spontaneity of life and our concept of a development project. At some point, we found ourselves in conflict with nature because it had aspirations we no longer saw as compatible. Hard to pinpoint, this back-and-forth conflict does not place the enemy in the opposing camp but seeks to articulate a freedom of ecological coexistence as opposed to human ideological rigor.

3.4
Expressing care for the living world through aesthetic resolution

The status of a natural monument was meant to protect this place; however, it can also put it at risk. An ill-considered eco-restoration would harm the ecological process that resulted from abandonment and the presence of industrial remnants, which are not recognized as heritage, yet without which Bullicante wouldn't be what it is: under the lake, there are still cement trucks providing shelter for fish.

This illegal private ruin is in fact a laboratory. Today, we should avoid its restoration, which would cause new environmental damage, adding another disaster to the one that created this ecosystem. That's the contradiction we are facing today. The current stage of the project requires various skills: biological, geological, regulatory, social... To ensure the spread of these ideas, we aim to keep the place open, and here fencing becomes a crucial issue, because allowing access changes certain dynamics. The great value of this site comes from the fact that nothing has been done to it, but when you create a situation of doing nothing, it becomes an act, whether you intend it or not. Once the question of intervention and what needs to be done arises, we enter a different aesthetic realm.

The role of art is not limited to representation; it's also about social education and construction. Thinking about aesthetic resolution helps us envision how minimal constructive, narrative, or educational actions can shed new light on things. The poetry of places shaped beyond human intention reminds us that the beauty of life surpasses our imagination.

Based on an interview with Stalker (Giulia Fiocca and Lorenzo Romito)

↑ ©Mario Paloni

↑ ©Giordano Pennisi — scattomancino.com

The Lago Bullicante
questions about *the l*
and about the recogn
environmental damag
standpoint. These ar
matters that current
to address, allowing
the name *of private p*

aises
gal status of life,
tion of
e from a legislative
the urgent
aws find difficult
lestruction **in**
operty.

↓ © Pierre Kattar

Art and science go hand in hand in exploring this mytho-eco-logical landscape.

The unprecedented landscape of Lago Bullicante is part of a system of landscapes emerging from the most neglected areas of the metropolitan territory. These are the creative epicenters of what we mapped with Stalker as Current Territories back in 1995. The manifesto that accompanied our first exploratory tour described "abandonment as the highest form of care" for landscapes.

Unique and unpredictable, they are also remarkably in line with the history of the Roman landscape, which is characterized by the mythological idea of a city built on the ruins of the Golden Age. Reclaimed both by the wild nature of Latium and the historical perspective of the Renaissance, it has always coexisted with the ruins.

Wild nature takes over the remnants of a weary era to shelter life forms that are alien to its codes and aesthetic order. In doing so, it triggers a series of possible relationships between itself and what has survived from the past. It also accommodates beings that have come from elsewhere. With these ingredients, nature becomes a mytho-eco-logical framework for unfolding the possibility of a fresh start after the end of an era. Rome is rich in wild landscapes and ruins where a variety of epochs, cultures, and species live together. The precariousness and uncertainty of the present contains countless potential worlds, among which the future might find an unpredictable path: an environment in which humans lose control of space and time – something literature often portrays as happily disorienting (like in Greek Arcadia and Virgilian Latium).

→ ©Pierre Kattar

GO È BENE DI TUTTI
NIALIZZAZIONE!

From biopolitics to biodiversity

It is relevant to draw a parallel with ecological transition. Urban nature is now a focal point in ecological studies due to its capacity to foster biodiversity, a rare and essential characteristic amidst the planet's dramatically widespread loss of living diversity. Places where urban nature can reinvent itself away from human pressures are invaluable. We must find strategies to preserve them, involving political struggle, artistic expression, and direct action. Radical approaches are probably needed, alongside the steadfast patience of a gardener.

Within the ecologically creative dimension of abandonment, the recent and rapid growth of biodiversity in this place has coincided with the end of its anthropic, industrial, and urban history. The depletion and economic exploitation of the area, combined with the significant loss of human control and dominance over the environment, mark the end of a cycle of capitalism that breeds neglect. The industrial production of viscose is environmentally polluting and socially alienating. It is precisely the abandonment of the factory that has allowed for the spontaneous refuge of other life forms in a heavily urbanized area. As a result, first multi-species ecological networks have started to be rebuilt, and the architectural structures that used to facilitate industrial exploitation got transformed into geomorphological features matching the site's geological complexity.

↑ ©Mohammad Khavari
↑ ©Pierre Kattar

Thirty years of empathy and struggle with the lake

This is when humans start getting re-involved in the realm of action – no longer as generators of dominance and entropy from above, but as allies from below to the spontaneously generated emerging ecosystem. As a catalyst for animal and plant communities, and thus biodiversity, the lake also becomes a magnet for sociodiversity, drawing in an emerging human community just like it did for other life forms. Matched with the creative evolution of the ecosystem promoted by the lake, the empathy of this new community has sharpened people's eco-sensitivity, making it more diverse, complex, competent, and giving birth to a new ecological awareness that has propelled people into a long struggle for the recognition and protection of the lake and its ecosystemic future, managed through the Energy Park's Territorial Forum (Forum).

Lasting for nearly 30 years, this struggle has led to the expropriation of and media attention to a large part of the area – and, more recently, to the recognition of a portion of the site as a natural monument. The slow pace, partial publicity, and calls for protection – sadly not yet extended to the entire factory zone – have sparked a violent reaction from the owner of the last 7 hectares that still remain private. Faced with a process that marginalized them and laid the groundwork for non-buildability, and even expropriation of the area, the owner systematically bulldozed thousands of trees and shrubs on their land. This destruction of an environment that – precisely because it remained inaccessible and abandoned – was an extremely important nesting site and a critical ecological buffer towards the most polluted and densely populated areas of Via Prenestina, illustrated the absurdity of the situation: to preserve the real estate interest of the site, let's trash its entire ecological value! Having nothing left to protect, the struggle would have made no more sense.

Just leaving certain places alone can become an integral part of a project.

↑ ©Pierre Kattar
↑ ©Fulvia Bernacca
↑ ©Giordano Pennisi – scattomancino.com

A reversal of roles: the lake as an implementing agent

Let's acknowledge the richness of biological and social self-organization forms: it is the lake, and not the humans, that should be recognized as the driving force behind a system with this level of complexity. This is why the proposed project/action does not aim to regain control over a highly effective ecological process, but rather to understand, share, document, narrate, perceive, socialize, and support the non-human process of ecosystem regeneration – exactly where the ecosystem has been repeatedly damaged by humans. It is precisely this aspect that gives meaning to the recognition, even partial, of the site as a natural monument, grants the project its experimental status, and makes it of high collective interest due to its role in fighting the human-induced loss of biodiversity.

Recognizing a non-human, non-living entity such as a lake as the creator of a landscape becomes part of contemporary debate and challenges our ability to place this creator at the center and understand its dynamics. The lake doesn't argue; it just acts.

The lake is not alone; it's part of Earth's living system. The act of personifying it, giving it a poetic identity, making it an author, even a legal entity, makes more sense than ever. There is a precedent where a sacred river in India was recognized as having rights. Why not Bullicante? Other animistic cultures see bodies of water as friends, even relatives. Some even view water as the mother of all humans. From a contemporary science perspective, this isn't far-fetched. To date, we know of no life without water, and therefore the sympathy for Bullicante, this lake that came to life so unexpectedly, ceases to surprise us.

An agency for ecological regeneration

The ecological and social process triggered by the emergence of Lake Bullicante has known many successful battles that gave us tools and methods for protecting, using, and respectfully managing the creative future of this emerging ecosystem. However, we also remember the lost battles, and the threat of losing an ecosystem that is vital for the whole city is looming over us. Whether we win or lose, we must learn from this unique process of transforming the city–nature relationship, paving the way for major shifts in urban planning, environmental laws, research, education, and social behavior.

With Lake Bullicante, we are exploring ways to bring about the fundamental changes that are necessary to avoid succumbing to climate disruption. Municipal administration can play a role by recognizing and encouraging this type of agency in each of the emerging urban ecosystems. This includes offering local institutional actors – including residents, activists, researchers, and educators – the shared management of these common resources, as well as the support needed to redesign institutional rules and practices with ecological considerations in mind, facilitating their implementation and preventing further environmental damage.

While waiting for institutional action, we suggest giving a name and purpose to this much-needed agency that addresses the urgent need for urban eco-social regeneration: DAFNE, Damage to the Environment and Formation of New Ecosystems.

— Lorenzo Romito

↗↗ ©Mohammad Khavari
↗ ©Pierre Kattar

↑ ©Pierre Kattar
↑ ©Pino Ramacciato

↓ ©Giordano Pennisi – scattomancino.com

3.F The Transformer

– Saint–Nicolas–de–Redon

Imagining a place for innovation and building it together

The Transformer of Redon started as an educational initiative in collaboration with the ENSP de Versailles (the Versailles National School of Landscape Architecture). For many years, this action research project has been the basis for on–site learning activities and has significantly contributed to the development of the project culture on the ground.

The Call to Create approach has allowed us to consistently optimize our resources and the ways of sharing this complex, flood–prone terrain that has, little by little, grown into a model for many other initiatives. With a fifteen–year track record of experimental work and collective organization, the project is evolving toward welcoming new members and audiences. What makes this collective effort interesting is its ability to grow and adapt to new situations, both on–site and in long–term governance.

Mission Nature restoration on an industrial brownfield site
Location Saint–Nicolas–de–Redon, France
Geographical coordinates 47°38′46.8″N, 2°05′03.3″W
Size 350 hectares
Status Industrial brownfield
Annual budget 42 000€ ex–tax
Implementation 2003 – ongoing

— Team
Client The Loire–Atlantique Departmental Council, Françoise Verchère
Project stewardship Collaboration with landscaper Gabriel Chauvel and Les Amis du Transformateur (The Friends of the Transformer)

— Institutional partners
The Loire–Atlantique Departmental Council: agreement, grant; the Municipality of Saint–Nicolas: free use of administrative space and kitchen, participation in some of the projects; the Municipality of Redon: allocation of land for the shared garden; La CCPR (Community of Municipalities of the Pays de Redon); Le GIP (Public Interest Group) pays de Redon; L'AIRE (Intercommunal Association for Employment Reintegration), integration through economic activity program.

— Partner associations and other local partners
Partnerships with schools, vocational training centers, integration programs, environmental education organizations, social and cultural associations, private owners of grazing land, and farmers.

Les Amis du Transformateur also collaborate with the associations that share the site and the building where the offices are located: Noria et Compagnie, Eco–building Training Center, and Un Vélo pour l'Afrique, a group that repairs and refurbishes bicycles.

Photo credits Les Amis du TransFo (unless otherwise specified)

**The Transformer follo
it** *sees* **waste as raw m
sorting things properl
value, and it only has
find whatever is miss
biodiversity – all of it
types), worksites, and
It becomes a better th
and a better practitior**
thinking. **The Transfo
that it** *writes* **as it acts**

ws a few rules:
aterials, it *knows* **that**
y gives them
to look around to
ng. It *sets*
- free. **It** *loves* **soil (all**
having fun.
nker through *practice,*
er through
rmer likes to think

.

3.F

The Transformer, *nature restoration on an industrial brownfield*

Created in July 2005, the association Les Amis du Transformateur (Friends of the Transformer) enables and oversees the return to nature on the site of the former Sébilleau joinery works, a protected natural area since 2003. The site is now owned by the Loire-Atlantique Department. Under an agreement with the department, the association supports, promotes, and guides the transformation process. It works to develop the site's biological diversity and facilitate the flow of floodwaters from the Vilaine river to the nearby marsh. It also manages a number of private and public hedgerow sites. To do all of this, the association runs several workshops: Beekeeping, Cattle Breeding, Collective Vegetable Gardening, Orchard, Nature Projects, Cooking, Poetic Nature Arts, and Public Events.

Les Amis du Transformateur

3.1 Considering the landscape project as a negotiation platform

Our starting point was an industrial wasteland, the former site of a wood-processing company that had operated in this area since the beginning of the 20th century before it went bankrupt. Abandoned for a while, the land was flooded a number of times, and for nearly fifteen years became a lawless area, a sort of illegal dump for the town of Saint-Nicolas-de-Redon. After a series of floods in 1995–2001, local officials started wondering what to do with this land. In 2003, a professor from the Versailles National School of Landscape Architecture (ENSP) who lived near Redon, had the idea to bring his students to the site for what he called regional workshops. The students came up with development ideas, sometimes realistic, and often quite insightful.

Concerned about the land, its owner, the departmental council, accepted the students' proposals. They almost gave carte blanche to the Versailles faculty. Some discussions did occur, however, but mainly between the volunteers and the school, regarding various choices for the site's development.

Goals have been set between the council and the school: firstly, to bring nature back to this damaged site, and secondly, to use this area, prone to flooding from the Vilaine, as a flood retention basin.

3.2 Building community by gardening together

Right from the outset, there were many discussions between students, professors, elected officials, and neighbors about the proposed developments. In 2005, an association was formed to help with practical issues and facilitate interactions with the departmental council. This association is still active today, counting about one hundred members, mostly volunteers.

These days, the relationship with the departmental council isn't as smooth – however, we have a management contract with them, making this relationship more official. Another change has come from the members themselves. Initially, they were often landscapers or people interested in the overall project for the site. Today, the members are more local and more consumer-like. The association is organized into workshops, and one of the risks of this setup is losing sight of the Transfo as a larger, more complex project. Some people come only for the training and then leave after two years. This helps spread the practice but is absolutely not the same in terms of commitment.

We keep opening up to new audiences, including schools. We are working with the LPO (Bird Protection League) and a number of environmental groups. We are in touch with other cities like Bordeaux, which is looking to replicate some of our experiences. We are also exploring new ways to engage people without requiring them to become members.

↑ © René Perron

↑ © René Perron

↑ Belvedere ©S. Argant

↑ Seed trap ©S. Argant

3.3
Turning the project into a score that unfolds over time

The Transformer is clearly a long–term project. The initial period of intense reflection started with the early involvement of the Versailles School and the architecture schools of Rennes and Nantes. Then came about ten years of development work, which have taken precedence over other activities. During this time, half of our members were landscapers, professors, current and former students. Back then, the Transfo had a national presence rather than a local one, while local residents had a distorted, or even negative, view of our actions. Over time, the local population has joined us and now outnumbers the landscapers.

The most significant change involved the association's strategic direction. Once the landscape was set up, it had to be kept alive, which wasn't easy. Managing a landscape can become a monotonous job, and some members lost their initial enthusiasm because there were no more big ideas or projects to get inspired with. Some of the original members were replaced by the new ones who were happy to keep the place alive. The association has opened up to other people, forming ties with the associations who were close to us either geographically or ideologically, and who wanted to share and promote our work. We now organize numerous visits and host associations or elected officials interested in how we manage a reclaimed brownfield.

3.4
Expressing care for the living world through aesthetic resolution

Aesthetics has always been an integral part of the project. The association is organized into various workshops, including one specifically called "Arts," which demonstrates the importance given to this aspect. For instance, in the Bosquito area, we arranged the recovered rubble in an aesthetically pleasing way.

Bringing nature back to this site can happen in different ways: we either let it come on its own, help it along, or manage it. For example, the large platform is an open space that we want to leave as it is; we mow the land and have brought in a herd of eight Nantaise cows.

Aesthetics is closely linked to practical choices. Thus, to ensure flood management on the site, it was necessary to build dikes and moats to retain and evacuate water. Initially, the departmental council planned to tear down all of the buildings, to avoid blocking the water flow and return the site almost to its original state. Historically, these were marshes, lying one meter below water level and filled in to accommodate business facilities. Going back to the original state would then imply removing seven hectares of fill to a height of one meter. However, we had established a fundamental principle of not removing anything from the site. Nothing goes in, nothing comes out. We have been working with existing materials for over fifteen years. In a way, this is the second meaning of the word "transformer." The Transformer is a place for experimenting and transforming waste into building materials.

↓ ©Flavien Guidoux

The transformation of an industrial brownfield into a natural area

In December 1991, after a tough decade, the joinery company called Société d'exploitation des menuiseries Sébilleau (Semès) ceased all industrial activities at the Saint-Nicolas-de-Redon site – leaving behind a vacant 5.5 hectare-area, several buildings including a 2,800 m² hall and a 1,620 m² warehouse, a large asphalt platform, and heaps of different materials.

In January 1995, and then again in 1999, 2000, and 2001, severe floods affected all industrial and commercial structures on the site.

In 2001, the Loire-Atlantique Department decided to help protect those inhabiting the territory through applying the policies for sensitive natural areas. In partnership with the town of Saint-Nicolas-de-Redon, they commissioned the Versailles School of Landscape Architecture (ENSP) to conduct a study on the future of this industrial wasteland. From 2003 to 2005, the ENSP held a series of "regional educational workshops" with fourth-year students.

In response to the departmental council's query about the future of this site, the ENSP students proposed a development and management plan, and carried out a number of experimental projects on-site to test those ideas. They recommended a gentle and cost-effective approach to encourage natural reclamation. Only pollutants had to be removed, while other materials were meant to be kept on-site and repurposed for various uses (such as building dikes to protect the neighborhood in June 2005), or serving to support vegetation recovery.

In 2005, the Loire-Atlantique General Council purchased the site, now designated as a Sensitive Natural Area. Established in July of that year, the association Les Amis du Transformateur entered into an agreement with the General Council. The following objectives have been set: to manage and enhance sensitive natural areas within the municipality of Saint-Nicolas-de-Redon, to create conditions for public access and reception, and to document and disseminate the experiences gained on the site.

↗ Société d'exploitation des menuiseries Sébilleau, in the 1970s
© Robert Sébilleau's private collection
→ The flood of 1995, a photo from the Ouest France newspaper, photographer unknown.

GROWING SPECIALIZATION IN GARDEN MAINTENANCE

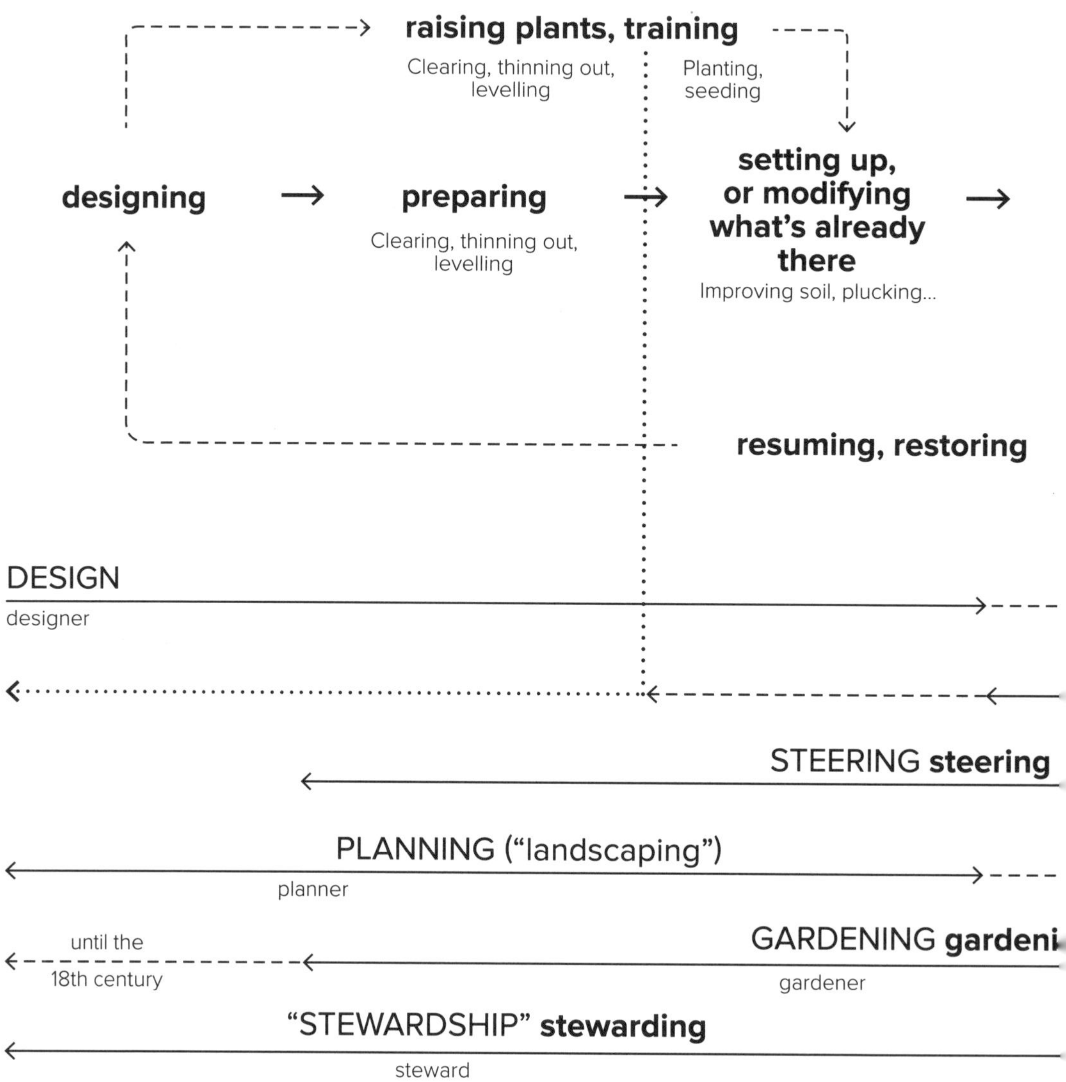

↑ For a long time, the multiple tasks involved in creating a garden – now handled by specialists of different educational and cultural backgrounds – all used to belong to the noble profession of gardening. The Transformer has been a major opportunity to try out a contemporary return to that unitary gardening ambition.
©Diagram by Marc Rumelhart revisited by Flavien Guidoux, Coloco

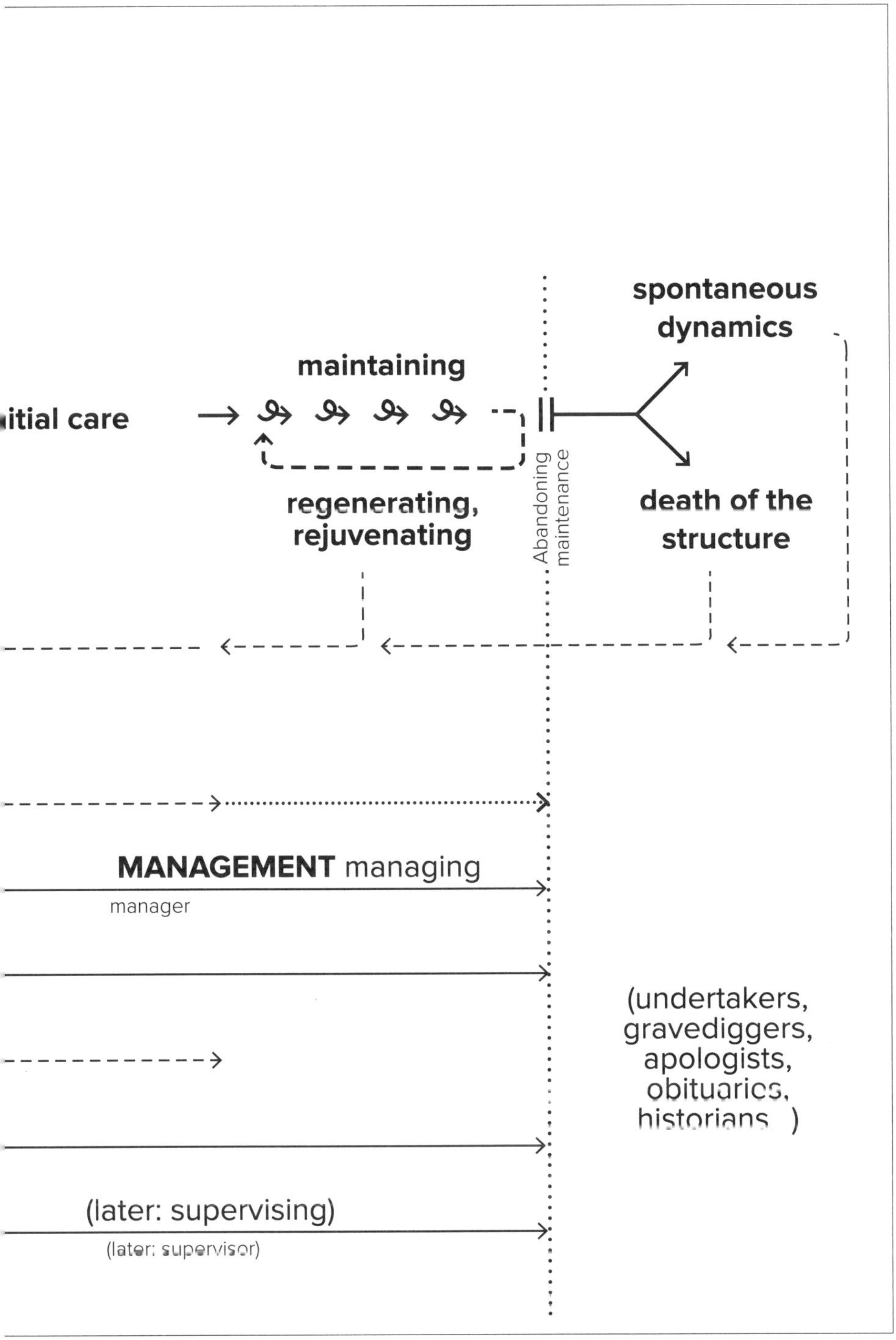
itial care
maintaining
regenerating, rejuvenating
Abandoning maintenance
spontaneous dynamics
death of the structure
MANAGEMENT managing
manager
(undertakers, gravediggers, apologists, obituarics, historians)
(later: supervising)
(later: supervisor)

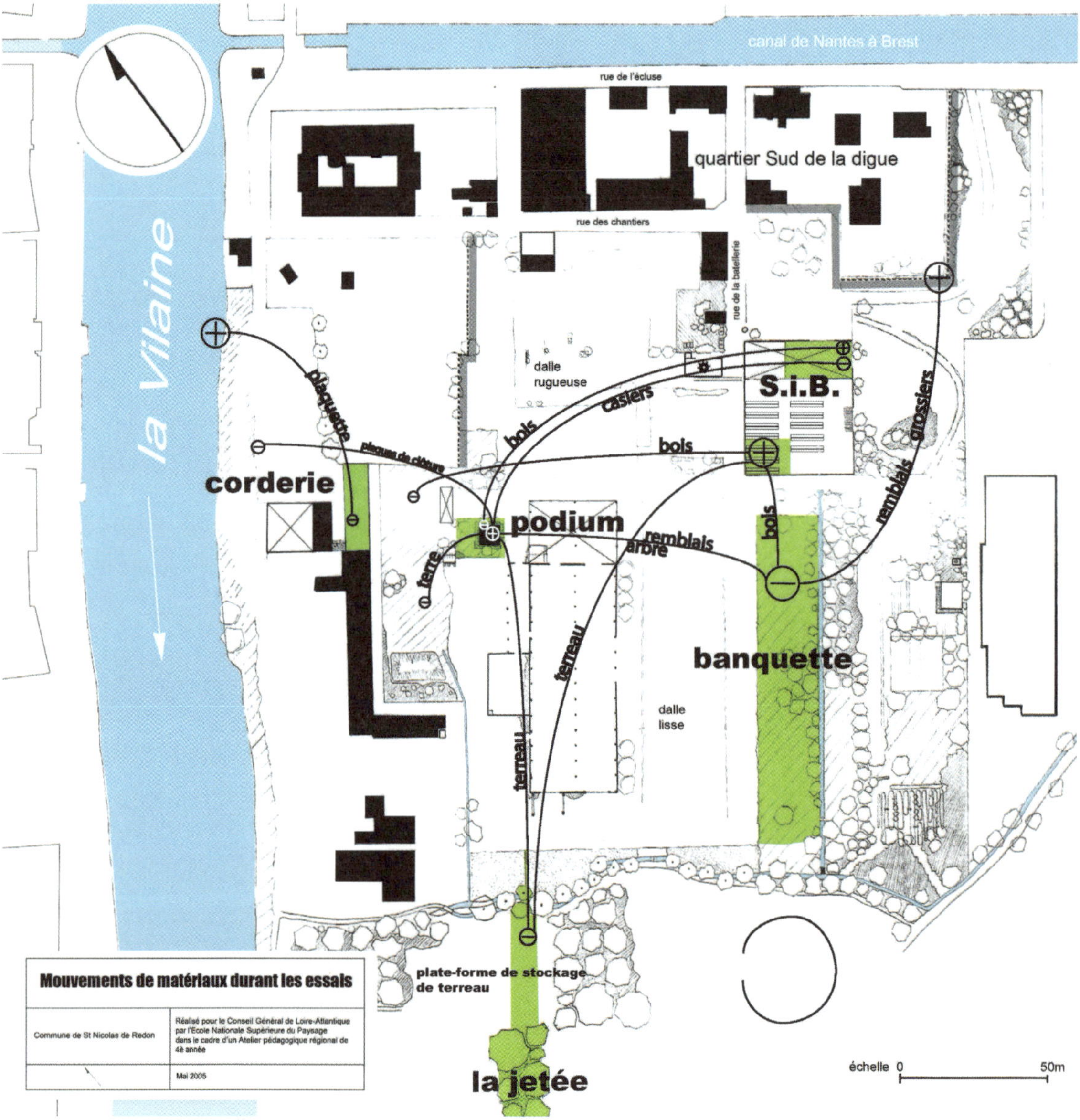

↑ Material flow during the testing phase
© L'ENSP Versailles

The Transformer *wastes nothing* **and** *creates* **through transforming everything.**

The Podium

We experimented with the concept of trees in the city, and thought of ways to introduce them as simply, minimally, and least labor-intensive as possible. The Podium is a building – the former canteen – where we have piled all the inert waste from the site and planted a tree on top of this pile. The roof has been removed, and today our sycamore maple is thriving.

Originally, the waste was up to the roof. Since then, the tree has gone down a meter and a half, growing and sinking at the same time. We did a similar experiment in another location – the drying shed – but we didn't clear the ground. After five years with no progress, the project was abandoned, and the materials piled in the drying shed were taken to the landfill as a one-time exception.

We have also sown and planted trees in a large former workshop known as la Société industrielle du bois (the Industrial Wood Company). The roof has been removed, the metal framework retained, and today the trees coexist with the framework.

↑ The Podium in its initial and current state
→ The Podium under transformation

The Bosquito

The numerous experiments carried out during the initial educational workshops of the ENSP Versailles and in the years that followed have shown that inert soil trapped under a concrete or asphalt slab remained fertile.

After multiple trials, we have carried out a project involving urban trees. On the Transformer's platform, we set up a small grove – hence the name Bosquito – and hosted a conference on the subject. Planted on a tough mix of fill, concrete, and asphalt, the Bosquito's purpose is to enhance biodiversity, which is why the site is closed to the public. In keeping with our reuse strategy, we utilized the fill materials from the site to build the protective perimeter.

The project follows a scientific approach. We have planted 432 plants across 27 plots, with each plot dedicated to one of the nine selected species: pedunculate oak, small-leaved lime, wild service tree, wild cherry, black locust, aspen, silver birch, white alder, and sweet chestnut. The Bosquito's progress is monitored every two years, with the site being visited by research teams from the University of Angers.

This ongoing experiment has already shown the potential of urban substrates, sparking creative ideas and practical approaches for phytoremediation with urban trees.

3.G
R–Urban
– Colombes, Gennevilliers, Bagneux, Paris, London...

Cultivating citizenship on creative soil

Delving deep into the innovations needed in these uncertain times, R–Urban has found itself at the heart of the city. Here, the conditions of proximity spark a Call to Create collectively. Commitment on the ground, together with the ambitions driven by ongoing inquiry, fuel the development of new project methodologies. Exchange and sharing guided by clearly defined values have turned R–Urban into an entity, a third party put forward by the collective, a vehicle for practices in constant evolution. Experimentation never stops, but convictions do solidify as we are living out this unprecedented relationship between location and activation. R–Urban is giving rise to new daily routines – convivial and fertile.

Mission Creation and setup of community–managed ecological transition hubs in several neighborhoods, with an aim to facilitate the shift towards resilient lifestyles.
Location Colombes, Paris, Gennevilliers, Bagneux, France, and London, UK, since 2011
Geographical coordinates 48°55'17.0"N, 2°17'21.0"E
Size Units from 25 m² to 300 m², parcels from 200 m² to 3000 m²
Budget Between 100 000 € and 1 500 000 €, depending on the location (from 150 000 € to 450 000 € per project and per unit)
Photo and image credits AAA

← Urban farming in the Agrocity of Colombes, 2012

— Team
Project owner Associated project ownership and participative project management: AAA with local partners from Colombes, Paris, Gennevilliers and Bagneux
Design / Strategy AAA
Institutional partners The European Commission; the municipalities of Colombes, Gennevilliers, Bagneux and Paris; la Métropole Grand Paris; the regional council of the IDF (the Paris Region), le Département 92, Ademe, Syctom, the foundations Carasso, Terre Solidaire, and Fondation de France. The Public Works collective (UK), a partner of R–Urban, has been developing a similar strategy in London since 2011. A new project is in the pipeline in Brezoi, a town in the Carpathian Mountains in Romania.

Popular ecology **at the**
block: we introduce
to enable *ecological tr*
in the middle of our n
places **for changing ou**
and *saving the planet,*
living beings, and dre
gaps **that support** *rhiz*

foot of a tower
co–citizen hubs
ansition **right**
eighborhoods, create
r daily lifestyles
co–build **with other**
am up urban
omatic **life.**

↓ Citizen Climate Day at the Agrocity and Recyclab R–Urban hubs, Bagneux 2021

3.G

R–Urban, *citizen–led ecological transition strategy*

Initiated in 2008, R–Urban is a citizen–driven ecological transition strategy that aims to address global crises such as climate disruption, pollution, biodiversity loss, and others through lifestyle changes. R–Urban offers sites and facilities designed to support collective resilience through daily activities accessible to all: urban farming, joint management of resources, biodiversity conservation, waste recycling, and community governance. By connecting its units (Agrocity, Recyclab, Ecohab, etc.) into a network, R–Urban encourages diverse populations to engage in a citizen movement for ecological transition based on life–affirming ethics, urgently needed in order to sustain a future–oriented society.

Atelier d'Architecture Autogerée

← Opening of the Agrocity in Gennevilliers, 2018

3.1 Considering the landscape project as a negotiation platform

The landscape that surrounds us is becoming increasingly artificial, designed, regulated, privatized, and polluted. How can we make sure it stays livable in the future? First, we need to stop imposing a purely human perspective on this landscape, which is not just our environment, but also home to many other species. We should look beyond a purely economic perspective adopted by a single type of allegedly superior order.

At the same time, we should maintain an ongoing dialogue between different viewpoints and goals, particularly those of living beings, and prioritize "planetary emergencies" (climate disruption, pollution, biodiversity, etc.). The landscape around us could then be seen as an example of living complexity due to its heterogeneity (soil, water, microbial life, insects, humans, birds, etc.) and its balance of natural cycles (seasons, diurnal/nocturnal life, rainfall/drought patterns, etc.). Additionally, we should promptly structure societal dynamics in a way that will let us find solutions to today's planetary problems.

↑ Disco–soup made with unsold products from Biocoop. The Agrocity in Colombes, 2013

3.2 Building community by gardening together

By engaging, almost daily, in ecological activities at a local level, users of R–Urban hubs create a community of active citizens focused on local ecological transition with a globally–reaching societal impact: a community of "citizens for the planet." From the outset, these units are designed to involve as many citizens as possible and to promote the knowledge and skills of people from various social and cultural backgrounds: from the North and the South, urban and rural, those with technological or traditional know–how. The infrastructure is publicly funded, while the activities started by resident groups forming thanks to the R–Urban project – cooking, gardening, culture, recycling, and others – quickly cover the operating costs. A small–scale economy, sufficient to maintain and develop each unit, is gradually being set up – a reasoned, non–consumerist, non–extractive ecological economy (ecolomy). Small–scale collective activities of R–Urban hubs pay attention to each square meter of land and to each presence of living things, but also to the seasons, weather, rainfall, biodiversity, waste, resources, reuse, decontamination techniques, and water conservation... This is a community to imagine, explore and build together.

↑ The Agrocity in Colombes, 2016
The communities that grow around each R–Urban unit are backed by different proactive citizen groups: cooking, gardening, composting, chicken coops, beekeeping, rainwater management, eco–construction, waste management, and more.

3.3
Turning the project into a score that unfolds over time

The strategy for supporting the medium– and long–term growth of R–Urban while using resources wisely is based on networking different units that operate on the principles of self–management, resource sharing, and citizen volunteering.

Meanwhile, to tackle systemic societal challenges, R–Urban promotes additional programs, aiming to gradually change all of the urban practices and lifestyles: urban farming, solidarity economy, reuse and recycling, short supply chains, cooperative housing, etc. Relying on small–scale units, this strategy enables the integration and implementation of daily ecological practices in almost any urban setting: historic neighborhoods, city centers, suburban areas, large housing estates, etc.

Built using reversible eco–construction techniques (C2C – Cradle to Cradle), R–Urban hubs can be adapted or rebuilt in different ways. The hubs can also be relocated, creating "rhizomatic project dynamics." This characteristic defines what we call "constructive resilience" and "resilient urban habitat." This resilient aspect is enhanced by the diversity of citizens and users involved (young couples, large families, retirees, students, people changing careers, and others), as well as the flexible forms of their involvement.

Ultimately, the R–Urban strategy helps create a resilient collective vision around ecology, which, unlike today's over–hyped trend, can contribute to building a positive future for the society.

3.4
Expressing care for the living world through aesthetic resolution

How can we share this new perspective on the "landscape of living beings," the perspective cultivated in R–Urban units? How do we pass on these insights and values? How do we effectively highlight the stakes involved in this landscape? Simple layout, clear setup, and transparent operations are key to easily engaging people in activities and project management, and to passing on knowledge to new project leaders. Part of the R–Urban strategy, "aesthetic resolution" is the opportunity for dialogue between forms, realms, and living beings. Akin to "planetary landscapers," through their daily understanding of living organisms and their dedication to nurturing life and transmitting this understanding to others, "R–Urban users" learn to make the right choice of materials for repair and fitting, and to plant in a way that benefits oneself and biodiversity alike.

In the R–Urban approach, aesthetics is never an explicit goal; rather, it emerges as an implicit result of balancing various parameters (programmatic, ethical, economic, contextual, resources, resilience...). This "implicit aesthetic" of a continually negotiated balance sensitizes us to the marginalized and excluded, makes us attentive to small things, encourages us to move from the ground up, negotiate diversity, and respect otherness. It represents a return to (re)sources, a dialogue with plants, a reconnection to rhizomatic dynamics: R–Urban provides us with a language of returning to life and bringing life back to our cities and societies.

↑ The Agrocity at night, 2015

↑ The Agrocity in Gennevilliers, 2019

R-URBAN

Eco-citizen hubs for ecological transition in our neighborhoods!

What kind of landscape are we seeing today? Glaciers are melting and beginning to threaten coastal cities on all continents. Pollution is not just a big city problem anymore – it's affecting mountain villages, too. Microplastic particles reach marine waters, get swallowed by fish and, in turn, by humans... In these circumstances, we must radically rethink the very notion of landscape! Let's question the landscapes we have created, figure out how to approach them differently, question the ways we live in them, and teach others about them! Our lifestyles – what kinds of landscapes are they producing today? Alarmed by numerous scientific studies (reports from IPCC, WWF, etc.) that have been warning us for years about impending "planetary catastrophes" (climate, pollution, biodiversity, resources, etc.) and noting that the measures taken are not enough for addressing these increasingly imminent risks, in 2008, AAA conceived and initiated R–Urban as a strategy letting everyone do something every day to try and stop these disasters from happening. We are convinced that acting locally and multiplying the actions that involve all inhabitants of the planet will necessarily influence the course of history. That way, we will be able to preserve a habitable planet for future generations who would otherwise be forced to live in a polluted and food–depleted world, marked by frequent heatwaves and more.

← The Agrocity of Colombes, a life–affirming presence amidst urban neighborhoods, 2014/2019

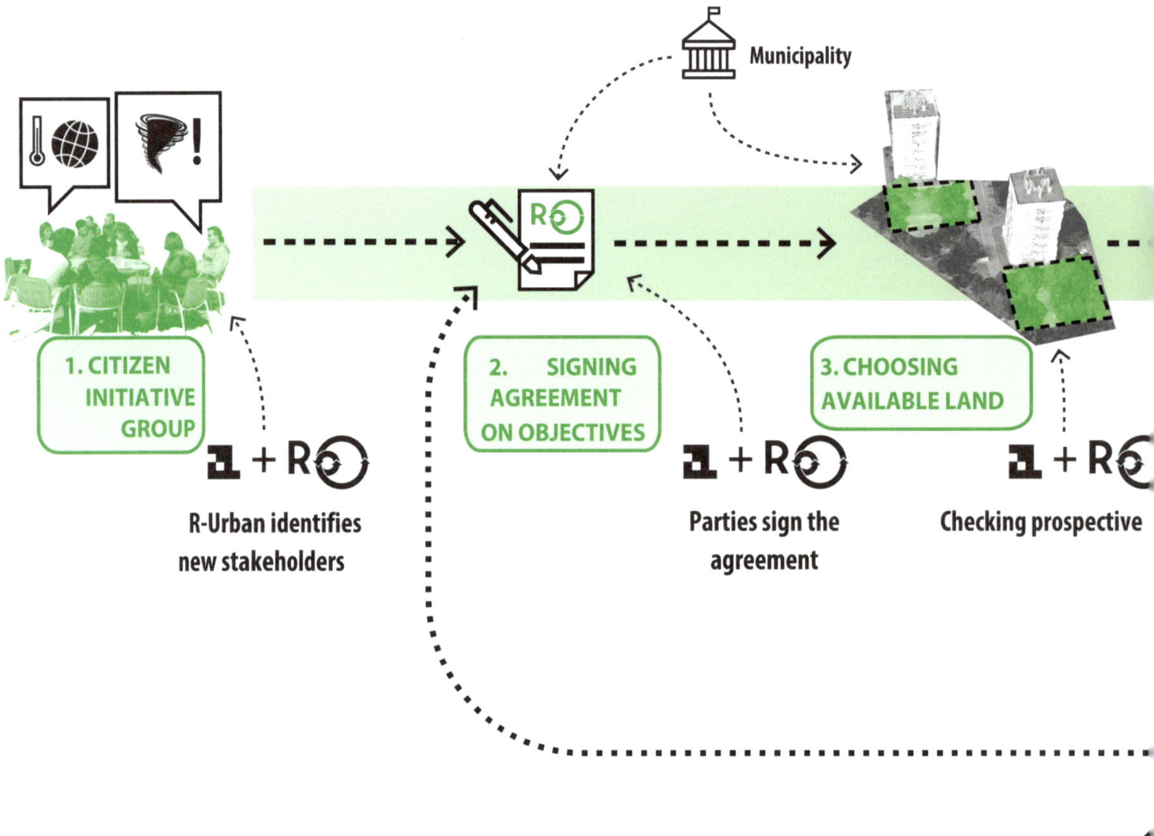

↑ Diagram of R–Urban process and partnerships, 2015

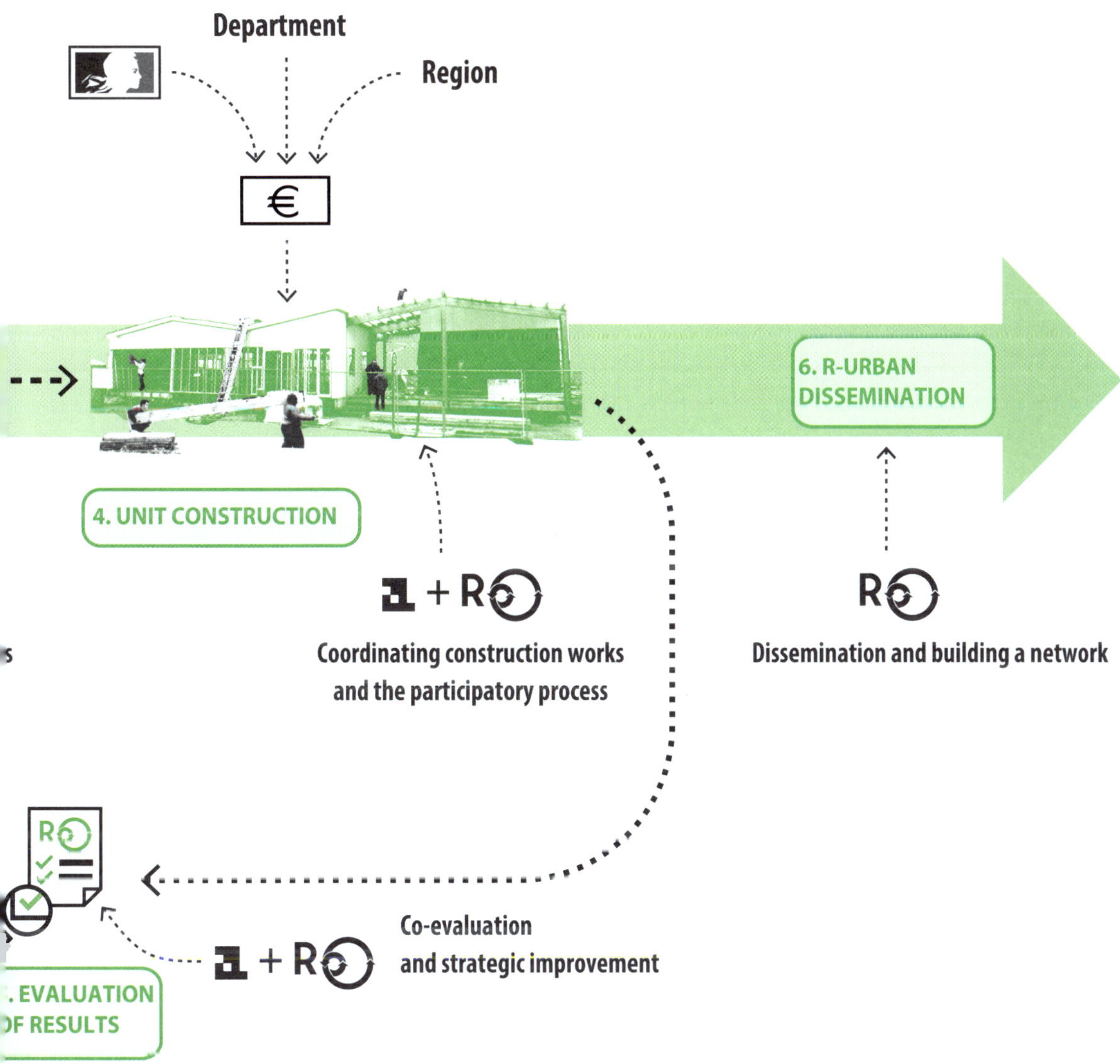

Department
Region
6. R-URBAN
DISSEMINATION
4. UNIT CONSTRUCTION
Coordinating construction works
and the participatory process
Dissemination and building a network
s
. EVALUATION
OF RESULTS
Co-evaluation
and strategic improvement

The Agrocity: the gateway for returning to our roots

R–Urban hubs are designed to integrate ecological principles such as reducing CO2 emissions (both in construction and use), cutting down on water and energy consumption, minimizing and recycling waste, preserving biodiversity, and using reclaimed materials.

One of the R–Urban hubs established in the Île-de-France (the Paris region), the Agrocity is aimed at encouraging citizen–driven and eco–friendly urban agriculture. The hub includes a community garden, an experimental vegetable micro–farm, educational plots, a space for processing and selling vegetables via a small café and community shop, cultural and educational areas, a chicken coop, a DIY workshop, and more.

Built in 2012 on a temporarily available site in Colombes, the Agrocity was designed with reversible land use in mind and incorporated the principles of resilience (lightweight, flexible, and removable construction systems). The building was created to be reversible and durable beyond the availability of this specific site. This approach anticipated the political uncertainties that came later, highlighting the difficulties faced by our society in responding to social and ecological emergencies.

Following the change in municipal leadership after the 2014 local elections, the Agrocity was threatened with eviction, which sparked a wave of protests. After two years of legal battles, in February 2017, the Agrocity was dismantled, but, with our intervention and the help of the municipality of Gennevilliers, the unit was rebuilt in a neighborhood of this town adjacent to Colombes. Following the cradle to cradle approach, we reused 95% of the materials from the original construction. Besides the relocation of the building itself, moving the Agrocity involved re–engaging some of the users, and transporting part of the productive soil and cultivated plants from the initial site. Former users of the Agrocity in Colombes have continued their engagement and met the new users in Gennevilliers.

Similar to the Agrocity in Colombes, a protective biodiversity strip has been created to welcome various "newcomers" to the site, offering them a secure habitat. Hedgehogs started passing through the garden; birds and insects came here attracted by the diversity of plants. Seeds and plants grown in the Agrocity greenhouse have found their way to other gardens, and gradually, a rhizomatic community has developed, based on the cooperation not just among humans but all species.

↑ The Agrocity in Colombes, 2015
↑ The Agrocity before demolition, Colombes, 2017
↗ The site slated to host the Agrocity in Gennevilliers, 2018
→ The Agrocity rebuilt in Gennevilliers, 2019

FedEx

Building together with the living things

The 250 m² Agrocity building is made from 90% recycled components (wood cladding, reused drying panels for flooring, repurposed joinery) and bio-sourced materials (local wood, straw, plant-based layers). It was built in cooperation with local businesses, while some parts have been crafted together with users during participatory workshops. Several environmentally friendly systems have been put in place to test the building's capacity to reduce, recycle, and generate short ecological circuits: a compost heating system, compost toilets, a hydroponic growing system, a greywater filtration system, systems for rainwater collection and use, solar energy production, etc.

These systems play an important educational role as they are intended to introduce users and the public to new resilience practices (dry toilets, compost production, phytopurification of greywater, compost heating, etc.). We have created and made available several user guides, and some systems have been replicated by others. This is indeed an "open sourcing" approach to architecture, allowing ideas to evolve and spread. As a result, the Agrocity users have reduced their annual CO2 emissions by 0.33 tons per person, which is three times the target of 0.1 tons set by the French government. To ensure social expansion and democratic access to daily resilient practices, R-Urban and its partners have proposed a governance system based on the principles of the commons. This management method should also prevent potential social conflicts that may arise due to extreme phenomena caused by climate change.

R-Urban makes resilient daily lifestyles (CO2 emissions reduction, short supply chains, waste reduction and recycling, phytopurification of greywater) available to urban populations and uses a bottom-up process to develop an eco-friendly infrastructure for changing the current system. The relocation of an R-Urban unit allowed us to test new programs in different urban contexts and involve new users. At the same time, such relocations are an opportunity to reuse materials and building parts, significantly reducing the ecological footprint: for example, the ecological footprint of the Agrocity in Gennevilliers is ten times smaller than that of a conventional building.

A shared and cooperative daily life

R–Urban units allow for local action against global crises through everyday activities: sharing knowledge and skills, educational workshops, local products, shared resources and common goods, resilient practices, reuse and recycling, self–managed spaces, and more.

Photos from Colombes, Gennevilliers and Bagneux, 2012/2022
↖ Collective cooking workshop
↖ Repair Café, Recyclab, R–Urban
↗ Repair Café, Recyclab, R–Urban
↗ Agrocity Garden
→ Local projects from the Agrocity

Popular ecology at the base of tower blocks!

Within the R–Urban network, numerous branches spread, both material and immaterial: prototypes, knowledge, skills, emotions, life... These are shared among the hubs, fostering exchange, friendship, and solidarity. This rhizomatic logic creates a community of emerging practices around the R–Urban hubs, a "more–than–human" community where both humans and non–humans are active participants.

Bruno Latour talks about the need to develop a new, "terrestrial" approach to the Earth in relation to our livelihood. R–Urban hubs reclaim former agricultural lands in the suburbs for "terrestrial" practices, healing and repairing this land to ensure the resilience of a more–than–human community. The R–Urban project has tangibly demonstrated that resilience can only be achieved through collective management and transformation of our neighborhoods, made possible by establishing ecological commons.

→ Melliferous biodiversity zone for beehives near an educational henhouse, Colombes 2014

The urban landscape

The "urban landscape" is a central issue today – not only because it's the primary living environment for humans, but also because it causes multiple catastrophic imbalances in other natural environments (forests, oceans, glaciers, ecosystems, and living habitats). This is why R–Urban wants to be a catalyst for various local ecological efforts, providing practical spaces for action and negotiation between the major challenges and pressure points of the present day: short and long term, personal and collective, local and global...

To make this happen, everyone is welcome, all of their skills are useful, and their availability is invaluable, because everything finds its proper place under an open, diverse, and cross-cutting governance. In the heart of large housing estates and working-class neighborhoods, R–Urban allows us to act right where we live, collectively and locally negotiating the transition and the societal goals for a livable planet tomorrow. R–Urban enables societal adaptation to the unpredictable: we preserve structural flexibility, we expand or reduce, we transform, change, and relocate without disrupting ecosystems.

R–Urban units are spaces for learning to live differently, in community with living things, by managing resources such as water, land, seeds, compost, vegetation, food, energy, knowledge, space, time, or networks as common goods.

Using resources as commons is a "mechanism" to transform our everyday life – practices, habits, stereotypes, daily and weekly schedules, and the way we spend our free time – as a political choice. Changing everyday life can generate systemic change! Changing everyday life is a political tool accessible to all!

The Agrocity of Colombes was relocated to Gennevilliers in 2018. New users started to get involved, and some members from Colombes continued to manage activities at the new site. Despite the abrupt interruption caused by the Colombes city hall in 2017, the rhizomatic dynamics are going strong and spreading more than ever.

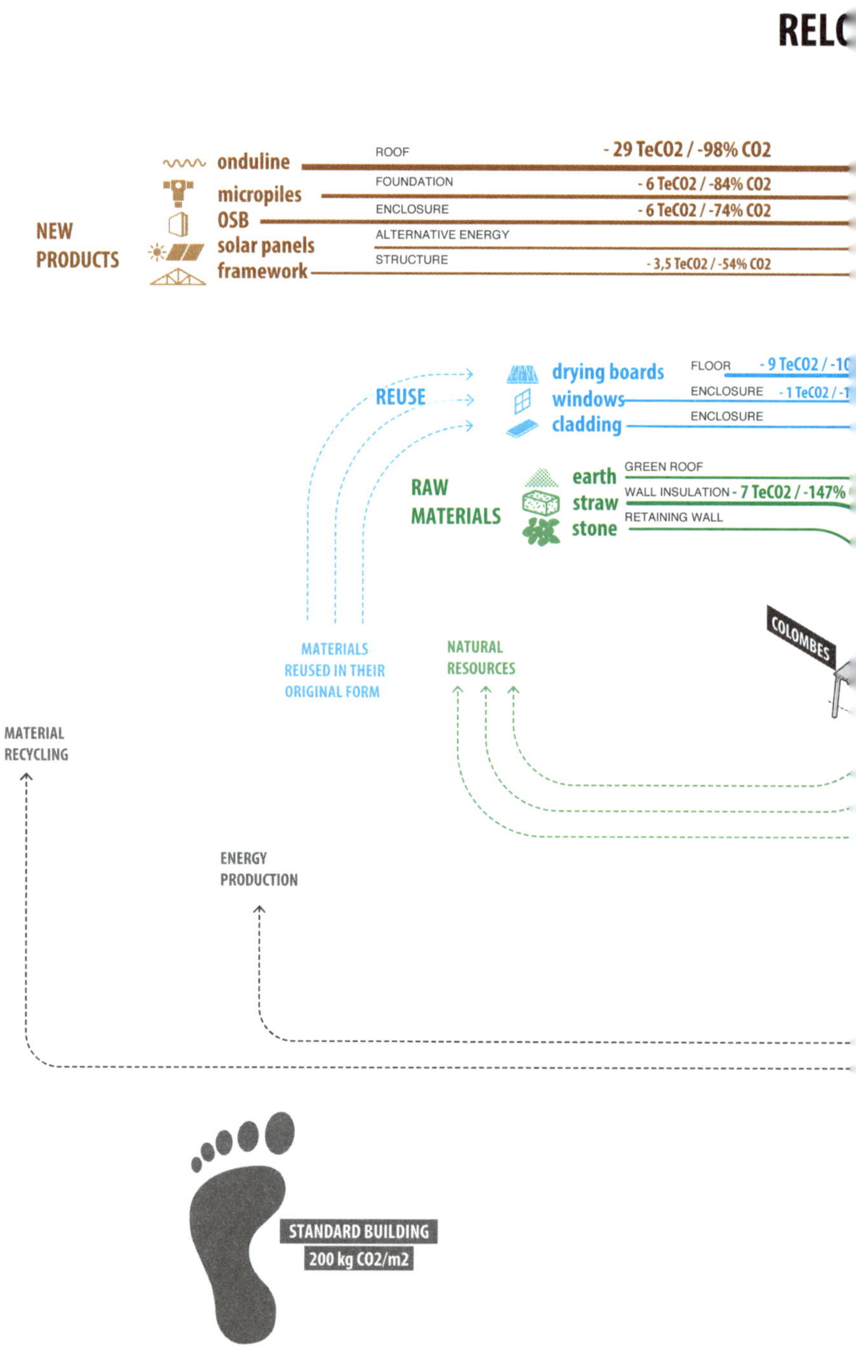

ATION OF THE AGROCITY / R-URBAN FROM COLOMBES TO GENNEVILLIERS
CRADLE TO CRADLE PROCESS

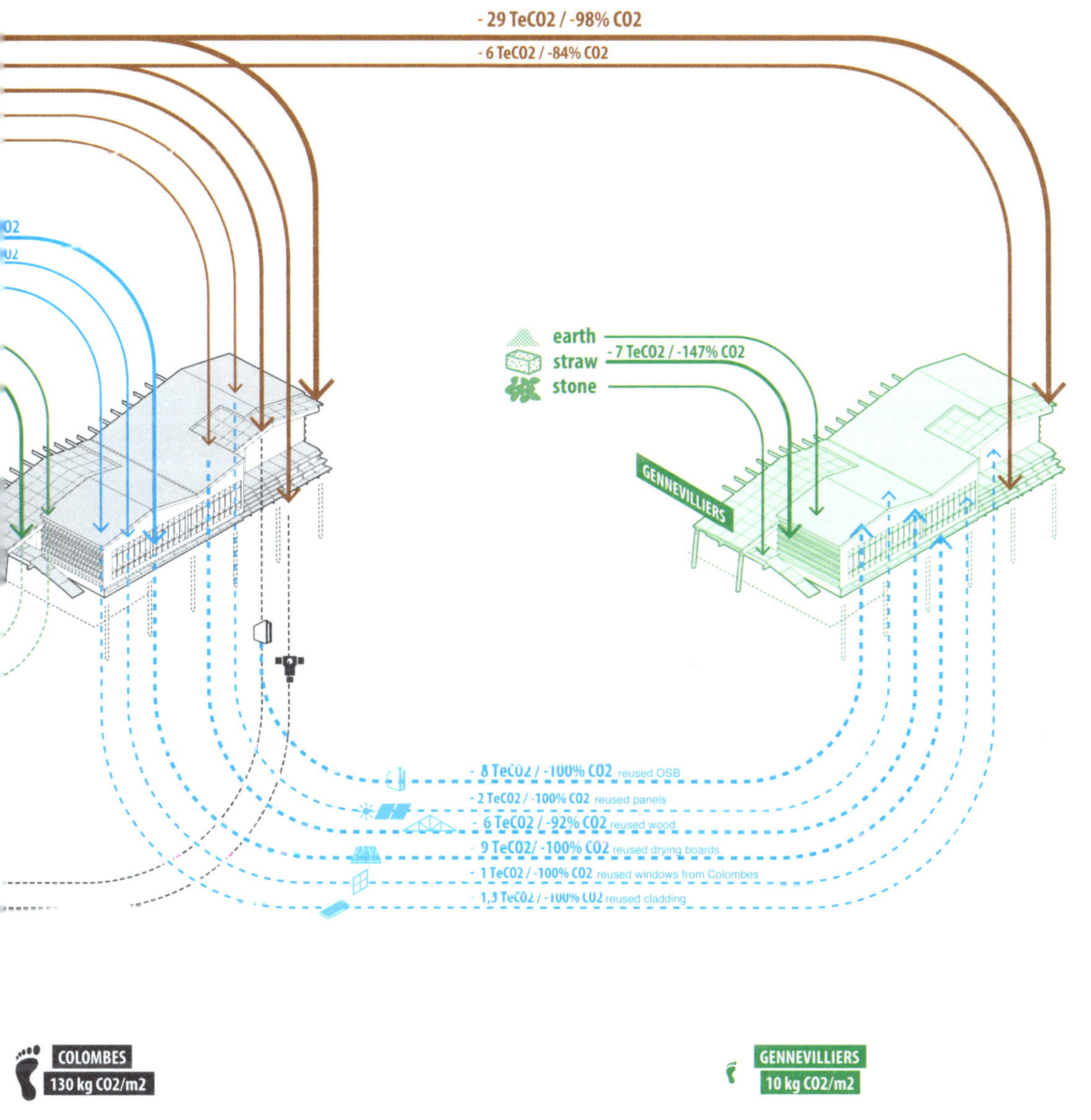

3.H
Vive les Groues

– Nanterre

Imagining a more fertile approach to urban planning

This initiative is enthusiastically transforming a piece of industrial wasteland into a vibrant place, ushering in a new urban cycle. Remediating soil, setting up a nursery, offering a number of experimental uses of the land – centered on life, it treats the living world as a common good and reinvents public and private frameworks and activities that normally precede the launch of a comprehensive development project.

The diverse commitments and project cultures of the stakeholders have led to conversations and, occasionally, clashes – serving as a laboratory where the dynamics of these types of scenarios have been unraveled, and possibilities explored to use them as models of *Putting Life first* in urban environments.

Mission Activation of transitional spaces
Location Nanterre, France
Geographical coordinates 48°53'22.0"N, 2°13'12.0"E
Size 9000 m²
Status Open public space
Annual budget 200 K€
Operating company Nouvelles Terres (TN+/ Yes We Camp/ BVAU/ABCD) and Vive les Groues (Yes We Camp)
Team Association Nouvelles Terres with TN+, Yes We Camp, BVAU, and ABCD Culture
Partner Daniel Soupe, nurseryman

← ©Julie Bourges

— Phasing
Since 2017 Occupation of the site
2017- 2019 Studies and contractual agreements for tree cultivation

— Implementation
March 2020 Stage 1, planting seedlings on the rue de la Garenne plot
2022-2024 Stage 2, transplantation of the trees and shrubs to the neighborhood's first public spaces. Growing production capacity
By 2026 Stage 3, transplantation to public spaces. Closure of the nursery
Photo credits TN+ (unless otherwise specified)

Trees and shrubs pla future neighborhood in the urban transfor Groues, crucial to get future *ecological challen* **and transplanting** *livi* **with the residents all to play an active part transition of our citie**

nted in this
vere a *major step*
nation of the
cing it ready for
ges. **Planting**
ng matter **together**
owed everyone
in the much-needed
s.

LE
JARDiNAGE
ça
se
PARTAGE

3.H

Vive les Groues, *activating transitional areas*

At 290 Rue de la Garenne in Nanterre, Yes We Camp, TN+, and their partners BVAU and ABCD have a temporary occupancy permit granted by Paris–La Défense to set up activities that will support the urban transformation of the Groues district, one of Greater Paris's most promising areas in terms of urban development (600,000 m² of GFA planned over 90 hectares). Our proposal responded to the request for EOI launched in 2016, which our group has won with a series of ideas for the site, including a hall for various collective activities, a micro–nursery to locally grow trees for the urban development project, and a broader plan encompassing the entire neighborhood.

Jean-Christophe Nani, TN

3.1
Considering the landscape project as a negotiation platform

Bringing life to the heart of the Groues and outlining the masterplan

Our plan involved temporary activities aimed at the Groues' current users and beyond, and the activities supporting the neighborhood transformation. It formed part of a global prefiguration strategy managed by a SCIC (a collective interest cooperative) bringing together various stakeholders such as residents, the municipality of Nanterre, developers, urban planners, and project leaders.

Set up with our tools and shared spaces at number 290, we are looking to make an impact throughout the whole area and to become the operators/supporters of the changes ahead.

The area we are focusing on includes the parcel at 290, linked to other plots from the same prefiguration program, and complete with open circulation areas, some private spaces in the heart of the Groues, as well as the urban areas to be built up within the designated perimeter.

Aiming to produce plant materials for future urban projects, we suggested creating a variable-size participatory nursery that would be open to the community, with a possibility of expanding beyond our parcel to include vacant areas in the neighborhood.

While technically the parcel at 290 is managed by Yes We Camp, the programming and interventions at the neighborhood level are being developed and implemented by The Groues Council, a cooperative entity created specifically for this purpose.

3.2
Building community by gardening together

The project's social goal: bringing people together around nature and communal living

A true host site and constituent assembly of the project, the Groues nursery crystallizes multiple individual interests into a decision-making body that guides the prefiguration efforts for the entire neighborhood. The community thus formed aims to improve the citizens' everyday lives by offering a place that acts as a welcoming ground for numerous initiatives, a space for meeting and sharing, and a production site for the city in transition.

Young plants are planted with local residents, especially the children from the neighborhood who adopt these plants and follow their growth until they are finally installed in public spaces. With help from Daniel Soupe, we have put together a preliminary catalog of species that could potentially thrive in our nursery. We have also defined the final plant palette in partnership with the developer Paris-La Défense, the landscape architects in charge of the planned public spaces (In Situ and Ter), and the technical team of the municipality of Nanterre.

To address the pollution problems on the site, we partnered with the Société du Grand Paris. The soil obtained from them – officially classified as inert waste – turned out to be a real boon for us. We were able to fertilize it and make sure the site was safe for people to visit.

Today, Vive les Groues brings together many project leaders, offering them a welcoming environment focused on life and sharing.

↑ ©TN+

↑ ©Julie Bourges

↑ © Yes We Camp

3.3
Turning the project into a score that unfolds over time

Matching the nursery's timeline with the urban project

The adaptable layout of the nursery fits well with the long-term planning and the mechanics of the urban project. The fifteen years leading up to the "horizon 2030" set by the masterplan is about how long it takes for a tree to mature, while the ten years allocated for prefiguration allow us to bring some nature to the neighborhood right away.

The micro-nursery of the Groues is more than just a source of plant material – it's a hub for building connections and developing new uses. It fosters a sense of togetherness by defining and consolidating various practices related to the living environment. It promotes the well-being and uniqueness of the neighborhood through an innovative approach, in line with the spirit of the Groues. The evolving layout of the nursery supports the project throughout its long timeline. With transplants, it spreads across the area based on the opportunities and available space, eventually shaping the key landscape features of the masterplan. The nursery's productive process is seen as a sum of symbolic actions related to use, facilitation, and urban quality, and contributing to a broader reflection on public space.

Last but not least, applying the nursery concept to the Groues neighborhood aligns both with the circular economy approach and the goal of activating the area.

↑ © Yes We Camp

3.4
Expressing care for the living world through aesthetic resolution

An aesthetic of rationality as a tribute to the terroirs of the Paris region

With our means limited to our own resources, the design of Vive les Groues follows a highly pragmatic approach. The layout may look almost random, but in fact it is carefully planned to meet the nursery's operational needs. The spacing between and within rows is calculated to allow the passage of the equipment necessary for the maintenance, transplantation, and final removal of the plants.

The trees are planted on mounds that are intentionally free-form, representing the various terroirs of the Paris region. The nursery celebrates these terroirs by using soils from the region's different construction sites. With multiple micro-projects taking place within the plot, a collection of microcosms comes together to form a living system.

Right across from La Défense, the kids' vegetable garden is set up in a meadow that has been left untouched so that herbaceous plants – many of them ruderal and commensal – could thrive. There are beehives and a compost area where people can be trained in beekeeping and composting techniques.

We have even got a campsite, a yurt, and a banya. In summer, crops are cultivated between the rows of the nursery's trees, which helps enrich the soil and maintain the paths.

Everything we are doing here is focused on well-being and life, resulting in a particularly striking landscape just opposite La Défense.

Acclimatizing **trees t**
environment: the tr
their time in the nu
the specific conditions
they will be transpl
Addressing climate
suitable species is
the *planting strategy***.**

the urban
es and shrubs use
sery to *adapt to*
of the site where
nted.
change and finding
major part of

PREMIERE VERSION DE L'IMPLANTATION
(version provisoire)

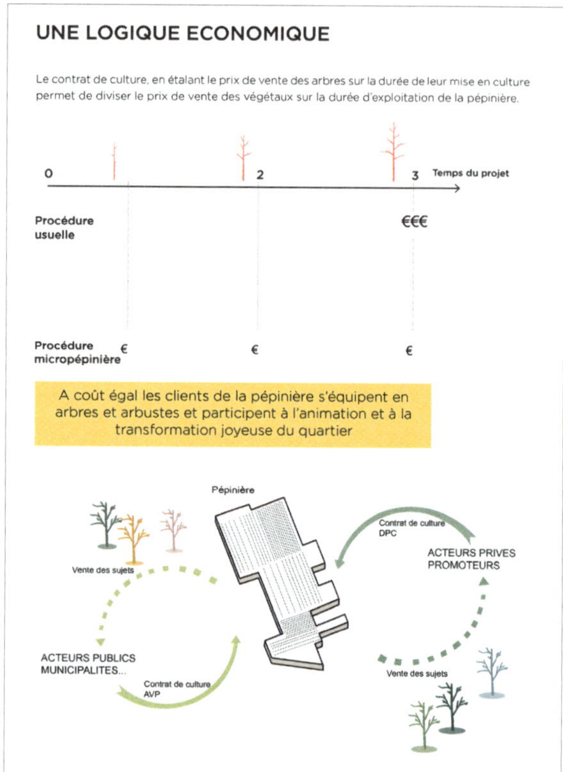
UNE LOGIQUE ECONOMIQUE
Le contrat de culture, en étalant le prix de vente des arbres sur la durée de leur mise en culture permet de diviser le prix de vente des végétaux sur la durée d'exploitation de la pépinière.
0
2
3
Temps du projet
Procédure usuelle
€€€
Procédure micropépinière
€
€
€
A coût égal les clients de la pépinière s'équipent en arbres et arbustes et participent à l'animation et à la transformation joyeuse du quartier
Pépinière
Vente des sujets
Contrat de culture DPC
ACTEURS PRIVES PROMOTEURS
ACTEURS PUBLICS MUNICIPALITES...
Contrat de culture AVP
Vente des sujets

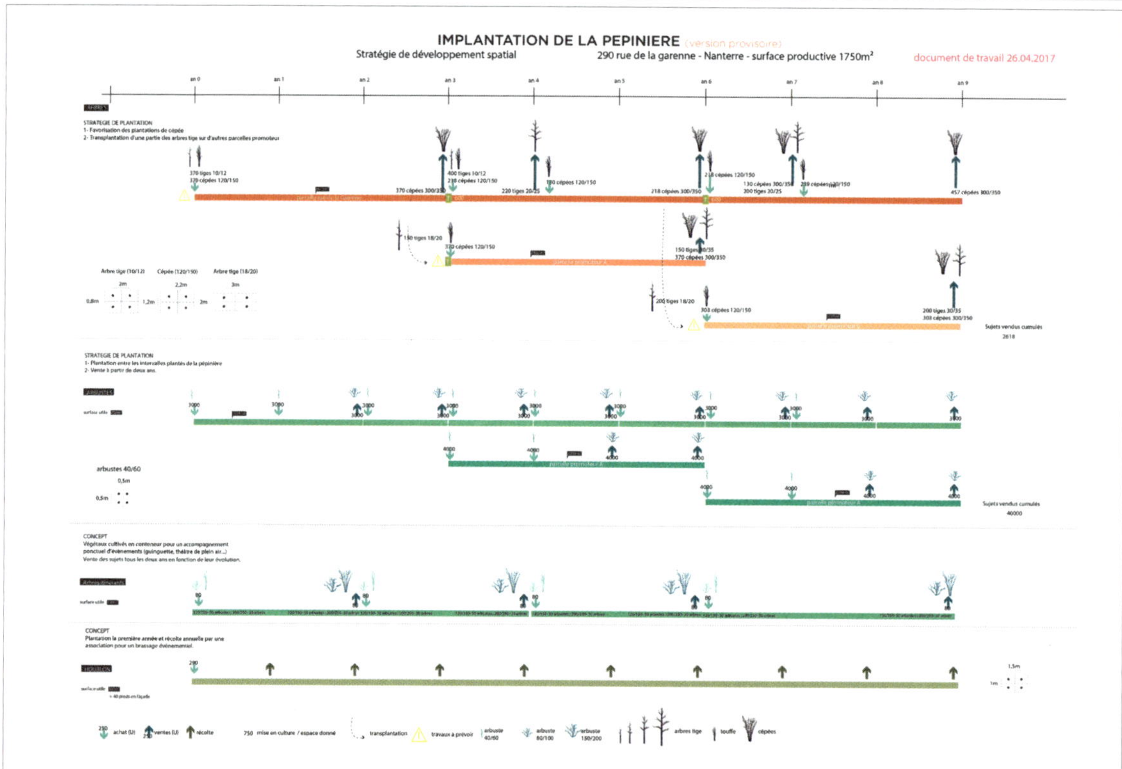
IMPLANTATION DE LA PEPINIERE (version provisoire)
Stratégie de développement spatial
290 rue de la garenne - Nanterre - surface productive 1750m²
document de travail 26.04.2017

FONCTIONNEMENT DE LA PEPINIERE

Des végétaux de taille différentes sont initialement implantés. De ce fait, lors de la première vente d'arbre trois ans plus tard, plusieurs gabarits sont à disposition cette stratégie peut s'adapter en fonction des besoins formulés lors de l'élaboration du catalogue des essences.

La production de végétaux est pensée selon deux cycles de croissance :

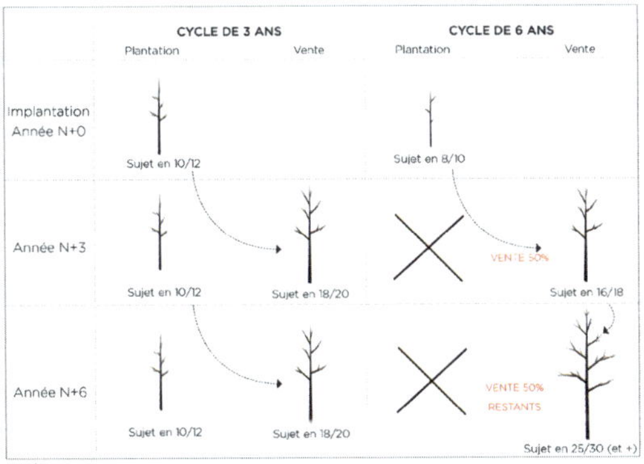

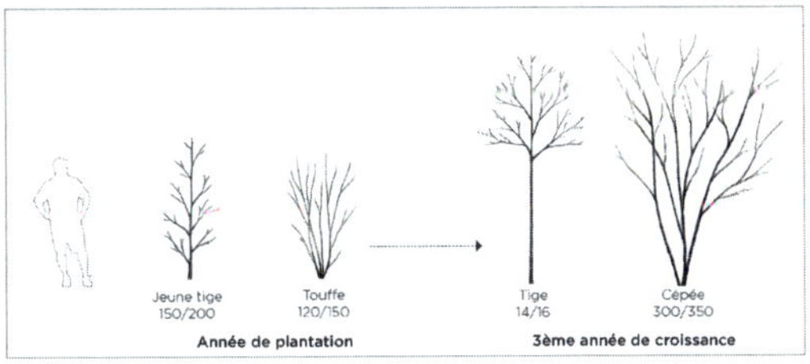

PRODUCTIVITE

Lors de l'implantation, 6 typologies d'arbres sont plantées. Trois tailles différentes (6/8, 8/10 et 10/12), pour deux techniques de développement : l'arbre tige et l'arbre en cépée.

Pour les arbustes, ceux-ci, placés en interligne, seront vendus tous les deux à trois ans.

TYPE DE SUJET DISPONIBLE

	Arbuste 60/80 (et +)	Tige 12/14	Tige 14/16	Tige 18/20	Haute tige 20/25 (et +)	Cépée 200/250	Cépée 300/350	Cépée 400/500 (et +)
Implantation Année N+0								
Année N+1								
Année N+2	✓							
Année N+3	✓	✓	✓	✓		✓	✓	
Année N+4			✓	✓			✓	
Année N+5	✓			✓	✓			✓
Année N+6	✓	✓	✓	✓	✓	✓	✓	✓
Année N+7			✓	✓			✓	
Année N+8	✓			✓	✓			✓
Année N+9	✓	✓			✓			✓

LA PÉPINIÈRE DES GROUES : PRINCIPE DE FONCTIONNEMENT

PLANNING DES TRAVAUX SUR LA PARCELLE DE LA COOP DES GROUES

(quantités indicatives)

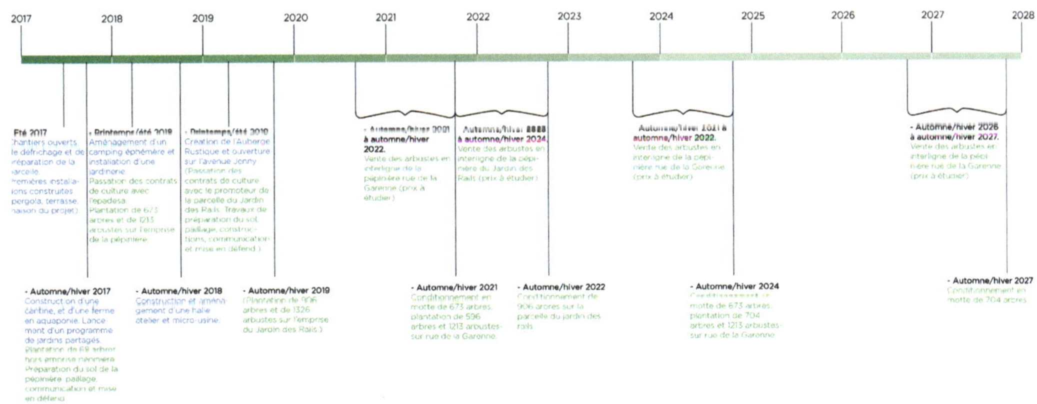

The nursery

In year Y+1, the fertilized soils of the Groues nursery hosted more than 150 trees commissioned by the developer, Paris–La Défense, for the future public spaces of the ZAC (Comprehensive Development Zone).

Schémas © TN+

Representing the nursery's integrated approach, its soils have been created from inert materials recovered from metropolitan construction sites. These materials were then amended and enriched with microbacteria, selected according to the type of soils and the intended plant palette.

We had to work out a new form of contract with the developer, the one that would focus on the supply of goods and services, in full compliance with public procurement laws. The resulting agreement between Nouvelles Terres and Paris–La Défense is a bespoke cultivation contract that challenges conventional practices.

→ The plaque in the photo reads:
New Soils
Once discarded as waste, these soils from construction sites in Île-de-France are now repurposed as fertile ground for the nursery.
A total of 4,000 m³ of soil has been delivered and distributed across the cultivation areas.
This project was made possible through a partnership with the Société du Grand Paris and Eiffage, with support from the Nord Sud architecture studio and the environmental consultancy Tribu.

nou-
-velles
terres
Issues de chantiers franciliens, une seconde vie est donnée aux terres considérées comme déchets de chantier : elle seront le terreau fertile sur lequel sera plantée la pépinière.
4 000 m3 de terre ont été acheminés et répartis sur l'ensemble des terrains à cultiver.
Un partenariat établi avec la Société du Grand Paris et Eiffage avec le soutien de l'atelier d'architecture Nord Sud et du bureau d'étude environnemental Tribu.

Initial transformations

The next steps focused on creating fertile soil to both contain the existing polluted soils and provide a suitable substrate for the future trees.

VIVE LES
GROUES

The transformed site

Today, the site hosts a range of initiatives such as a gardening school, a greenhouse for growing vegetables, a yurt, DIY workshops, and the Compost School. The nursery's trees form the backdrop of an ecosystem centered around the exchange of skills and knowledge.

JARDIN

Opening the site to public

The site was opened in stages, depending on when various facilities became available. Initially limited to non-polluted areas, public access has been gradually expanded through a series of events that marked the project's growth.

Appel d'Air

Appel d'Air, an artistic project led by La Société du Grand Paris and entrusted to the artist Thierry Boutonnier, is one of the initiatives hosted at the Vive les Groues site. Sixty-eight Paulownia trees intended for the public squares of the future Grand Paris Express stations are being grown on-site and transplanted with the help of local residents.

↗ © Yes We Camp
→ © TN+
↓ The Appel d'Air event
© Julie Bourges

3.1 Biodiversity School

– Boulogne–Billancourt

Welcoming diversity into our daily environment

This building is intended to accommodate life – both on the roof, designed as a continuous fertile surface, and on the meticulously crafted façades where water runoff and wall textures enable habitats for the greatest possible variety of species.

In this innovative experiment, a building incorporates the habitats of the non–human species that live alongside us, including in urban environments. By making possible a close connection with the Third Landscape, the project fosters the development of countless relationships.

Monitoring the vegetation over time reveals interesting dynamics and provides insights for maintaining biodiversity.

Mission An ecosystem as an educational tool
Location Boulogne Billancourt, France
Geographical coordinates 48°49'35.4", N 2°14'22.0"E
Parcel size 6 766 m²
Building size 6 596 m²
Program School complex with 18 classrooms (elementary and preschool) and a regional–standard gymnasium
Budget 18 M € ex–tax

— Team
Client SAEM Val de Seine
Designer ChartierDalix Architectes
Implementation EVP (structure), Cferm (MEP), F. Bougon (cost consultant), F. Boutté (High Environmental Quality consultant), Atelier d'Écologie Urbaine (ecology consultant), Biodiversita (biodiversity consultant)
Ecologists Aurélien Huguet and Jean–Louis Ducreux (AEU)
Gardeners GPSO

— Phasing
2010–2010 Design development
2012–2014 Implementation
2016 First survey of the flora on the planted areas and walls carried out by botanist Audrey Muratet
2017–2020 The Biodiversity School's roof is included in the GROOVES survey conducted by the ARB (Regional Biodiversity Agency)
September 2020 Participatory fieldwork: manual loosening of soil and addition of substrate; re–sowing of the meadow and the facades
May to October 2021 Naturalist assessment carried out by Écolo GIE under the guidance of Aurélien Huguet

Photo and image credits ChartierDalix, Takuji Shimmura

Combining an 18-clas
and a gymnasium wit
that encompasses the
facades, this pioneeri
a conversation about
systems **and embodies**
return biodiversity to the

sroom primary school
n an ecosystem
school's roof and
ng project starts
ccommodating living
the desire to
heart of urban areas.

3.1

Biodiversity School, *an ecosystem as an educational tool*

Emerging from an innovative concept, this building places two programs within a 'living' envelope designed to accommodate various species of fauna and flora. The challenge was to create a rooftop ecosystem, a patch of wilderness that would extend onto the building's textured, habitable exterior facade. Aiming for smooth transitions and trying to minimize gaps, we created connections between solids and voids, and between different topographic levels. The result is a building turned into a piece of extruded land, a kind of urban canopy, a vertical landscape where local nature can grow freely, protected from humans and by humans. The ecosystem takes time to evolve, and it subjects the building's appearance to the laws of nature.

Chartier Dalix

3.1
Considering the landscape project as a negotiation platform

When we have to design a building or a place, this leads us to reconsider its uses, the program, and the boundaries between public and private areas. It is by fostering programmatic inventiveness – a quality often missing from the brief – that our role takes on its full meaning.

In search of alternative architectural situations, we are looking to negotiate with the project's explicit and binding specifications. By identifying "hidden" programs, we can offer those who will inhabit this space a new freedom of use; with this freedom, they will regain involvement and responsibility, which will boost their desire to take ownership of the place.

In Boulogne, the goal of high-density construction, along with wanting more greenery in the neighborhood, called for a way to merge different programs within a 6,700 m^2 plot (the total area allocated for the school, courtyard, and gymnasium). We were recommended to place vegetation on a portion of the roof, but chose to extend planted space to the entire building so that it would become an integral part of the project. Our decision resulted from a forward-looking interpretation of the program and the contingencies of the site. We immediately saw the opportunity to organize the project around the layering of programs, and thus create a symbiosis between the school, its uses, and new spatial combinations that would be equally suitable for children, wildlife, and plants.

The idea of negotiating for alternative programs makes us rethink our relationship with time and nature. By proposing a complete ecosystem that brings humans and other living beings closer in a holistic way, this negotiation becomes political and cultural, touching on the deeper roots of our desire to shape the world.

3.2
Building community by gardening together

Architecture is primarily connected to the sensory, the human, and to nature; it supports the society and contributes to its evolution. We believe in the importance of strengthening the communal aspect – like in an ecosystem where everyone has their place.

In each of our projects, we want to create opportunities for enhancing the sense of community. Ironically, dense cities don't really support this, while gardens do have such power. A garden is one of the best mediators because it allows us to reconnect with the land, the earth, and with living things. It brings people together around a shared activity and revives the collective experience of "doing together." We want to design places that foster encounters, mixed uses, and knowledge-sharing, places that stimulate curiosity, make us rediscover mutual help, and celebrate the simple pleasure of togetherness.

The planted areas of the Boulogne school are intended for educational use, allowing teachers to organize various types of collective and participatory workshops. The balconies can be accessed directly from the classrooms. This close relationship with an ecosystem becomes central to the schoolchildren's daily lives. They interact with biodiversity throughout the week, all year long. The drawings that line the school's walls show this: observing and interacting with nature on a daily basis fuels their imagination. This creates a bond of habit, a familiarity arising from proximity. The planted roof provides the school with a unique environment in terms of ecology and education, with both aspects interwoven in a mutually beneficial symbiosis.

3.3

Turning the project into a score that unfolds over time

As a result, the building becomes more than just a shelter for humans: it serves as a carrier of nature, culture, and experience. This approach challenges both the concept of time and the idea of a "finished" building.

Colonization by the living world introduces uncertainty and randomness. The fleeting and perishable aspect of nature calls for rethinking our views on completion and finalization. In this perspective, aging becomes an essential factor: upon delivery, the new building is bare and empty, but as time goes on, vegetation grows, creating a living environment. Colonization also entails a certain wear and tear on the built surfaces, which goes against traditional maintenance practices and the positive perception of a newly completed facade. Taking this variable into account means coming to terms with a vision where a building's quality depends on its aging and even deterioration. A certain fragility is therefore acceptable, and even desirable, as it opens up a vast field of possibilities for the installation of living organisms.

In this temporal perspective, the evolution of the areas of exchange between the ground and the roof, the exterior and the interior, the evolution of inhabited walls becomes an integral part of a certain aesthetic. We need to change our views on what is clean or dirty, and reduce our need to control aging.

At the Biodiversity School, time – free from the constraints of schedules and deadlines – becomes an essential part of the architecture. This forward-thinking approach to design has turned the school into a real, full-scale tool for experimentation. The building acts as a prime observatory of the mutual influence between living organisms and built spaces in a dense urban environment.

3.4

Expressing care for the living world through aesthetic resolution

We should consider the subjective dimension of aesthetics. For us, talking about aesthetics means giving more thought to the state of living things, their well-being, and vitality. The beauty of a garden is first and foremost about energy, harmony, "good health", and about the physical aptitude developed by plants. Aesthetics is therefore not a fixed state, but an outcome that is subject to fragility and change.

Developing new urban functions in Boulogne made us think about what cities will look like in the future. Placing living things on buildings, we question the basic principles of architecture in a way that connects poetry, education, and nature through new aesthetic approaches. This project is designed as a piece of inhabited landscape rather than a mere building. Facades and roofs are imagined as thick, nurturing bark, capable of hosting fauna and flora. The topography that blends the ground, the facades, and the roof is an invitation to redefine each of these elements. The roof hosts a forest, educational gardens, and animals; all of this is easily accessed thanks to a continuous grass-covered ramp that also serves as the schoolyard. Each architectural element has multiple functions, even the deep and rugged enclosing wall that incorporates birdhouses and supports spontaneous vegetation.

Treating the building as an ecosystem creates a true laboratory for testing new forms of expression. Architecture and integrated living organisms are seen as parts of the same body that harmoniously complement and enrich each other.

↓ The roof hosts a forest, educational gardens, and animals

Pascale Dalix answers Coloco's questions about the **Biodiversity School** in the context of *Putting Life first.*

PASCALE DALIX This school offers a way of welcoming living things, but also represents a specific approach. I believe there are no limits to accommodating living things in our projects – this can work for any size and any program, with different methods and different kinds of proximity that we want to create with the living world.

PABLO GEORGIEFF What was your initial intention?

PD From the start, the client wanted the building to support biodiversity. Aurélien Huguet, an ecologist, spent two years on site to identify the species that could potentially be involved. His work helped determine many factors, from the size of birdhouses and entrance holes to the choice of plant species.

PG One can never be certain if nature will settle in.

PD That's true; we had to create the right conditions for it to happen.

PG What was your design approach? Did you have to adapt your usual process?

PD We designed the building as an architectural project. The brief only asked for biodiversity on the north facade and a bit of the roof. We decided to extend this idea to the entire building: instead of having some facades with biodiversity and others without, we designed a comprehensive system across all dimensions, making it the core principle of the building. It may seem obvious today, but it wasn't part of the original plan.

Then came the architectural work. The classrooms encircle the recreation areas. The building has a gentle slope and a ramp that goes down to the playground on the first floor. Boulogne is pretty dense. The building gives back to the neighborhood what it has taken from the ground, the nature it has 'borrowed'. It carries a landscape that won't ever be there.

For the third goal, we wanted students and teachers to be able to find their way around the school and to always know where they are. This means they should always have a view of some part of the garden, meadow, or forest.

So, initially, the work focused more on the landscape and morphological design. We thought of the landscape and the building as a kind of small geography. It's interesting to work on the building's 'skin,' its envelope. Moreover, the entire shape of the building is designed to accommodate biodiversity. We wanted to create a connection with living things: to welcome, observe, experience, and so on.

PG Kind of like a topography. How did you organize the spaces on the roof?

PD We organized the roof into two main zones. One is a sort of oak–hornbeam forest – though without oak – rather, beech–hornbeam; a truly protected area, marked by a small looped path. It's a spot that children are supposed to observe but not to enter. This wooded core is surrounded by shrubs (hazel, raspberry, rowan, etc.) leading into a mown meadow. Next to it is an educational garden for the children; they even have chickens there. Teachers use it as a real educational tool. The focus for the 18 preschool and elementary classes, as well as the after–school program, is on environmental and ecological topics. This changes depending on the directors and has evolved in various ways.

PG Before living organisms came in, the terrain you designed had to support a substrate. How did you handle the heavy load of soil and water on the structure?

PD In this project, we have three different soil depths: 30 to 50 cm of substrate (earth) under the meadow, and 120 cm under the shrubbery and the forest. The depth variations were created with insulating blocks on the gym's slab. The loads are quite heavy: 1 ton per cubic meter of wet soil, plus the additional operational load. The entire school has a concrete structure. The forest is above the gym, where 3–meter thick beams create the longest span.

PG Three meters of concrete – that's a bridge!

PD It's worth mentioning that the gymnasium is approved for regional competitions, with a span of 30 meters.

PG Did you choose the types of plants based on the roof's waterproofing?

PD Yes, that's why we didn't plant oak trees.We realized that oaks take 80 years to mature, while waterproofing only lasts 10 to 20 years. So we chose the species accordingly, matching their life cycles to the end of the warranty. The time to fix the waterproofing will also be the time to replace the plants. We had to align the life cycles of the plants with those of the building.

→ The building blocks have numerous gaps, grooves, and recesses that encourage the spontaneous growth of pioneer vegetation.

PG What really stands out when you look at this building is its inhabited facade.

PD When designing the wall, we imagined a kind of mineral–like crust made of concrete. When it comes to thermal and water inertia, concrete has the advantage of behaving like stone, and you can work with it in depth.

We realized that, to achieve the result we were looking for, to truly welcome life, all species must be present (including cavern–dwelling species that prefer darkness). There were big debates during construction; we were almost forced to use shotcrete. That would have been a total failure because shotcrete deteriorates and would not have allowed us to work with a greater thickness. But it was precisely this inertia that interested us, which is why we needed blocks between 30 and 40 cm deep. What's more, arranged in a staggered pattern, the blocks enable a large variety of settings: east or west sunlight depending on the block's design, but also overhangs, cornices... By recreating the different situations that exist in nature, we could accommodate as many animal and plant species as possible.

We designed the blocks based on the different façades and heights, figuring out what could grow and where. We also considered the path of the water, making the blocks polished on their face and sandblasted on their edges. This sandblasting has grooves that help guide the water to flow over the edges and stick to the areas that are more suitable for algae and moss. The blocks also incorporate insect hotels and around 90 birdhouses.

The parts are molded from standard concrete. Using a simple technique, we created a formwork with varying angles. There are about ten different types of blocks.

Our goal for these blocks was to create something experimental and natural, waiting for life to develop. The fauna and flora that settle here can handle extreme stress; they will die for a month, then resurrect thanks to a three–week torrential rain... Our approach relies on time. The succession of seasons creates a first substrate, then a second, then a third, and so on. Birds also help by bringing seeds.

PG Did you plant something at the building's delivery, or did you just have a substrate, waiting for the seed bank to express itself?

PD We waited, and after a year and a half or two years, we tried placing small pots and micro–plugs here and there. It was not about creating a vertical garden, but rather a delicate seeding process. The plants died out in some areas and thrived in others. Two years after the building's delivery, the GROOVES research program, launched by the Regional Biodiversity Agency (ARB), detected 114 species: 44 issued from the original plantings, and 70 more that arrived spontaneously. A really encouraging proof of the site's colonization!

Our inventory continues: new species of bats and tits have shown up... The living environment is gradually taking its place, but we need to be careful and protect this dynamic.

PG Do you have a management contract for this project?

PD Our office is currently working with the municipality of Boulogne to develop a management plan for the roof for the upcoming years. Meanwhile, we are running experimental operations to test some processes that would also be suitable for the educational teams. In 2020, ecologist Aurélien Huguet found a preserved meadow in Marly that was similar to the one on the school roof and could survive drought without irrigation. We went there to collect seeds and re–seeded the roof meadow. As for the forest, which had been somewhat damaged, – especially the soil that got compacted by children's trampling – we planted ground covers, added mulch, and marked the path with barriers to manage the kids' movement.

These initial actions will help us fine–tune the management of this environment, and the ecological experiment will be continually monitored to match its uses.

PG How do you reconcile the presence of living organisms with human habitat?

PD Living things are not just for making the project look 'nice'; they are a connection system between the building and the landscape. The landscape is more than a backdrop for the building. We are driven by three key reasons. The first one is environmental, dealing with thermal issues, rainwater harvesting, and bringing back small–scale biodiversity. The second is architectural. Often, architectural elements have only one function: waterproofing just waterproofs, insulation just insulates. In this building, each element has multiple functions, and each function is enabled by several elements.

None of the elements does just one single thing; the project is an ensemble that forms a system. When a roof, which typically just covers, becomes flat and accessible, it also becomes a floor. If planted, it becomes a garden. As a third function, it can even become a terroir. With added topography, it becomes a hill, a geographical feature, etc. This approach challenges architectural fundamentals, letting us think about architecture in a different way, with new functions leading to new forms. For us, it's also a very stimulating design tool.

PG It's a new way to bring parameters into your process and to work with different people and problems.

PD This is the third reason behind our motivation: working with the parameters of living systems. Take, for example, water. Algae were the first living organisms. The issue of water is a real paradox: water is the building's main enemy, so we have to protect against it. But at the same time, water is essential for growth and sustaining life. So, when you are designing a building that aims to accommodate living organisms, things get a bit schizophrenic: on the one hand, you're protecting yourself from water, and on the other, you need it.

This raises several questions, especially about the price we'll have to pay. A water-retaining roof is great, but we need to be sure about the waterproofing system underneath. As for the façade, what is the desired look in the long term? Are we going to tolerate drips and stains, which are the first signs of spontaneous vegetation?

A façade like the one in Boulogne is not under constant maintenance. It means that growth won't happen immediately; it will take time and may not occur exactly where we want it. It also means there is an expectation and a reversal of the conventional situation where the façade is supposed to be finished on the day of delivery. In our case, on the day of delivery, the façade is just bare. We then wait for it to degrade, to be colonized by microalgae, then by mosses, for birds to find refuge there, for plants to establish themselves for a season and then die, creating the bed for the next generation, etc. This is also a different way of thinking about the building, which will be colonized and thus subjected to a kind of aggression, to evolution – while a traditional approach to architecture implies that a façade should be renovated every ten years to make it look new again!

It's about trusting evolution and the effect of time. And it's a new way of seeing things, both for the architect and the people living around.

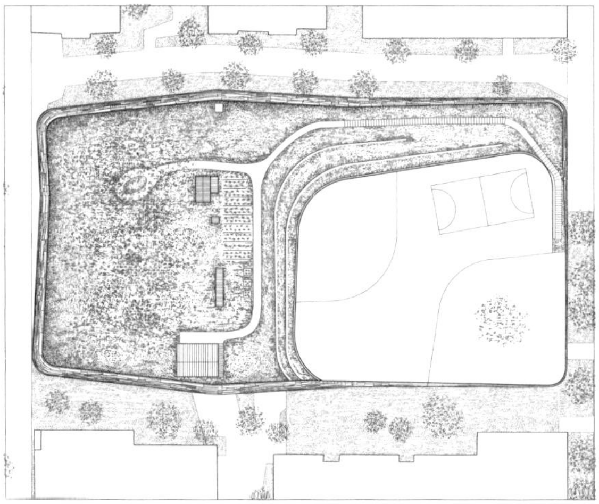

↑ Rooftop plan

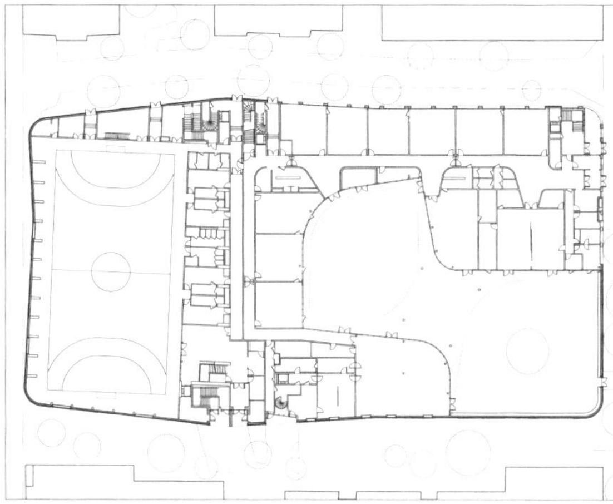

↑ Ground floor plan

Roof and balconies

Similar to the school spaces, the planted areas smoothly transition one into the other. The classrooms are bordered by continuous balconies, connected to the roof through a grass–covered ramp. The overlapping of the balconies, as well as the ramp's gentle slope, help species (both plants and animals) move from one level to another. This makes it easier to integrate biodiversity, both within the project and on a wider scale.

The characteristics of the planted roof were defined with ecologists Aurélien Huguet and Jean–Louis Ducreux[1] during the conceptual phases of the project. The oak–hornbeam forest, a typical forest configuration of the Île–de–France region, served as the primary model for the distribution of species and helped determine the right soil thickness for each zone. However, the system had to be adapted to the project's constraints: for example, oaks were removed from our list of species because their taproots could damage the building's waterproofing[2].

The roof, which is about 2,000 square meters, is divided into three main zones with different soil depths. These variations are needed to recreate forest conditions and control tree growth, especially around the edges of the roof. Controlling the composition of substrates and the precise amounts of soil makes it possible to predict and manage the forest's morphology.

↑ The building has two defining elements: the façade with its concrete 'bark' and the planted roof

↑ Similar to the school spaces, the planted areas smoothly transition one into the other. The classrooms are bordered by continuous balconies, connected to the roof through a grass–covered ramp

The planted roof

The plant composition on the roof is organized as follows:

– The forest core (550 m²): The center of the planted roof has a 1-meter thick layer of substrate and hosts 220 trees that are the tallest species on our list[3]. With the soil depths available, these trees will grow to 10–15 meters tall. This central zone consists of hornbeams, lindens, and maples, as well as smaller species like small-leaved lindens and interstitial groves. Dense planting provides great conditions for the roots of the transplanted species. However, this density will change over time due to natural selection, as not all planted species will survive over the long term. The forest core, which is home to many birds, has birdhouses installed among the trees.

– The fringe of shrubs and undergrowth transitioning between the forest and the meadow (about 500 m²): This peripheral zone around the central forest has a soil thickness varying between 1 m and 0.5 m. Tree heights decrease as the soil gets thinner. This intermediate belt protects the forest core and gradually transitions to prairie vegetation. It has 350 trees of 18 different species, mainly hazel and berry bushes, with heights ranging from 0.6 m to 2.5 m. The varied vegetation in this zone serves multiple purposes. From an educational perspective, schoolchildren can learn about the nutritional systems represented by plants like wrinkled blackberry, red currant, and raspberry bushes. Additionally, the diversity of species enhances the young users' sensory experience. The plants can be touched, smelled, tasted, but they can also scratch or sting. For birds, this shrub area with its berries, thickets, and shade provides a valuable food source.

– The mesophilic meadow (about 850 m²): With different plant varieties (perennials, grasses, legumes), this area has a 50 cm thick soil layer[4]. Here, the plants stay low. This zone plays a crucial role in the ecosystem, hosting many insects, which are also accommodated nearby in special insect hotels, placed in the educational area for observation activities.

Extending from the system of ramps and balconies, a grassy area of about 1,100 m² gently transitions into the meadow. From the bottom to the top of the ramp, a 30 cm layer of soil supports various grass species like perennial ryegrass and fescue[5].

Next to the prairie, over 100 m² have been set aside for the educational garden, where children can engage in planting and experimenting. This area can be used for different educational projects. To ensure the programs coexist well and avoid damaging the rooftop ecosystem, a set of guidelines was given to the teachers after a few months of using the garden. For example, it was advised to keep the chickens in a covered and enclosed area as much as possible to limit their impact on the rooftop system (trampling, hunting for worms) and to stop pigeons from getting to their food.

1 Aurélien Huguet defined the preliminary program, and then Jean-Louis Ducreux worked with us to integrate all the ecological data into the project.

2 Oak trees are not allowed on green roofs according to current French regulations (Unified Technical Document No. 43).

3 The list of selected species includes 20 specimens that can grow to 4 meters or more; 50 specimens expected to reach between 2.5 and 3 meters, and smaller species that reach maturity at 0.8 to 2 meters.

4 To provide optimal conditions for insects, the vegetation in this area follows the prescriptions of the Arrhenatherion elatioris code CORINE 38.2 "Low Altitude Hay Meadows" from the National Inventory of Natural Heritage (INPN). The seeds were then selected based on specific conditions (maintaining the density of 20 to 30 seeds per square meter).

5 The grassy zone includes 20% perennial ryegrass, which grows slowly and is suited to short mowing; 40% Brockton fescue, which is highly resistant to trampling and stays short; and 40% Greystone fescue, also highly resistant to trampling, with upright growth and winter hardiness.

→ The gymnasium supports the forest

The inhabited wall

The enclosing wall composed of concrete blocks forms an envelope linking the different parts of the project: the school program, the planted areas, and the development of local biodiversity. This prefabricated shell is inspired by old stone walls that have lots of irregularities like interstices, recesses, and crevices, providing ideal conditions for various animal and plant species to thrive.

We chose concrete for two main reasons. First, for its stone-like texture, as we wanted to replicate the morphological conditions of an old wall that would gradually be colonized by moss and vegetation. The physical behavior of concrete is similar to that of stone: it erodes on the surface while maintaining a stable structure and demonstrating optimal longevity. The surface erosion of the material is seen as a positive factor, as it facilitates the growth of surface vegetation.

Secondly, for its malleability. To make sure the system works comprehensively, we wanted all the birdhouses and insect hotels to be built right into the blocks. Concrete allowed us to achieve the functions of a stone wall, while easily molding custom prefabricated building blocks with all necessary openings.

The wall is designed as a multi-variable envelope system and a coherent geometric structure. Its lower part remains vertical for 3 meters, then gradually leans inward to offer more angles, overhangs, and thicknesses, especially for fitting in the deepest birdhouses.

The blocks are arranged with faces tilted at different angles. The resulting formal variety combines with the multiple setups created by the blocks across the entire facade. The wall's geometry is not just an aesthetic choice, but a complex mix of technical and ecological information with a single purpose: provide the maximum number of possible conditions so flora and fauna could settle in sustainably.

The positioning of the blocks creates exposed areas, shaded zones, overhangs, and ledges, offering multiple niches for different species of plants, insects, or animals. For instance, spaces between the blocks make perfect shelters for pipistrelles.

The grooves in the upper parts of the blocks play a major role: they form gaps and provide microsoils that help pioneer vegetation take root on the facade.

The concrete wall is meant to recreate the conditions of an old stone wall while offering unique, optimal situations enabled by the malleability of the material. However, these conditions need time to develop. The blocks keep evolving, and their weathering makes them increasingly effective for supporting biodiversity.

The inhabited wall has the following facilities:

Facilities for fauna

— Birdhouses: Built into the thickness of the blocks and designed according to the recommendations of ecologist Aurélien Huguet, the birdhouses meet the specific needs of local bird species, such as nesting altitude, the amount of light, interior space, and entrance dimensions.

— Insect hotels: These are located in the lower part of the wall, from 0 to 3 meters above the ground. They consist of a series of cylindrical holes in the concrete blocks, with diameters ranging from 3 to 15 mm and a depth of 10 cm. Their purpose is to provide shelters for various insects, some of which are beneficial to the garden in terms of pollination and pest control: bees, bumblebees, earwigs, lacewings, ladybugs, etc.

Facilities for flora

— Integrated Planters: 26 planters measuring 47 x 16 cm and 6 cm deep have been provided on the upper face of certain blocks, based on environmental conditions such as humidity levels or sun exposure. They host a total of 360 local species, arranged according to the plants' needs.

— Grooves: The upper and lateral parts of the blocks are grooved to direct rainwater from the roof to the ground, so that it could water the vegetation on the wall. This natural, guided irrigation system requires no maintenance or additional watering, and is enough to sustain the ecosystem in place.

— Vertical Cables: Steel cables have been stretched vertically to encourage the growth of climbing vegetation. This strengthens the "biodiversity connection" between the base of the façade and the planted roof, enhancing the overall colonization process.

The façade requires no maintenance. This way, the evolution of the ecosystem is supported, observed, and monitored, but not controlled. The inhabited wall is designed to create favorable conditions for certain local species, but it also allows for unforeseen developments. The shape of the wall offers various settings that encourage spontaneous colonization processes.

Monitoring and management plan

After the building's completion in 2014, we initiated regular visits by ecologists to document and assess changes in the ecosystem. The green roof is an artificially created environment that cannot be viewed as a natural ecosystem and requires regular monitoring. The conclusions from these visits will help improve our understanding and management of the ecosystem. Our role in supporting these changes puts architectural experimentation in a long-term context.

Since 2020, the objective has been to increase the biological potential of all present environments (meadows, woods, and façades) by using ecological engineering techniques innovatively applied to architecture. Every two years, we carry out enrichment activities (mowing, reseeding, and direct planting), together with the children and under the guidance of Aurélien Huguet. In 2021, a comprehensive assessment by Aurélien Huguet Ecologie and Ecolo GIE identified more than 350 species on the premises. Some were introduced during the planting, while others are native and have moved in on their own.

The gradually developed educational activities are changing how the rooftop is used. Regular discussions with teachers and facilitators are held to evaluate the impact of these interventions and adjust the overall balance. In 2023, we restructured the wooded area, created vegetable gardens, and planted a lilac orchard with informational panels about the different environments. At the same time, we are drafting a charter for teachers, leisure center facilitators, specialized preschool staff, and parents. This document will provide guidelines for the proper use of the school's green spaces, aiming to help everyone understand the balance involved in the design and sustainability of these ecosystems, so they can enjoy them without causing harm.

↑ The prefabricated building blocks were transported and put in place one by one

It's a prototype that h *and lived in*. **The scho observation, analysis of how a building can proposed concept is n be exported to just an a** *unique solution* **tailo site and program, and to local data and spec constraints.**

as been *colonized*
ol encourages
and understanding
welcome life. **The**
ot generic and cannot
y context. It offers
red to a particular
designed according
ific technical

3.J GardeNation

— Paris

Shaping a project through needs, uses, and practices

A team of landscape architects, researchers, and artists spent several months in one of Paris's most iconic squares, engaging with the territory, the street, and the night, and exploring the myriad ways to cross this major public area. The challenge was to reimagine Place de la Nation's six hectares, based on what people do in this vast and diverse space.

During the several–month–long Call to Create, the square was being transformed through collaborative action, which led to the revision of the development plan. Through a sequence of core steps, the team was able to build a shared vision with the municipal services in charge of the project, and reclaim the 'car space' for lots of potential uses, including the successful transition from a traffic circle to a park.

As an end result, thanks to this methodology, the city saved nearly 40% of the initially estimated 20-million-euro budget.

Mission Co–design, co–building, and redevelopment of the Place de la Nation
Location Paris, 11th, 12th and 20th arrondissements
Geographical coordinates 48°50'53.5"N, 2°23'47.1"E
Size 61 000 m²
Status Public space
Budget 12 000 000 €
Phasing 2016 – 2019

Team Ville de Paris
– Secretary General's Office, Jean Christophe Choblet
– The Mayor's Office, Michele Zaoui
– Department of roads and trasportation
Department of green spaces
Team Coloco & Co
– Atelier Coloco
– Bfluid, expert in mobility and the gender approach to public space, Sonia Lavadinho
– Vertigo In Vivo, expert in cultural projects in public spaces, Pascal Le Brun–Cordier
– SAA Architectes – Jean–François Authier, licensed architect and urban planner
– OGI Ingénierie – Laurent Straboni, engineer and head of communications

← © Yann Monel

Public space belongs
Spend enough time h
awareness, and you v
the *intangible qualitie*
the physical space. Y
become one of space

to everyone.
ere, sharpen your
vill notice
s **layering over**
our project will then
and *community***.**

→ A draft map of the commons good
© P. Georgieff, Coloco

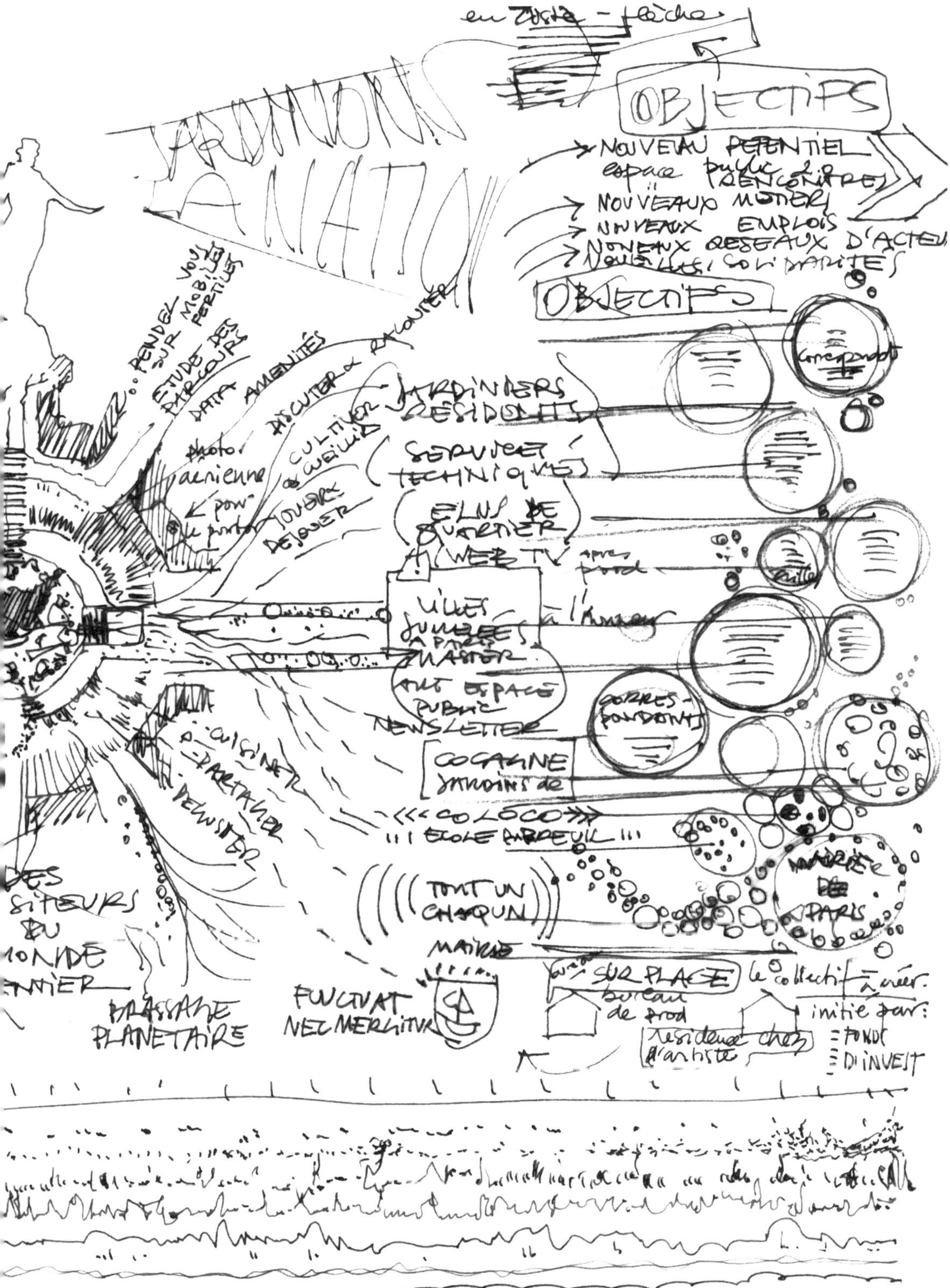

OBJECTIFS
NOUVEAU POTENTIEL espace public de RENCONTRES
NOUVEAUX METIERS
NOUVEAUX EMPLOIS
NOUVEAUX RESEAUX D'ACTEU
NOUVELLES SOLIDARITES
OBJECTIFS
JARDINIERS RESIDENTS
SERVICES TECHNIQUES
ELUS DE QUARTIER
WEB TV
VILLES JUMELEES
MASTER
ART ESPACE PUBLIC
NEWSLETTER
COCAGNE
<<< COLOCO >>>
TOUT UN CHACUN
MAIRIE
SUR PLACE bureau de prod
le collectif à créer initié par:
FONDS D'INVEST
FLUCTUAT NEC MERGITUR
BRASSAGE PLANETAIRE
DES VISITEURS DU MONDE ENTIER
PHOTO AERIENNE
DATA
AMENITES
DISCUTER RACONTER
CULTIVER
CUISINER
PARTAGER
ETUDE DES PARCOURS

3.J
GardeNation

"I had a dream. Bursts of soap bubbles, blown by a mischievous little girl with a water gun, were dancing in the air, reflecting a whole world in a kaleidoscope of lively scenes. It was clearly the same place, and yet each time a different scene popped up at the center of the picture. Gardeners dressed in white and carrying palm trees like statues of saints in religious processions, a group of women in suits picnicking on checkered tablecloths, right on the sidewalk, a blind boy leading a group of tourists, waving his pennant in the air, a hyena on a leash, held by a drag queen and laughing its head off, a group of high school students rehearsing a play – and another one, apparently having a serious discussion about something important, a shepherd on roller skates, rounding up sheep, a hundred of very young carpenters having fun building the biggest table on Earth, a Creole cook offering countless chilies to blushing diners, a guy in a tie suit playing the double bass in a stationary bus, a crowd gathered around some old men debating under a palaver tree, a group of elderly ladies, skillfully attacking the asphalt with pickaxes, street sweepers sewing golden sequins onto their work uniforms, a young man in a beret giving slang lessons, a docked galleon hoisting her white flag, which read: *Fluctuat nec mergitur*"[1].

Pablo Georgieff, Coloco

[1] ([she] is rocked [by the waves], but does not sink, the Latin motto of the city of Paris – t/n).

← ©Yann Monel

3.1
Considering the landscape project as a negotiation platform

The redevelopment of seven major Parisian squares, including Place de la Nation, was a politically assertive project with a very tight budget (30 million euros for a total of seven squares, with 22 million allocated for Place de la République alone).

The officials wanted the residents to decide what these spaces should look like – but the municipality of Paris is a large organization, and these working methods are not part of its culture. Besides, shifting from a top–down to a bottom–up approach is never easy. A new kind of public commission had to be invented.

An international workshop on participatory urban planning was organized, involving experts, municipal services, and elected officials, and introducing some very different working methods. It took a year to develop a plan and select the teams: multidisciplinary groups capable of building and testing prototypes and establishing relationships with the users.

The decision was made to use a purchase order contract: a framework with maximum amounts and unit prices per task, which the client would activate as necessary. In practice, frequent negotiations were needed to fine–tune the package. Detailed monitoring facilitated budget negotiations for each phase.

Project management was split between multidisciplinary teams on the one hand, and the Department of Roads and Transportation and the Department of Green Spaces and Environment on the other. This way of separating creative work and responsibility is far from straightforward, and sharing authorship throughout the project was no small challenge.

3.2
Building community by gardening together

At the start of the project, we only thought about involving residents – at best, citizens. But this kind of voter filter, prioritizing the people based in the neighborhood, is not suitable for major public spaces that are of concern to the whole city, and sometimes even the whole nation. Many of the square's users are neither residents nor citizens. This particular place is a site for political expression, for challenging authority, and for national rallies.

One thing we had to realize was that anyone passing through Place de la Nation could provide valuable insights for reimagining its design. Which led us to use a tool like sensitive maps, created on–site. This implied dedicating time to meet people, gathering various viewpoints, tracking desires, and identifying areas of calm and concern, as well as friendships, tensions, and routines.

For this to happen, being present is essential; it's a case where the quality of your work depends on the time you dedicate to it. This might seem wasteful from a purely technical perspective, but knowing how people actually use a space can show that expensive interventions aren't always necessary. For example, the decision to keep, rather than remove, a portion of the road in the center of the square and cover it with light–coloured asphalt became possible thanks to carefully observing uses and making prototypes. The amount spent on research was increased, but this allowed saving significant costs for the project as a result. The success of the square in terms of visitor numbers and the diversity of available uses demonstrated the effectiveness of this approach.

↑ ©Coloco

↑ ©Ana Bloom

3.3
Turning the project into a score that unfolds over time

When working ambitiously on public space, one races against the political calendar, as the work must be completed within the current term. As a result, one tends to stick to familiar routines and stay within the known territory, because innovation can put public services under stress. One needs to keep in mind the timelines for procedures, contracts, permits, and appeals. It's worth noting, though, that no appeals have been lodged for any of the seven squares' projects, which is quite exceptional.

It is however possible to follow the timelines and phases of a classical project management process, while at the same time co-designing and co-building prototypes and testing them on-site. In this project, despite a significant transformation of the initial draft, the deadlines were met, and the projected budget was revised downward.

The new approach has also prompted some questions. When applying these methods, is the remuneration based on a percentage of the construction costs still relevant? Should we come up with new rules for public spaces and landscaping to promote cost-saving through rewarding frugal projects? This crucial question may be a call for revising the Public Project Management Law.

Lastly, when working with living things, the issue of extending support for plants and communities beyond the construction period is paramount. The necessary forms and resources for this are still to be put in place.

3.4
Expressing care for the living world through aesthetic resolution

Working on a manifesto for a new Parisian aesthetic, the Paris City Hall is addressing the issue at an institutional level. When non-standard items such as bike lanes, terraces, or plazas, arrive in public spaces, this disrupts the Second Empire aesthetic to which a certain demographic is attached. They regard Haussmann and Alphand as the ultimate peak, and see any novelty that does not reference them as almost sacrilegious.

But perhaps we need to define the concept of a new aesthetic in the context of the 21st century. While in the 19th and early 20th centuries the notion of aesthetics shaped the complex idea of taste and beauty, today it has gone beyond the concept of "the beautiful" as "that which pleases universally, without a concept."

We do not question the importance of proportions, color, material, and harmony, but what makes a furniture piece or an urban project aesthetically pleasing is whether it lives up to its promise and provides a true experience. This is especially relevant for contemporary urban planning, which puts the user first. Contemporary urban aesthetics is a synthesis between good, harmonious design that defines an object's identity and its capacity to make people want to engage with it, walk through it, occupy it; the capacity to reassure, and the practicality of use.

Jean Christophe Choblet – Secretary General's Office and the Department of Roads and Transportation of the Municipality of Paris

↑ ©Ana Bloom

↑ ©Ana Bloom

CONSTRUCTION

CO-DESIGNED WITH
SCATERS
BOWLERS
HIGH-SCHOOL STUDENTS

PHOTO EXHIBITION
TABLES
WHEELBARROWS
SEATING FOR SKATERS
SEATING FOR BOWLERS
MISTING SYSTEM
URBAN FURNITURE
PROTOTYPES
SKATE RAMPS

RECEPTION

SITE LOGISTICS
TOOLING
VILLAGE MANAGEMENT
SCHEDULE
SUPPLY
OPENING/CLOSURE
ON-SITE MEDIATION
CO-DESIGNING

1500
PARTICIPANTS

EVENT

OPERATION DIVAN
« WALKING
ENCYCLOPEDIA »
WORLD MUSIC DAY
NATION SKATE TEAM
KIDZ IN SADDLE

2500
PARTICIPANTS

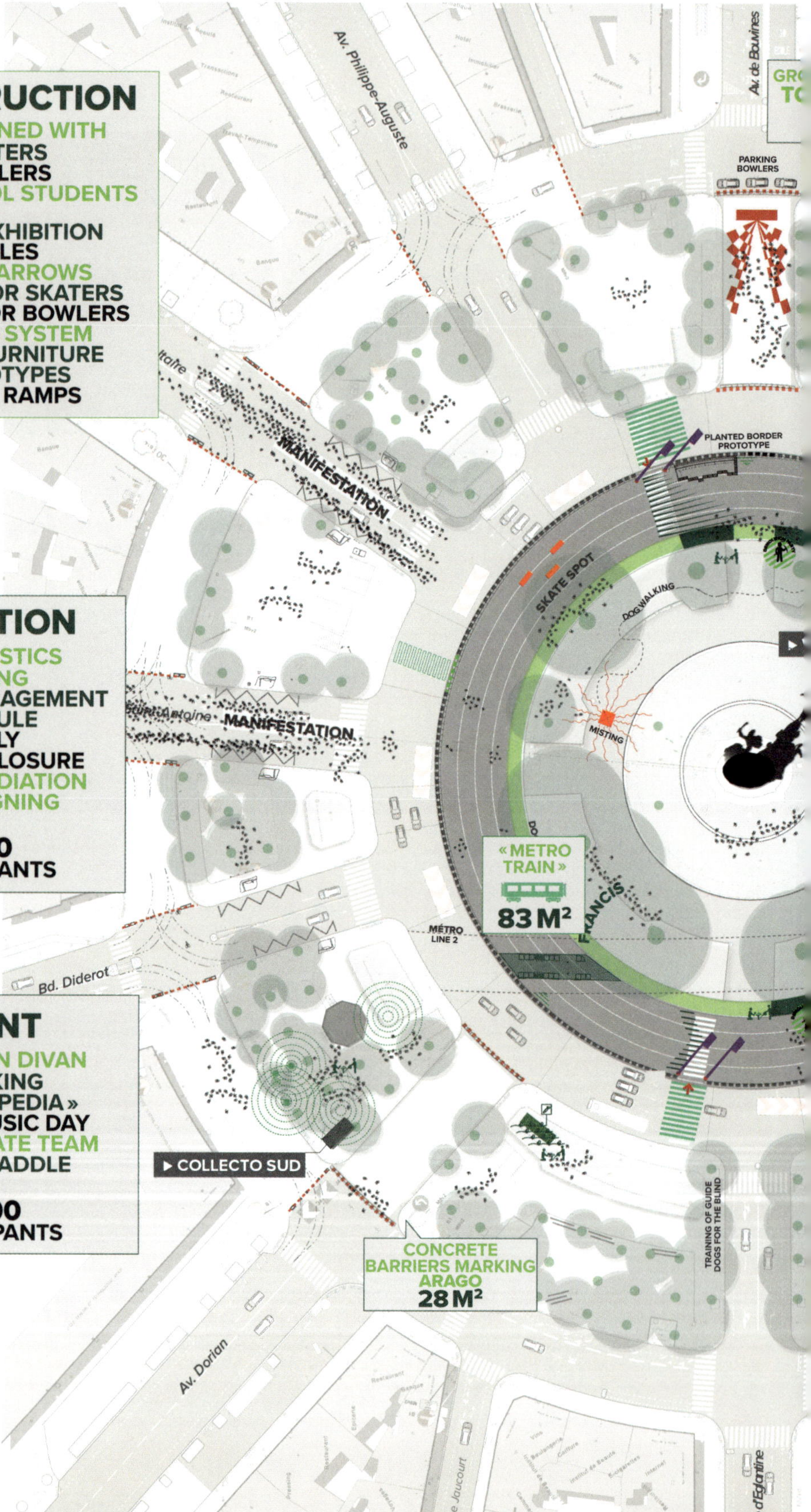

www.coloco.org

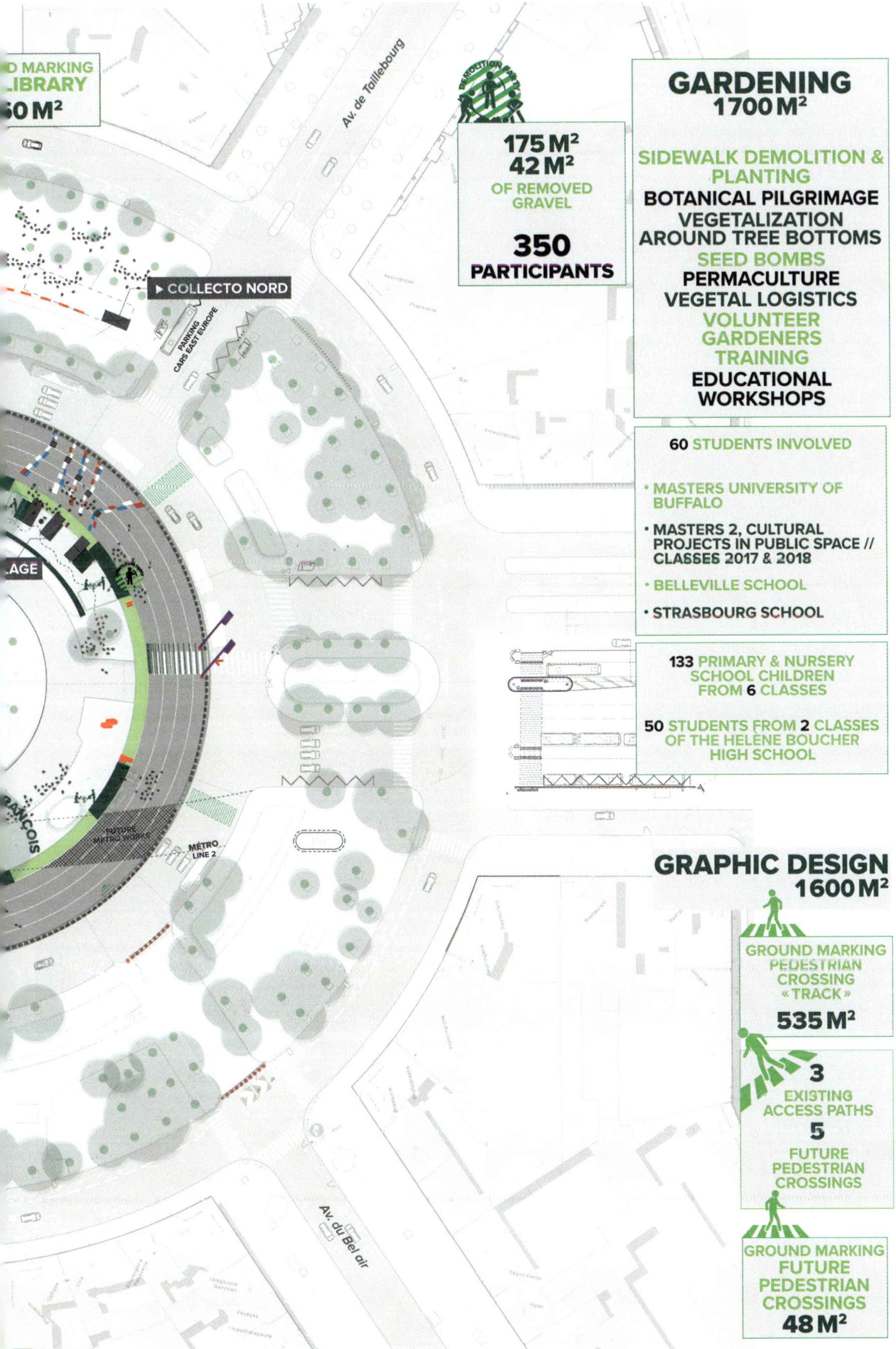
D MARKING
LIBRARY
50 M²
Av. de Taillebourg
DEMOLITION PARTY
175 M²
42 M²
OF REMOVED GRAVEL
350
PARTICIPANTS
GARDENING
1700 M²
SIDEWALK DEMOLITION & PLANTING
BOTANICAL PILGRIMAGE
VEGETALIZATION AROUND TREE BOTTOMS
SEED BOMBS
PERMACULTURE
VEGETAL LOGISTICS
VOLUNTEER GARDENERS TRAINING
EDUCATIONAL WORKSHOPS
▸ COLLECTO NORD
PARKING CARS EAST EUROPE
60 STUDENTS INVOLVED
• MASTERS UNIVERSITY OF BUFFALO
• MASTERS 2, CULTURAL PROJECTS IN PUBLIC SPACE // CLASSES 2017 & 2018
• BELLEVILLE SCHOOL
• STRASBOURG SCHOOL
AGE
133 PRIMARY & NURSERY SCHOOL CHILDREN FROM 6 CLASSES
50 STUDENTS FROM 2 CLASSES OF THE HELÈNE BOUCHER HIGH SCHOOL
ANÇOIS
FUTURE METRO WORKS
MÉTRO LINE 2
GRAPHIC DESIGN
1600 M²
GROUND MARKING PEDESTRIAN CROSSING « TRACK »
535 M²
3
EXISTING ACCESS PATHS
5
FUTURE PEDESTRIAN CROSSINGS
GROUND MARKING FUTURE PEDESTRIAN CROSSINGS
48 M²
Av. du Bel air

We use various diagnostic methods to broaden our understanding and capture the complexity of the public space.

We don't just invite people to a one-and-a-half-hour meeting or ask them to complete an online questionnaire. Such methods 'professionalize' citizen participation because, typically, they involve only those with direct interests, like the owners of apartments facing the square, or political activists. Which is not necessarily a bad thing, but these individuals only represent a small fraction of the users. In contrast, spending significant time on-site with no rush and being available for discussions at different times, rather than simply conducting a consultation, helps build a real connection.

This approach is much more effective, even though it is harder to quantify. It focuses on quality rather than quantity and is the opposite of a multiple-choice questionnaire that lacks human interaction. Here, we deal with real-life situations and make room for people's complexity. A person who comes here every day to walk their dog has many stories and observations that won't fit into a questionnaire. Such people often have valuable knowledge, including on-site expertise, which traditional consultation and technical diagnostic methods miss entirely. Adding this extra source of insight to conventional working methods improves the quality of public spaces, but also changes the traditional methods themselves.

→ ©Ana Bloom

New aesthetic

To create a new Parisian aesthetic, there are two main things to keep in mind:

— Material quality in the urban space

Identify a set of rules, objects, materials, and colors that constitute the harmony and identity of Paris. This toolkit will serve as a foundation, with a possibility of adapting the arrangements to each specific situation.

— Design process

Every stage – design, implementation, experimentation, and evaluation – should involve gathering the residents' opinions on the urban project.

It's crucial to bring to the fore the creative process, the one where beauty becomes a battleground. Similar approaches, though hard to standardize, are emerging in contemporary art. This requires skills from both the client and the designer, as well as a team's commitment to the project. It's worth fighting for, because – just like the Second Empire style with its inventory of elements – it's a tradition and know-how that is unique to Paris and that makes it, according to many, the world's most beautiful city.

Finally, there are places like pétanque courts or wild-looking plant borders that can sometimes be even a bit ugly, but where nothing needs to be done, because their value is in the life they support. Attention must be focused on the margins. What's happening here will show that a space is cared for, and not neglected. That's a challenge, because the fantasy of a perfect order – the one that would choke a city – is hard to shake away.

↓ Summary of the wishes expressed during the consultation

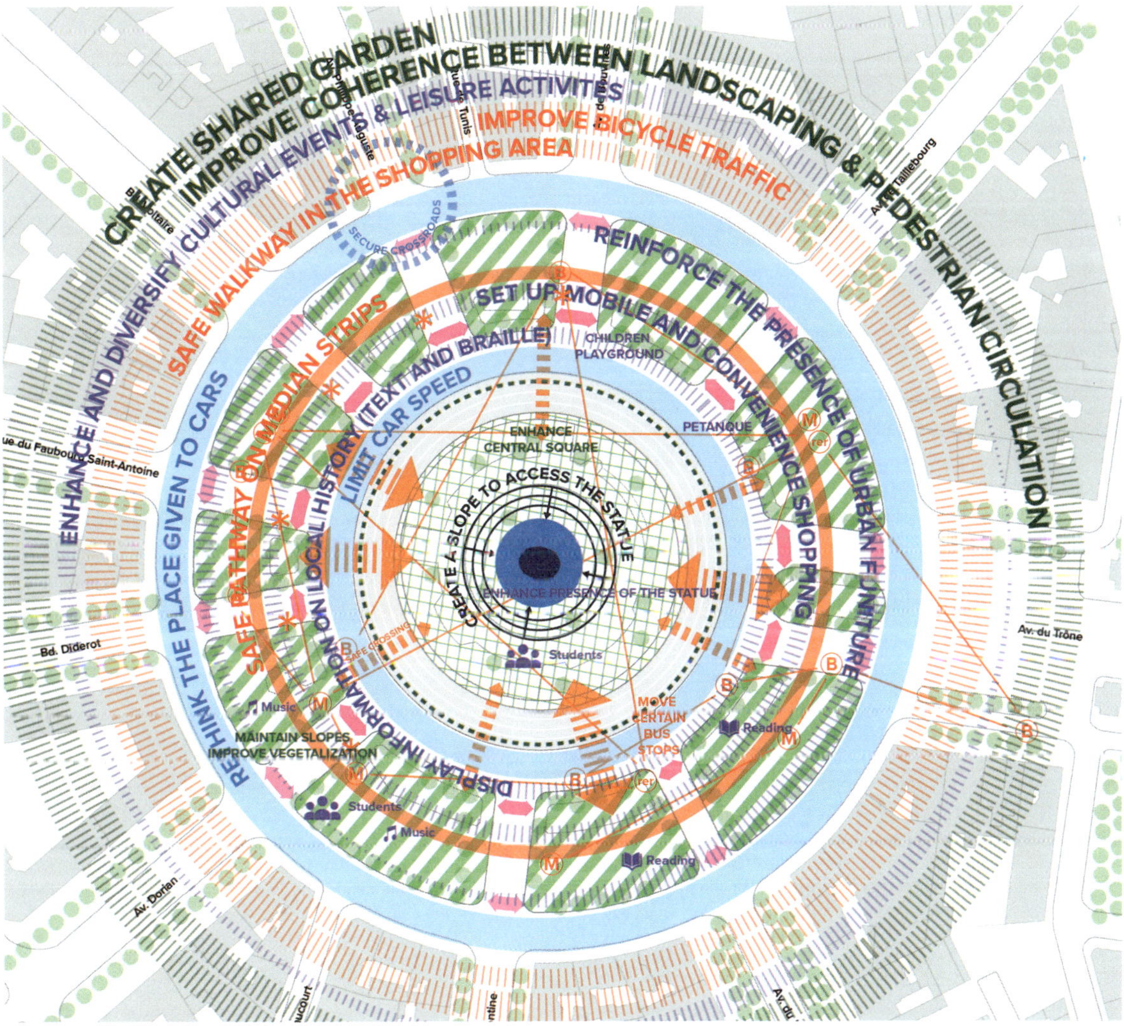

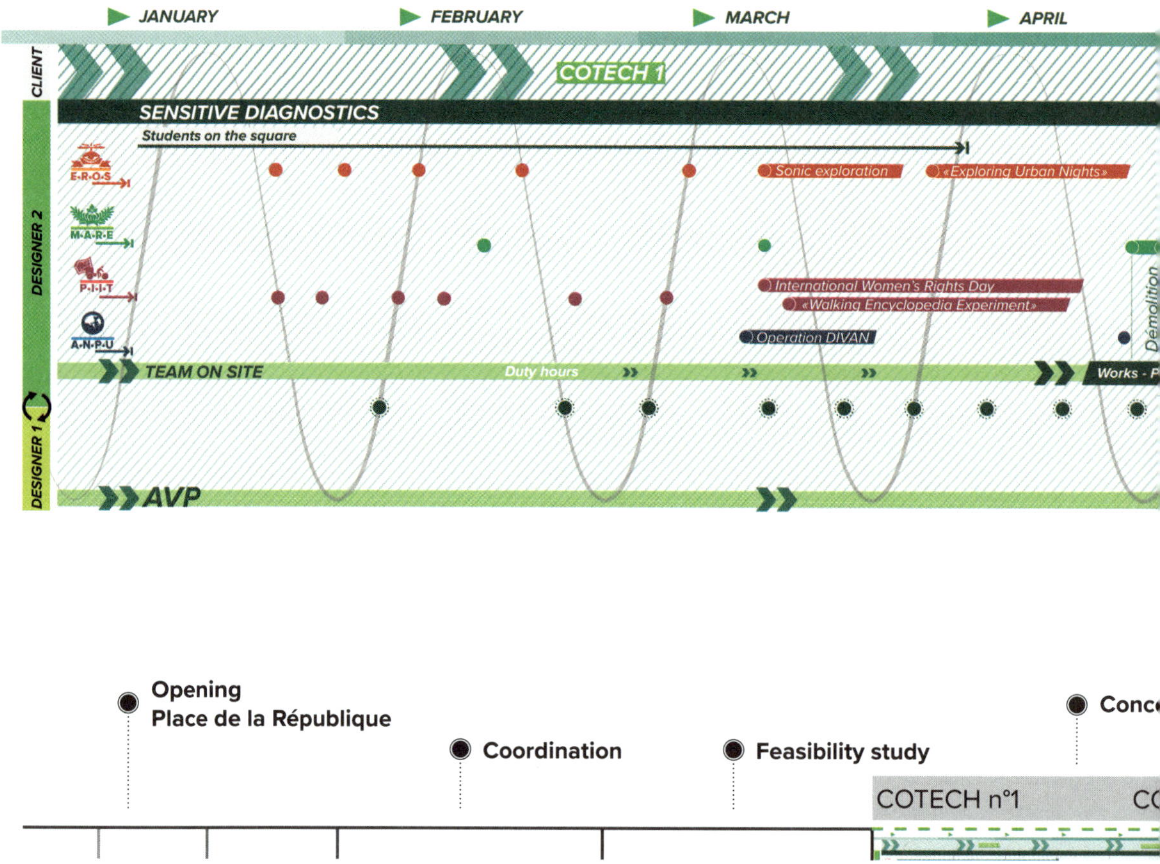

↑ Construction project timeline
© Coloco & Co score

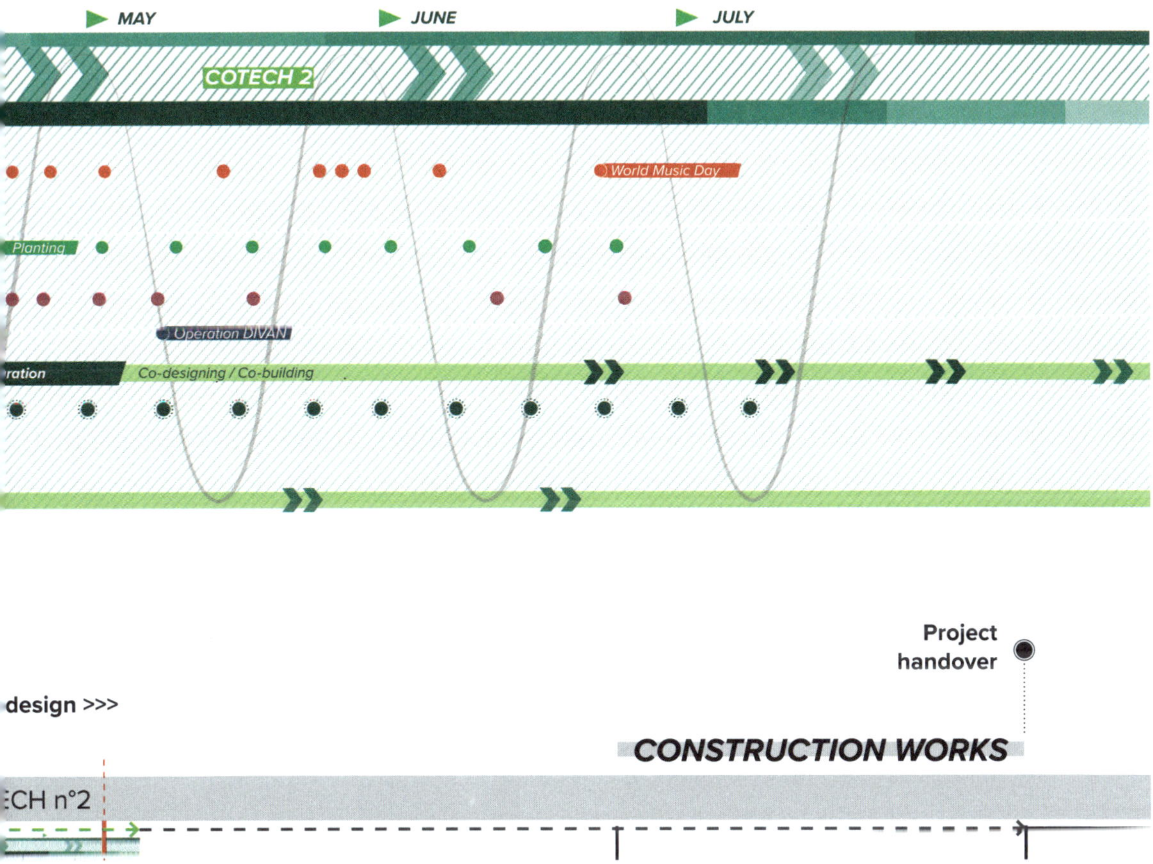

MAY
JUNE
JULY
COTECH 2
World Music Day
Planting
Operation DIVAN
ration
Co-designing / Co-building
Project handover
design >>>
CONSTRUCTION WORKS
ECH n°2

Call to Create

The *Call to Create* is one of our foundational concepts. The idea is to declare that we are embarking on a project to which everyone is invited.

This is different from traditional project management because it involves less control: instead, we are inviting people to collaborate and build together. In such projects, design is secondary: there is no initial blueprint, only responsiveness to opportunities and constraints. The *Call to Create* is precisely an invitation to be part of the creative process with its ups and downs, trials, errors, and discoveries. Designing a space by incorporating the opinions, ideas, attempts, and contributions of many different individuals requires committing yourself to the project and leaving behind the mindset of being the sole author.

Working together takes time, both in terms of explaining and coordinating the project. It's always much longer than working alone or with a team of professionals in a structured hierarchy. But this collaborative process offers more than just efficiency: for everyone involved, it's a step towards greater independence of thought and action.

← ©Nathan Rivin

The gardeners' village

Designing and building the project with the users at its core

To achieve this, we set up "the gardeners' village" – a technical term for a base camp – which allowed us to spend over a hundred days on-site, meeting users in their everyday settings and at their own pace, rather than just through formal consultations. This made a big difference, as it enabled direct interaction with both the lived experience of the place and the diverse range of individuals who use it and pass through it daily, and many of whom do not typically attend formal meetings. We conducted a 'sensitive diagnostic' to gather their feedback on how the space works in terms of social interactions (including generational and gender issues), practices, comforts and discomforts, and then displayed this information on-site, as required by the project brief.

Prefiguration

Next was the prefiguration phase, where we reduced the traffic lanes from 8 to 4, creating a 6,000-square-meter pedestrian space by expanding the central part of the square – as decided during consultations and studied by the Department of Roads and Transportation. This space was made available to the people right away, so we could see how new ways of using it and new ways of meeting there started to emerge.

This was a real-life draft of the project, which we could tweak as uses evolved. We translated it into drawings that have been revised and discussed countless times. This was done mostly on-site, just like two-thirds of the 220 meetings.

↗ ©Ana Bloom

→ ©Pablo Georgieff

JARDINATION
JARDINATION
JARDINATION

Designed and built *co*
la Nation is a *collectiv*
idea of authorship is
it becomes secondary
The *Call to Create* **has**
end of the constructio
tending the gardens a
the countless activiti
capable of hosting da
purpose, we designed
as possible.

operatively, **Place de**
e work **where the**
so multifaceted that
to the final result.
n't ended at the
n: it continues by
nd engaging in
s the place is
y by day. For this
it to be as flexible

↓ ©P. Georgieff, Coloco

3.K Base 217

– Le Plessis–Pâté / Brétigny–sur–Orge

A laboratory of new practices

This project aims to balance the needs of living organisms with development goals. It shows a different way of handling large–scale schemes while limiting urban sprawl.

By focusing on landscape, agriculture, green and blue corridors, and, in particular, on stormwater management, the team intends to restore the geographical and natural connections in this human–altered, fully–serviced area.

This experimental territory space takes its time, seizes opportunities, and fosters interactions to actively make things happen, but also to let nature take its course. Base 217 is not a static oeuvre but an evolving park for living beings.

Mission Urban, landscape, and hydrological project management for the conversion of the former Airbase 217 into a park
Location The Cœur d'Essonne agglomeration, France
Geographical coordinates 48°36'19"N, 2°19'41"E
Size 300 hectares

← ©A. Magnan, Airborne Films

Team
Client SPL Air 217
Design/Strategy Urban planning: l'AUC, Safege
Landscape: Coloco, Gilles Clément, Atelier Thierry Maytraud
Institutional partners The project is co–financed by European funds, the state, the Île–de–France region, and the Essonne department
Implementation 2020–2025

To implement the *gui*
for a living environmen
balance between gar
nature take its course
plants grow **naturally**
landscape by *subtrac*

dance strategy
t **means to strike a**
ening and letting
. It involves *letting*
nd shaping the
ion.

↓ Students do the strategic pruning of the 'school fringe' — ©E. Pardon, Coloco

3.K

Base 217, a laboratory of the *Planetary Garden*

Base 217 is an extraordinary venture that promotes a practical and open approach. It's about fostering exchanges and synergies, as well as cultivating the capacity to evolve and adapt to challenges, particularly to climate change. The aim is not to deliver a finished project but to create the conditions for long-term success, relying on local stakeholders. We prioritize experimentation, testing, and temporary activation. Keeping options open for as long as possible gives the project time to solidify, allows the solutions to emerge, and lets us include the precautionary principle and the right to make mistakes. By adopting this approach, we can view uncertainty with optimism and experiment with Putting Life first. We can maintain and develop the site through meaningful actions for the sake of the landscape and the living world – welcoming new practices, preserving what's already there if it's compatible with intended uses, and, most importantly, planting and supporting the establishment of all forms of life.

Nicolas Bonnenfant, Coloco

← ©L. Foulon, Coloco

3.1
Considering the landscape project as a negotiation platform

The project to repurpose the former military airbase 217 brought together multiple stakeholders and institutions, each with their own interests but all aligning around the themes of the living world, water, and landscape. These themes have shaped the development scheme.

Natural enemies of airplanes and the first to benefit from the airbase decommissioning, birds have settled here in no time. This exceptionally large site became a magnet for various aspirations and projects. So, how do we balance everyone's interests while preserving the biodiversity potential of the vast, open meadows between the runways?

The experiments made by various players (landscapers, ecology and hydrology experts, the Bird Protection League, farmers, etc.) have highlighted some current contradictions and paradoxes of biodiversity. What kind of biodiversity, and for whom? How do we keep as many open spaces as possible for the species that suffer from the fragmentation of these spaces? Can we achieve this by steering away from the intensive maintenance methods practiced by the military?

How do we enhance habitats to welcome new species? How do we bring water back into the system that has been drained and dried out by infrastructure? All of these issues had to be addressed – in addition to preserving the already existing habitats and species, and enabling future activities on the site.

The creation of the Planetary Garden at Base 217 is both a significant ecological challenge and part of the "laboratory of new practices" that aims to demonstrate a new way of developing living environments with eco-consciousness and respect.

↑ ©E. Pardon, Coloco

3.2
Building community by gardening together

The project mainly relies on the dynamics of living systems and includes whole sections of productive landscape, which are partly integrated into the new park, helping enhance biodiversity. The community involved is large and diverse, but the project centered around landscape, water management, and biodiversity brings everyone together.

It's not easy to understand the site and its scale. Organizing small-scale planting, conducting discovery visits of man-made and natural heritage, setting up botanical signage and building an educational greenhouse that will serve as an outdoor school for nearby towns – each of these small initiatives offers ways to understand, bring to life, and pass on knowledge about living organisms. A blackthorn wasteland where we found a few walnuts, oaks, and hazel trees planted by birds is also a tool for discovery and learning. A path cut through this wasteland leads to a clearing where an oak tree has grown, sheltered from the winds by its thorny neighbors. This is the beginning of the story of a wasteland garden, which continues to develop as part of the project.

Another unifying element is water, a crucial resource for the garden. Once promptly drained for the airfield's needs, water now finds its natural path on this plateau at the junction of the Orge, Seine, and Essonne watersheds. Disconnecting the runways and future developments from the drainage network is one of the project's main challenges, and various stakeholders have come together to achieve this. Water becomes a resource instead of a problem.

↑ ©L. Foulon, Coloco

3.3
Turning the project into a score that unfolds over time

The landscape project of Base 217 is gradually developing from a network of ecological continuities set up according to the SRCE (Regional Ecological Coherence Scheme) guidelines. The goal is to quickly establish the main network (tree and shrub continuities, culverts and wildlife crossings under roads, refuge meadows, etc.), in order to create a functional system that will grow with each new project phase. The project evolves over time, as new players join in. The Masterplan for the living environment adapts in parallel with the maintenance plan for the already implemented parts. It also addresses the issues of adaptability and opportunities: how do we meet future ecological challenges without trying to freeze the region's typical ecosystem whose very essence is to adapt and evolve?

At the scale of the project, the ecological challenge involves using on-site resources and minimizing exports. One of the main features of the future park, the belvedere hill is being built as work on the site progresses. Creating this hill not only brings significant savings by limiting soil export or "landfilling," but is also part of the broader reflection on maximizing the reuse of local resources.

As opportunities like recovering the trees used in a fashion show, or transplanting spontaneously grown oaks, or others, arise, the project evolves and adapts to incorporate new elements.

3.4
Expressing care for the living world through aesthetic resolution

How do we showcase and enhance ordinary biodiversity that seems extraordinary in the areas dominated by intensive, standardized agriculture?

In this vast, mostly flat territory, the project adopts identifiable forms found in agroforestry and agricultural systems. These features highlight specific and functional setups for supporting biodiversity, acting as clear and structured markers of the attention given to it. They also serve as educational tools for understanding the environments, species, and life forms present at Base 217.

To aesthetically enhance these features, various fieldwork is undertaken, such as highlighting notable specimens, implementing a differentiated maintenance system that adopts geometric patterns across the meadows, carving paths through the wasteland... All of this allows us to integrate the existing features, and emphasize the scope of the environments that develop within the established framework.

↑ ©N. Bonnenfant, Coloco

↑ ©E. Pardon, Coloco

Plan with living things in mind. Create the *conditions to welcome life*, **build a landscape framework where projects can fit, and then** *help expand it*.

→ Structural pruning to create transparency
©A. Goncalves, Coloco

The General Plan of ecological continuities, phasing of the Maintenance Plan, and evolution factors for Base 217.

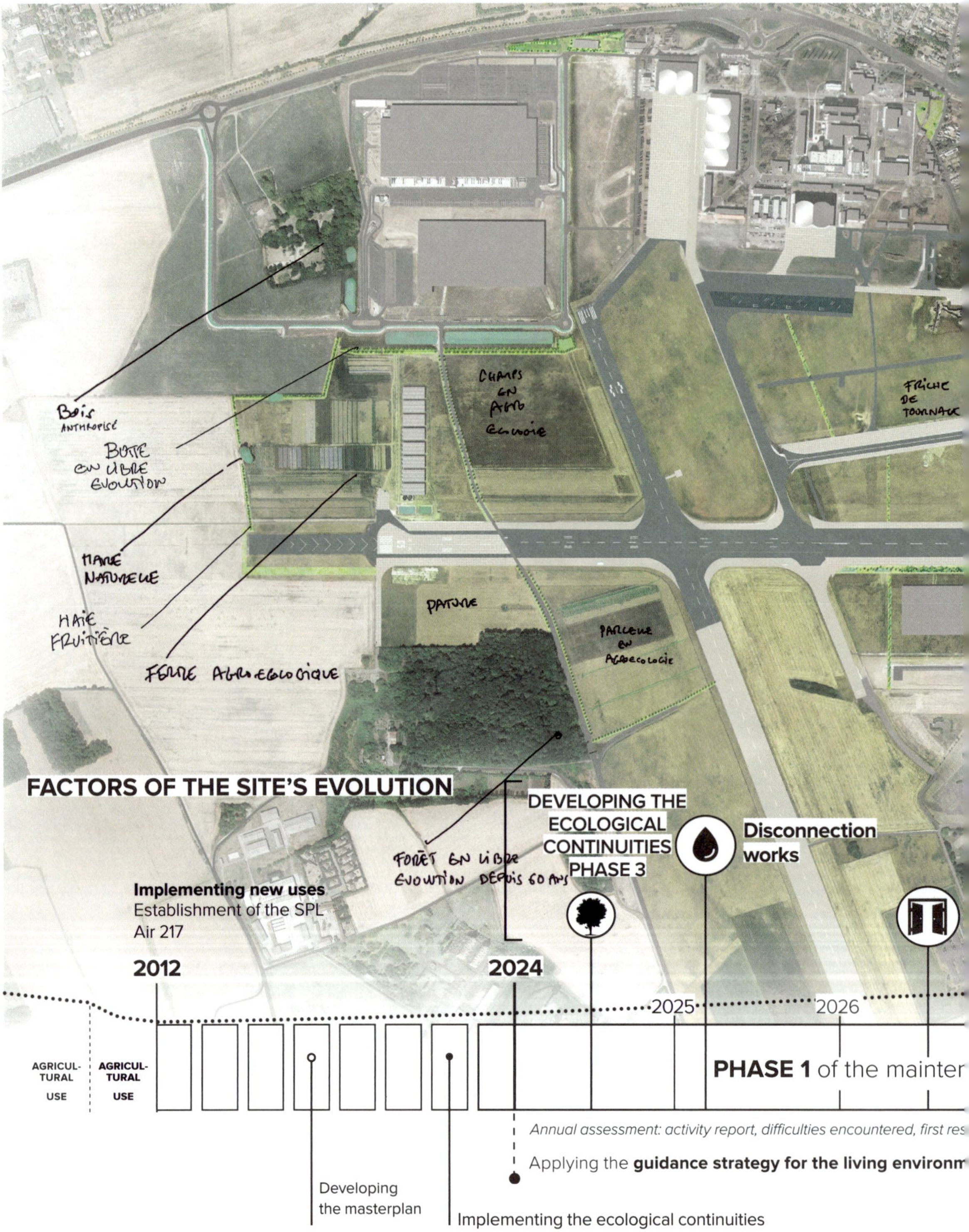

↑ ©N. Bonnenfant and T. Wambergue, Coloco

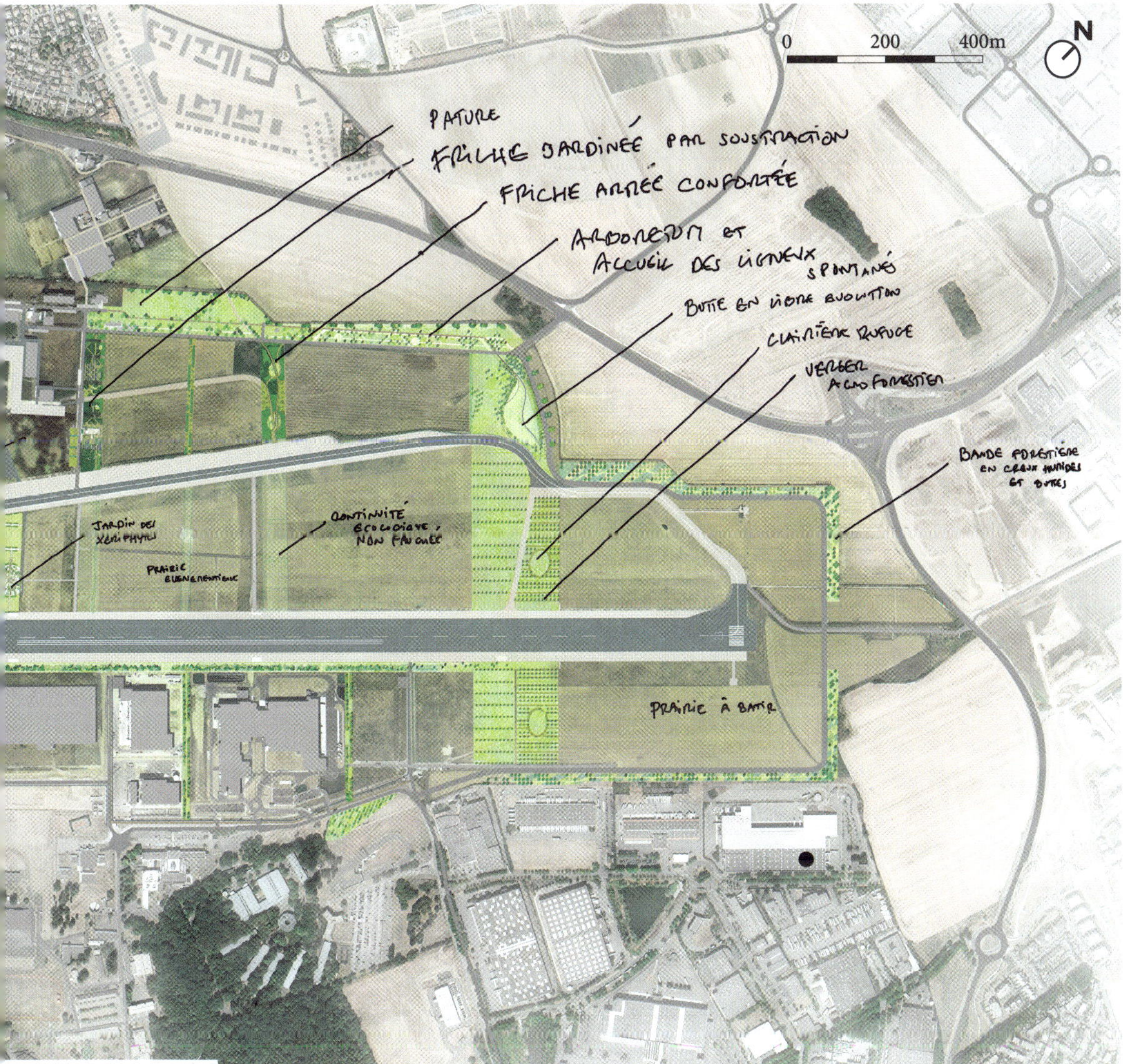

ening to the public?

INCREASE OF BIODIVERSITY

2028 **2032**

027 | **+ 4 years** | 2029 | 2030 | 2031 | **+ 8 years**

ce plan

PHASE 2 of the maintenance plan

bserved

Annual assessment: activity report, difficulties encountered, first results observed

(maintenance plan)

Multi–year assessment
– Redefining the operational strategy, readjustment in case of technical problems
– Identifying new issues

Final assessment
– Assessing the level of achievement of long–term objectives

Creating *plant successions* **in the airport infrastructures –** *even on concrete.*

→ ©R. Joubert, Coloco

Base 217, the territory of common good

Long bypassed and once forgotten, Base 217 is now a territory that is visited and flown over, a place where life must settle. The integration of living things as a new dimension of the Masterplan allows us to explore new horizons that had never been explored before. We all exist within the narrow space of the Planetary Garden, in this little biosphere, swimming together in the same waters that keep us alive. The water we drink has already been drunk by plants and animals before us, multiple times. This is our shared condition. The dragonfly, symbol of the Planetary Garden, is an insect that explores water both from the water and from the air. When there is no water, there is nothing.

Too often pushed to the background, trimmed and attacked in favor of the so-called efficiency or pragmatism of human practices, the space left for biodiversity, for life, for the water that is no longer just drained but allowed to find its natural spread as the rains come, must play a crucial role in the revitalization of Base 217. It acts as a link between the surrounding towns – a true common good that brings them together.

Each nearby town should have easy access to the park and reconnect with its geography. Reconnecting this island-like site is also about creating a dialogue between forested areas and open spaces. The park seeks to restore the natural connections of the territory that surrounds the former airbase. This means thinking about the project's water cycle – not only for the Base 217 site itself, but also for the whole hydrographic network, including the streams that feed into the Orge and Essonne rivers.

The water cycle – water-retaining soil and potential new wetlands that will help develop a rich, dense network of plants modeled on the ever-present but invisible water network – contributes to integrating the project into its urban context. The watercourses guide the design of paths and access points, facilitating mobility and integration of the former base into the city. They help unite territories and stakeholders around Base 217.

↗ ©T. Wambergue, Coloco
→ ©A. Magnan, Airborne Films

Collecting seeds to enhance meadows and open areas

The landscape of Base 217 is largely made up of vast open meadows. Legacy of the site's airfield past, these continuous plant formations, mostly composed of grasses, are valuable assets, and their maintenance is crucial for preserving the associated and endangered fauna. Given the fragmentation and decline of meadow biodiversity in the Île-de-France region, permanent meadows are considered to have heritage value.

To keep these meadows strong and growing, we use the seeds extracted through brush-harvesting the site. After identifying available species through a botanical survey and determining the best time for intervention based on seed maturity, the meadows are brushed to collect the seeds. This technique conserves the existing biodiversity while making good use of the site's resources.

↗ ©L. Foulon, Coloco
↗ ©E. Pardon, Coloco
↗ ©N. Bonnenfant, Coloco
→ ©I. Siegel, Coloco

Artificial soils vs. new habitats

The former airbase is a stopover for various species, particularly migratory birds. How can it become a haven for wildlife while maintaining its potential for developing activities?

To preserve as much open space as possible, all existing infrastructures (roads, concrete slabs, runways) have been reused. The project gradually builds around this mineral legacy, keeping the two runways and the central meadow as a common good suited for multiple purposes (events, farming, migratory bird habitats, land sailing).

The vast runway 23, inherited from the site's military past and easy to spot from the sky, is now a landing strip for migratory birds. Paradoxically, this fully artificial area is also becoming a home for wildlife. Integrating dry habitats for reptiles and preserving pioneer vegetation in the infrastructure's joints and cracks are some of the key aspects of the project.

↗ ©A. Magnan, Airborne Films
→ ©A. Kaki, Coloco

Water: resource of life and foundation of the landscape

Water has always been a key part of the site's history. It was a resource before the base existed, a constraint during its operation, and is especially significant today, "after the base." The presence of a shallow layer of clay allows the soil to retain water, which is good for farming and for the creation of fertile soil. To access water, a little digging is enough to open up a pond – as a result, there used to be a lot of natural and artificial ponds in the site's lower areas. The soil served as a conduit for the territory's water resources. When it became a problem for the airbase and had to be evacuated, they drained the plateau so that water could flow into the Orge and Essonne valleys – its natural outlets – via three small streams: from the Blutin to the Orge, from the Misery to the Essonne, and from the Écoute–s'il–pleut to the Seine.

Today, the redevelopment project brings new life to the site, and water–related priorities have changed. The new Base 217 will keep its water as an essential resource for reviving the soil and helping rebuild it, for nurturing new vegetated areas and supporting new agriculture – and also for developing biodiversity and facilitating its adaptation to climate change by providing natural coolness.

To achieve this, we need a small revolution, which is... do nothing! Just let the site reconnect with its geological, topographic, geographical, and hydrographic reality. The goal is to facilitate a contemporary approach to area development, in harmony with its natural context, especially the soil and natural water cycle (rain followed by infiltration; minimal runoff due to the lack of slopes; retention in the soil, above the clay layer, with slow circulation towards the Blutin or the Misery – all while fertilizing the land).

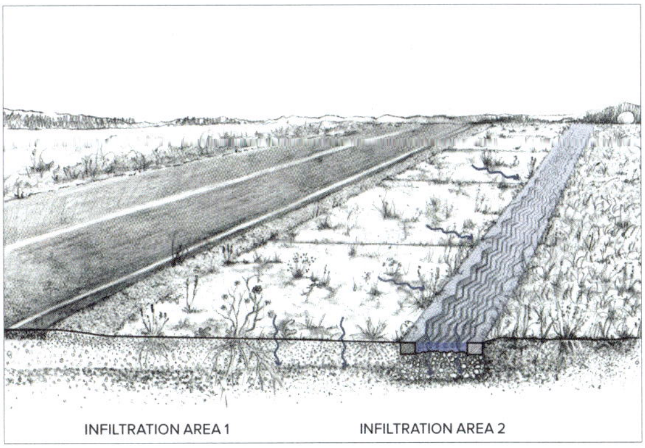

↗ ©E. Pardon, Coloco
↗ ©R. Joubert, Coloco
↗ ©E. Pardon, Coloco
→ ©S. Brenier, Coloco

Site management based on an agricultural model

Given the scale of the site, the layouts, shapes, and sizes of the newly-created spaces should be able to support multiple activities, facilitating their management and ensuring the longevity of the developments.

A significant portion of the project is managed through eco-grazing. Bringing sheep to the meadows helps respect ground nesting while keeping the landscape productive. A mowing plan allows for alternating between late-mowing areas and those where mowing is used for agricultural purposes.

By providing a variety of settings with different access levels, we aim to make agricultural uses, biodiversity, and public access work together. Thus, the orchard area transitions from a central refuge zone reserved for birds – with wild trees and shrubs as their food source – to a public pick-your-own orchard.

↖ ©E. Pardon, Coloco
↗ ©E. Pardon, Coloco
↗ ©I. Siegel, Coloco
↗ ©E. Pardon, Coloco
← ©A. Magnan, Airborne Films
› ©E. Pardon, Coloco

From a maintenance plan to a strategy for guiding the living environment

Isolated for military purposes and somewhat kept under a bell jar, this territory, with its vast open spaces long protected from urban development, emerges today as an exceptional asset. To continue building ecological connections, we need to enhance the flora and fauna heritage of Base 217 and increase biodiversity. The Guidance Strategy for the Living Environment has been designed to put into practice the intentions defined by the laboratory approach. This maintenance plan for biodiversity spaces involves working by subtraction in order to "guide" life. As a result, maintenance actions will be finely tuned to each use, intervening only where necessary and according to the needs of each living being. Tailored to each space, this differentiated management approach will allow for multiple plant layers leading people through a nuanced landscape, and provide varied habitats for non–humans. It also implies working closely with stakeholders on the overall management of resources (water, soil, air, plants, waste, energy, etc.). Although it takes more time and effort, this method ultimately proves to be more economical and better adapted, having a smaller ecological impact, and making place for new compensations, mutualizations, and associations.

Observing, making room, preserving, and gardening are our main actions to enhance this unique plant heritage.

Consisting of local species to be protected, the plant communities can also welcome future species adapted to climate changes such as prolonged droughts, increased precipitation, and rising average temperatures. Documenting the evolution of this landscape is also part of Base 217's laboratory approach.

Natural evolution of plant successions over time

Aiming to support the existing successions based on usage and changing climate, Base 217 is a laboratory for studying the evolution of living organisms.

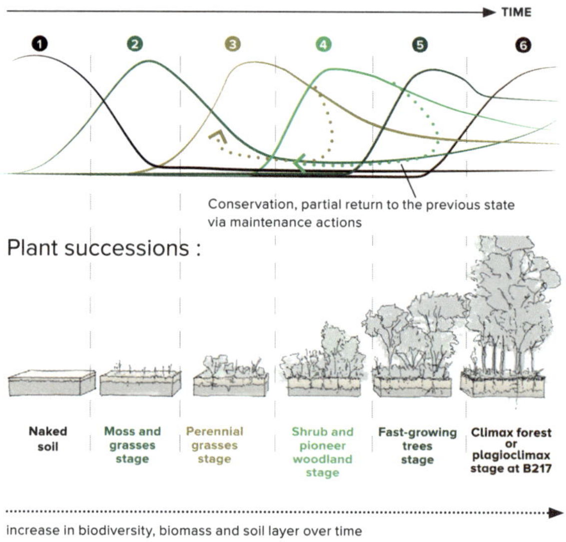

Developing a maintenance tool, adaptable by users and capable of evolving

We use action sheets that serve as the maintenance journal.

By sector:

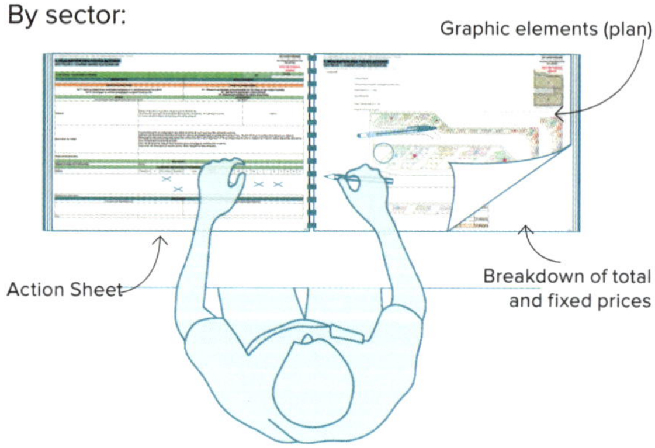

↗ ©N. Bonnenfant, Coloco
↗ ©T. Wambergue, Coloco

Maintenance: striking a balance between gardening and letting nature take its course

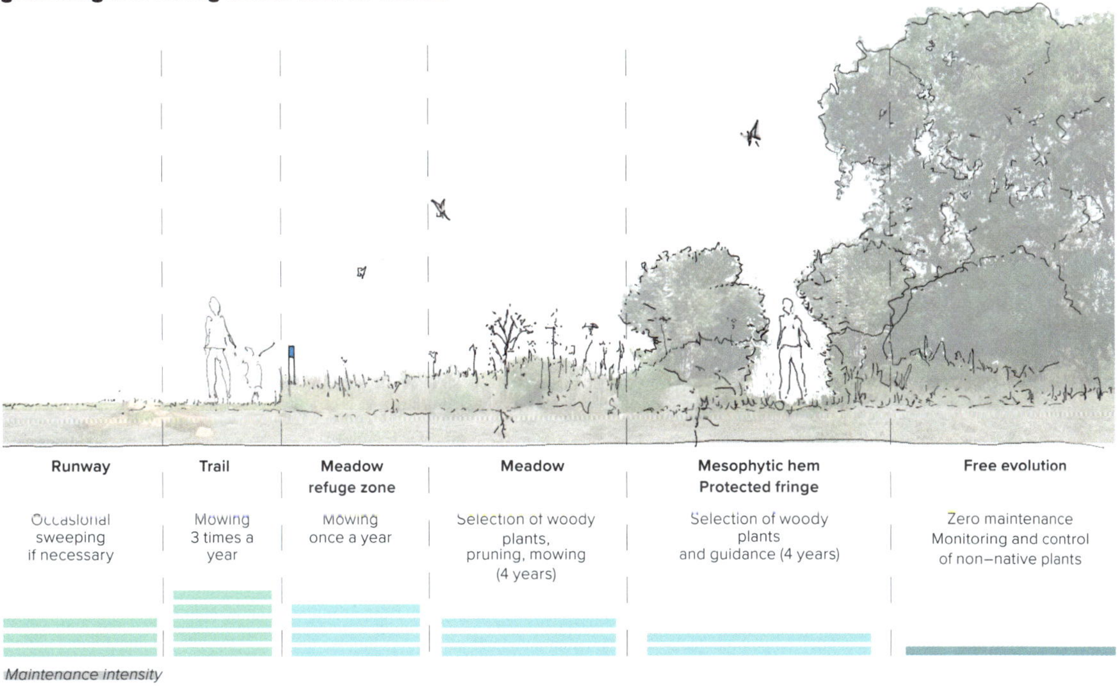

The intensity of maintenance activities depending on use

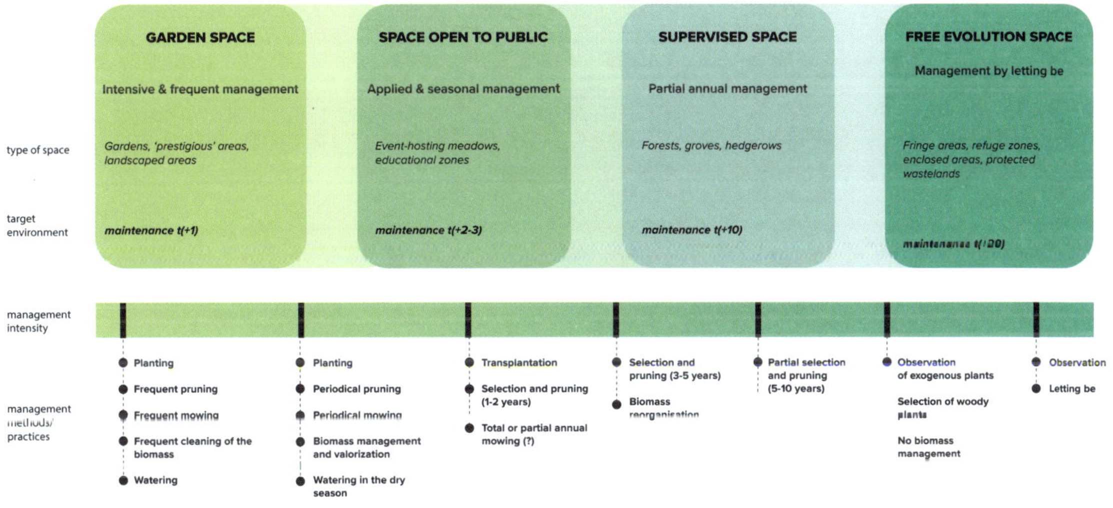

↑ ©N. Bonnenfant, Coloco
↑ ©H. Cassan, Coloco
↓ ©A. Magnan, Airborne Films

3.L
The Edges of Girona

– Girona

Transforming the metropolis with the help of its gardeners

Based on a project culture built in partnership with municipal management teams, this remarkable city–wide program has taken more than a decade to develop. A system of urban parks treated as a network of Gardens in Motion – the whole idea was a challenge to the usual models and practices used by the municipal community.

Working out new modes of management, organization, and commissioning required close, long–term involvement with people on the ground, taking into account their experiences and challenges – such as, for instance, a budget of €1/m²/year. A rare opportunity for practice–based reflection, the project proposed to deploy new strategies for engaging with living systems. To make this happen, education was crucial; it became the main focus for creating a shared vision at the project's core.

Mission Activation of transitional spaces
Location Girona, Catalonia, Spain
Geographical coordinates 41°59'00" N, 2°49'00"
Size 70 ha out of 600 ha under management
Status Urban open green spaces
Annual budget 180 000 €, 2,50 €/m²
Operating company EMF Martí Franch

— Phasing
(2009) 2014–2021 (2025) Implementation
2009–2010 Previous project "Itinerari de la Pedra de Girona"
2014–2015 Pilot project I "Montagne Pedreres"
2015–2016 Pilot project II "Fleuve Pedreres"
2016–2017 Masterplan
2018–2019 Project "Muralles"
2020–2021 Project "Pirulí"
2015–2018–2021 Project "Park Pont Major"
2018, 2019, 2020, 2021 Land Art Festival – Art & Gavarres
2022–2025 New framework agreement

— Team
Gemma Batllori, Héloïse Bouju, Sergi Romero, Mercè Pagès, François Poupeau, Meruyert Syzdkova, Marine Coudert, Estelle Andrieu, Luca Ciliani, Caroline Holz, Aya Itani, Jose–Luis Campoy, Lorenzo Majer, and Daniela Fuentealba.
Co–producers at the Girona municipal administration – Technical Services of the Environmental Department, Landscape and Biodiversity Section – Marc Rosdevall. Christian Geis, Ricard Jorquera and Victor Àguila.
The municipal "brigade" members – Jordi Batallé (curator), Ferran Navarro, David Cayuela, Agustin Romero, Dalmau Coll, Albert Muntalat and Raul Ruiz.

Photo credits EMF Martí Franch

The way people experi
of Girona has been co
by *carefully enhancing*
there, **adding subtle to**
and creating openings
vegetation.
The *tools* **needed for s**
and minimal. **They ca**
quickly, making an *im*
significant difference. **N**
aren't just preserved –
and amplified.

ence the Edges
npletely transformed
what's already
uches to the site,
in the existing

ich work are *simple*
n be put in place
mediate and
atural resources
they are *nurtured*

Bosc ribera
Bosc escleròfil
Flora exòtica invasora
i prats anuales
Aiguamolls
Prat alt
Prat baix
Còdols
Hospital
Universitari
Resclosa
de la Manola
Pavelló
Fontajau
El Ter
La Devesa
Sant Feliu
Catedral
El Onyar

3.L

The Edges of Girona, *promoting Girona's urban nature*

The Edges of Girona is an applied research project launched in 2013 by the municipality in collaboration with the landscape firm EMF. Since then, it has sparked a network of initiatives to reclaim, maintain, and develop the city's largely neglected peri–urban natural spaces, creating a multifunctional green infrastructure. The project reimagines Girona as a green and open conurbation, an "extended" city where nature is a vital resource available to everyone.

To make this ambition a reality, a replicable low–cost and low–tech approach has been developed over the years, using various intervention tactics. Differentiated management plays a key role: it delivers quick and tangible results, helping to renew the perspective on the Edges and reclaim the city's riverbanks and mountains.

Martí Franch

3.1
Considering the landscape project as a negotiation platform

The city of Girona is nested against the first slopes of the Gavarres mountains and crossed by five rivers. It enjoys a rich and diverse array of natural spaces, both within the city (the river system) and at its edges (mountains, agricultural terraces, and woodlands). Up until 2014, the management of these "naturban" spaces was handled by the Environmental Department with a simple approach that mainly consisted of trimming low vegetation twice a year to reduce fire hazards, and clearing illegal dumps.

The aim of the Edges project is to change how these spaces are viewed and managed. Using differentiated management as a tool, the project introduces a new approach to handling plant succession, allowing for greater biodiversity and a more varied landscape while also creating more opportunities for people to enjoy these spaces. Landscapers are working together with the municipal team to fine-tune this management and adapt it to different contexts, intensifying care in some parts and allowing nature to take its course in others.

By rethinking the management, the project changes the status of the Edges from neglected or hidden to valued spaces, both in terms of public use and in terms of their natural and landscape qualities.

In the next phase, through the work on the Masterplan, we focused on integrating these ideas into urban planning documents, to ensure the continuity of the Edges and their pathways.

3.2
Building community by gardening together

"Building together" is a leitmotif of the differentiated management approach in Girona. By closely integrating design and implementation through constant back-and-forth exchanges among landscapers, technicians, municipal brigades, and operators, a shared culture is being built, with the municipal management team acting as the co-authors of the project.

But beyond the gardeners, how do we grow the community around the Edges? Bringing new people into these spaces has been a priority since the project began: how can we introduce residents to these hidden areas? One strategy was to involve neighbors in mapping out the routes, with initiatives like "Camins de barri" (neighborhood paths) and participatory walkshops. Another consisted in encouraging city festivals to expand beyond urban areas into the Edges, with street art and land art projects bringing a fresh look at this large common "garden." In the coming years, one avenue to explore is developing a governance model for these spaces that will consider not only environmental management but also the input of cultural, social, educational, and sports stakeholders.

In the end, what makes the Edges unique is their ability to support extremely free, open-ended uses. By creating multiple pathways and providing simple, open-ended furniture, the project – unlike more structured urban areas – gives residents the freedom to define their own uses and engage with the Edges in their own way.

3.3
Turning the project into a score that unfolds over time

Establishing the Edges of Girona as a system of parks is a large-scale, long-term goal. It's not just one project but a collection of projects and initiatives that will allow the Edges to gradually unfold. The traditional project management sequence is ineffective for this purpose; a variety of other time-based tactics have to be used:

– Carrying out "Victorias Tempranas – that is, actions that deliver immediate, tangible results, quickly making the idea of the Edge a reality (like the first year's pilot projects, or land art festivals);

– Starting pilot projects before deciding on the overall strategy: the lessons learned from these prototypes will then inform the development of the general Masterplan;

– Returning to a project site multiple times to monitor and refine changes year after year – treating them like "gardens in motion." This means not all decisions need to be made at the start; they can be made as the sites evolve, vegetation grows, and uses develop;

– Letting the project spread on its own: the pilot projects helped the municipal team to sufficiently understand the principles of differentiated management, enabling them to independently expand the project to other areas. This handover makes the municipal team a true partner and co-author of the project;

– Appointing a "pilot" rather than an author. For the next four years, the Oficina Tecnica (Technical Office) represented by EMF will help the municipality manage and expand the Edge: extending differentiated management to new sites, revisiting what we have learned, updating the Masterplan, and building new partnerships.

3.4
Expressing care for the living world through aesthetic resolution

How can we change the way residents view these areas, so they stop being seen as marginal and instead become the largest public space in the city? How can we shift perception so that people start considering them as natural heritage rather than neglected places of little value and potential dumping grounds? As Alexandre Chemetoff might say, we need to "change everything without changing everything."

A clear and readable aesthetic creates a change in perspective, showing that these landscapes are now cared for. The intervention vocabulary is simple but easy to recognize: a neatly mown edge of a meadow, a marked difference between accessible lawns and woodland refuges, specific urban furniture... The project uses geometry but also works on human-scale relationships, framing views of the river or city, placing chairs in sunny spots and under particular trees, or providing spaces sized for families. The moves themselves are quite straightforward, but they need to be done with precision, paying close attention to the site in order to better reveal it.

This aesthetic, deliberate yet understated and sometimes playful, mediates between citizens and rediscovered natural spaces. It's what helps them see the city differently, expanding it and offering new ways to coexist with nearby living environments.

↑ As if only feet could see… It all started with repeated, often bushwhacking trips around the Edges, hunting for the site's hidden resources – all kinds of inputs that one never finds on official maps.

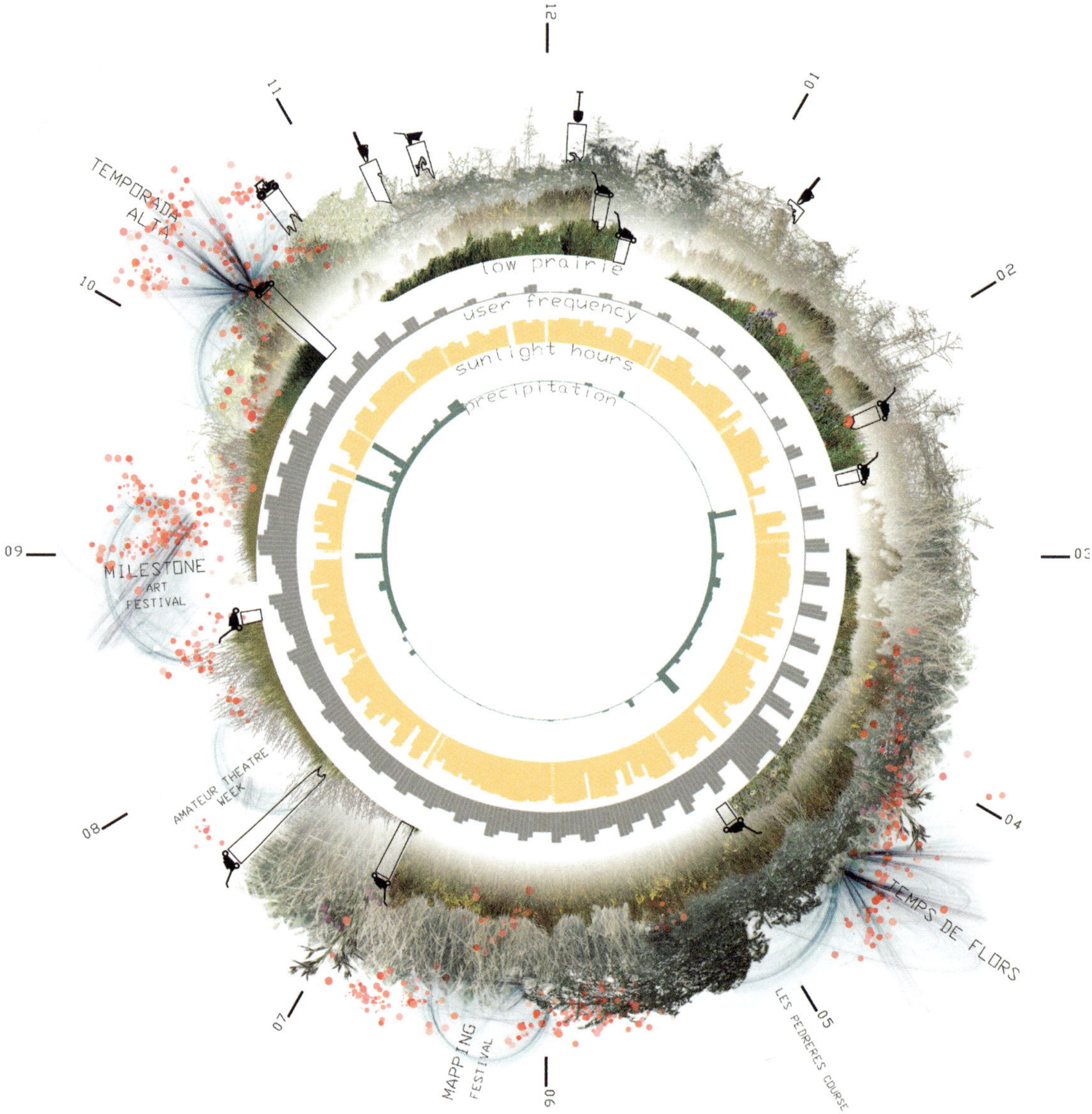

↑ Natural growth cycles and the synergies between differentiated management and the city's cultural calendar. Displayed in the middle of the diagram are natural factors like sunlight, rain, and user frequency. The management strategies are represented by pictograms on radial markers, while the effects of these strategies on plant growth are illustrated by the images of high and low prairies. Red circles represent major cultural events in Girona, as the project seeks to create synergies among these various uses and dynamics.

Based on *differentiated management* **and guided by** *ecological succession* **principles, this distinctive approach to landscape maintenance enables** *immediate diversification* **and better understanding of the Edges' ecology.**

USE BY TYPE OF SPACE
forest
1 / year
undergrowth
clearing
shrubland
1 / 5 years
high meadow
1 / year
low meadow
6-8 / year
MANAGEMENT

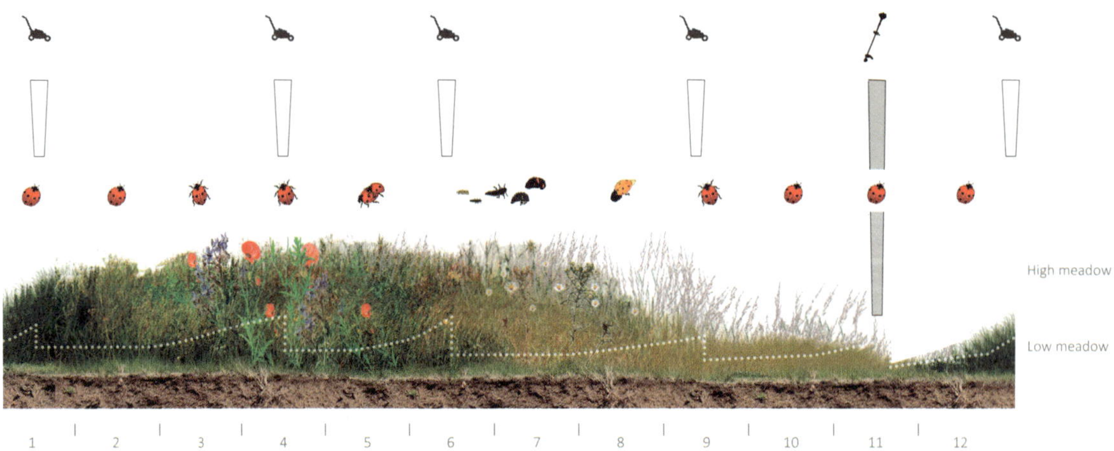
High meadow
Low meadow
1
2
3
4
5
6
7
8
9
10
11
12

↑ This drawing is made using a photo of the landscape mosaic created by differentiated management. It shows the management regimes related to shrublands, high meadows, paths, and "rooms," along with various species of associated wildlife.

↖ The frequency of maintenance shapes the transition between meadow and Mediterranean forest, the potential associated wildlife, and the opportunities for public use.

← This timeline shows the evolution of a Mediterranean dry meadow and the associated cycles of flora and fauna depending on the management regime. The dashed white line shows the impact of mowing six times a year to keep the meadow low and accessible, compared to a management approach that enhances biodiversity.

Incremental interventions in separate phases: a project that develops over the years. The four drawings presenting the first pilot project "Mina del Calvari" and its evolution between 2015 and 2019 illustrate the approach adopted by the Edges:

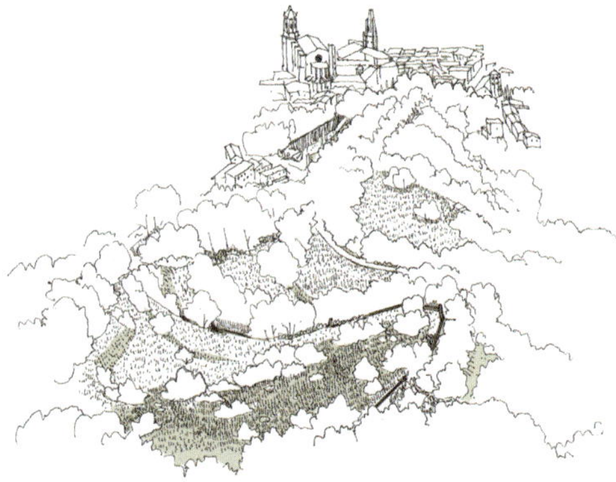

Until 2015, annual management consisted of 1 to 2 uniform trimmings across the entire site to reduce fire hazards and "clean up" the area.

In 2015, the "if/then" protocol for differentiated management was applied for the first time. This phase was carried out using the municipality's ordinary budget and together with the municipal management brigade, with no additional investment.

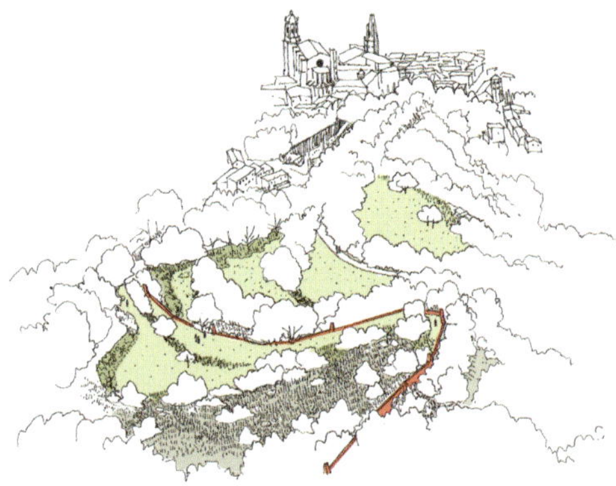

In 2015–2016, EMF mapped the landscape, as well as the natural and cultural resources of the site, and proposed a more detailed plan of differentiated management that went beyond the "if/then" protocol. The plan included creating new paths, opening up views between terraces, and improving the slope of certain trails. While this phase required design and supervision, the investment was minimal, with work done using regular maintenance funds.

From 2017 to 2019 and during the "Temps de Flors" festival, the city provided small-scale funding for targeted interventions, such as building wooden observation platforms, installing custom furniture, and opening new trails.

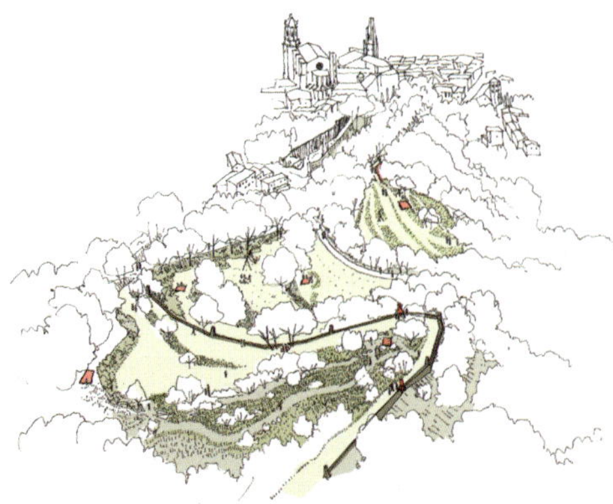

In three years, the area under differentiated management has grown from 11 to 20 hectares. Today, the managed space is quite large, and its management improves year after year, thanks to the experience gained by the brigade and the ongoing evolution of the ecosystem.

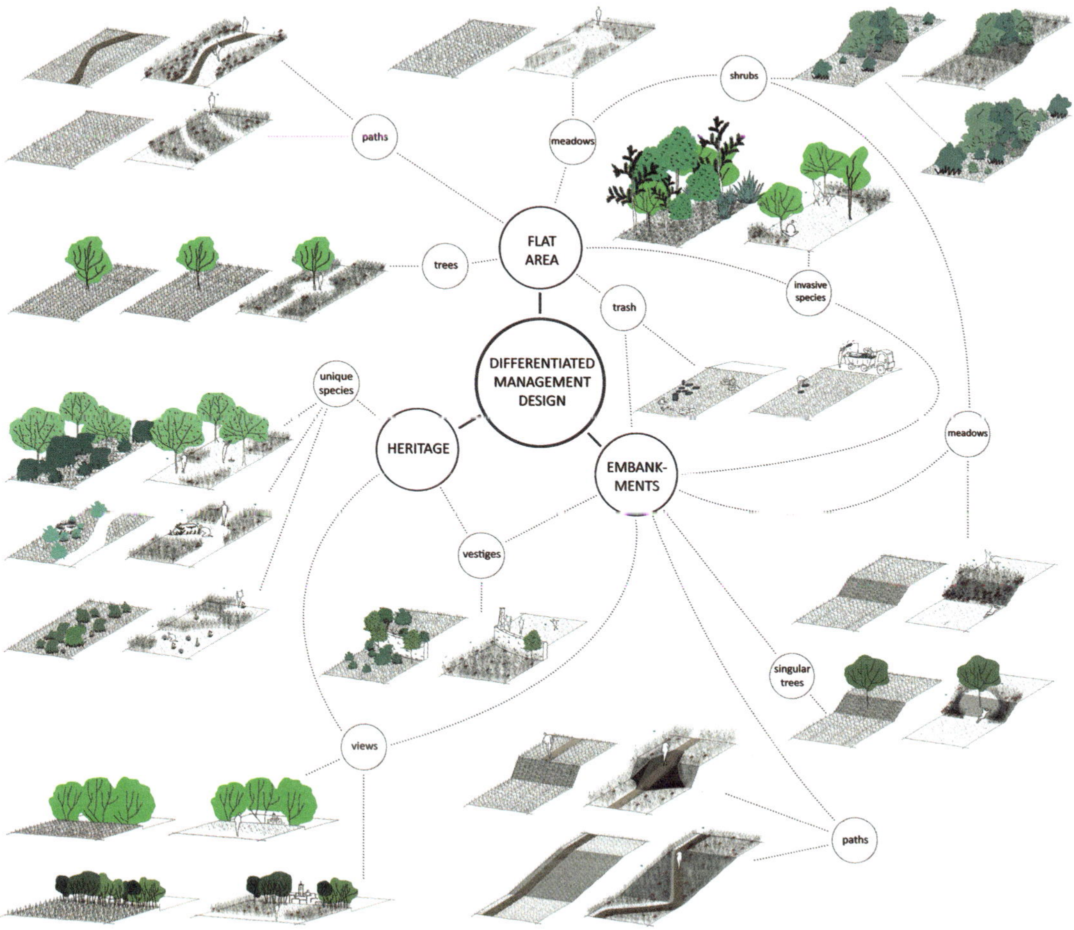

↑ The know–how gained from the pilot projects in differentiated management has been distilled into a simple, adaptable protocol based on the "if/then" model. The protocol can be replicated and updated each season. Environmental technical services, ecologists, and the municipal management team become co–designers, implementers, managers, and spreaders of the project, allowing it to grow on its own. The average cost of the interventions is around 2.40 € per square meter.

12 ways to look at the Edge

Recalibrating values

We want to change how we see the city so we can change the value system with which we assess and plan it. To achieve this, we are proposing 12 perspectives, presented as 12 plans, to explore 12 distinct and systematic values of the "edge" – values that have remained invisible until now. Combined, these viewpoints give us reasons to reconsider the city as a conurbation defined by the landscapes of its "edges."

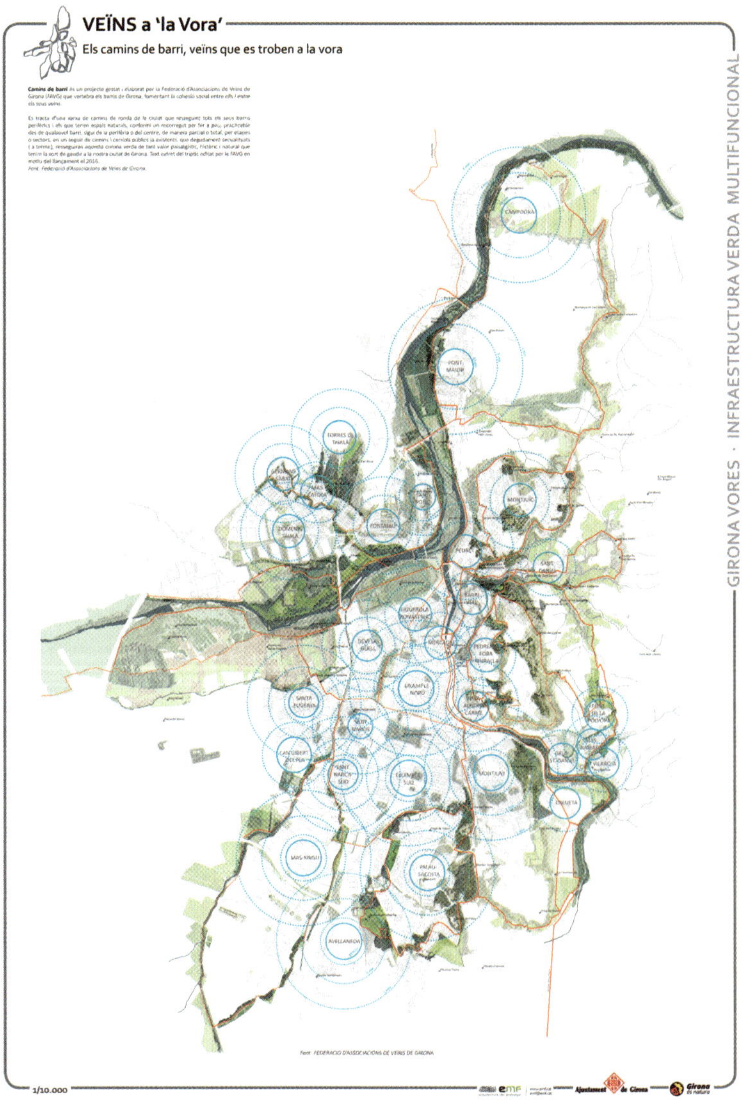

The Edge & health

The proposed health routes are grouped according to the 13 loops of the Edge. Serving as open-air health facilities, these loops come in different lengths for daily, weekly, or monthly use.

The Edge & risk prevention

Managing fire and water

The differentiated management of the Edge's agroforestry mosaic helps create robust low-combustibility buffers that protect the city from fires coming from the Gavarres mountains, and vice versa. Flood risks can be reduced by setting up flood retention zones within the Edge's riverine areas.

Well-being: a nature bath at the Edge of your neighborhood

The poster identifies urban areas located within one, five, and ten minutes from the natural landscapes of the Edge, showing how close nature is to the city.

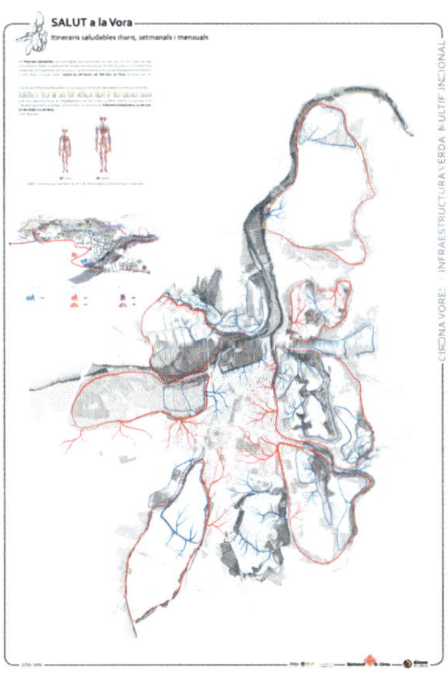

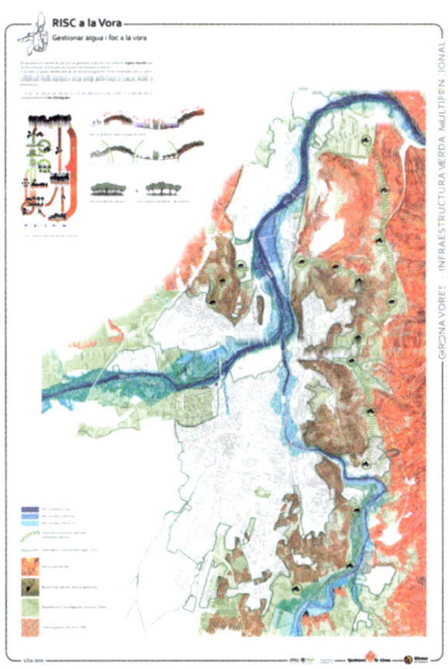

Seeing with new eyes. Sequential paths and catalysts of emotion

In Girona, the edge of the city is still mostly seen as a non-place, a forgotten area. One of the main challenges for the project's social sustainability is to find a new aesthetic, a new kind of beauty that would refresh people's appreciation of the Edge. But how do we achieve this?

In the pilot projects, we tried to change the currently underwhelming experience of the area by creating scenic routes enhanced with "confetti." Acting as storytellers of the landscape, the trails are orchestrated in a way that gradually reveals the site's views, ruins, or biotopes. The more immediate and practical aspect of engaging citizens is introduced through "confetti." The concept of "confetti" includes a wide range of ad hoc micro-interventions that help identify, highlight, and celebrate the uniqueness of a place; they serve as catalysts for discovery and emotional connection.

Unconventional uses: unexpected activities that energize the Edge

Every year, EMF and the Landscape and Urban Habitat Department of the Girona municipality reach out to different groups, encouraging them to discover and make use of the Edge through cultural activities. Taking cues from French festivals like the Bordeaux Panoramas, the idea is to move cultural and sporting events out of their habitual settings and invite them into the Edge. Various festivals have given it a try, including land art, floral art, orienteering, graffiti, and video morphing. This shifts the focus from changing the infrastructure / "hardware" to updating the "software" with new forms of engagement.

3.M Parc du Peuple de l'herbe (Grass People Park)

– Carrières-sous-Poissy

Designing complex habitats assembled like a park

Covering a hundred hectares, this territory extends over former sand quarries along the Seine. Life is once again thriving here, thanks to the recreated and enhanced habitats. The park embodies Putting Life first as a shared vision, with insects taking center stage. Acknowledging life forms other than human park-goers challenges us to profoundly rethink our planning practices, and ask ourselves: who are we working for?

In this project, the designers have successfully shown how respect for living beings can be shared by a collective. All project stakeholders have been able to take care of the habitats and make these "territories of life" available to others. We admire this compelling example of communal effort, in which design solutions and the resulting aesthetics convey a vital poetic force.

Mission Design and project management for the development of an ecological park on the banks of the Seine
Location Carrières-sous-Poissy, France
Geographical coordinates 48°56'58"N, 02°02'26"E
Size 113 ha
Status Urban park
Budget 14 M€

Photo credits Yann Monel (unless otherwise specified)

— Team
Client The Yvelines Departmental Council
Consultant team Agence TER (Lead Designer), Écosphère, INFRA services, Nez-Haut, Atelier d'écologie urbaine, Hydratec

— Phasing
Competition success 2010
Design and construction 2011–2017

This site is entirely m
highlights how *alive* e

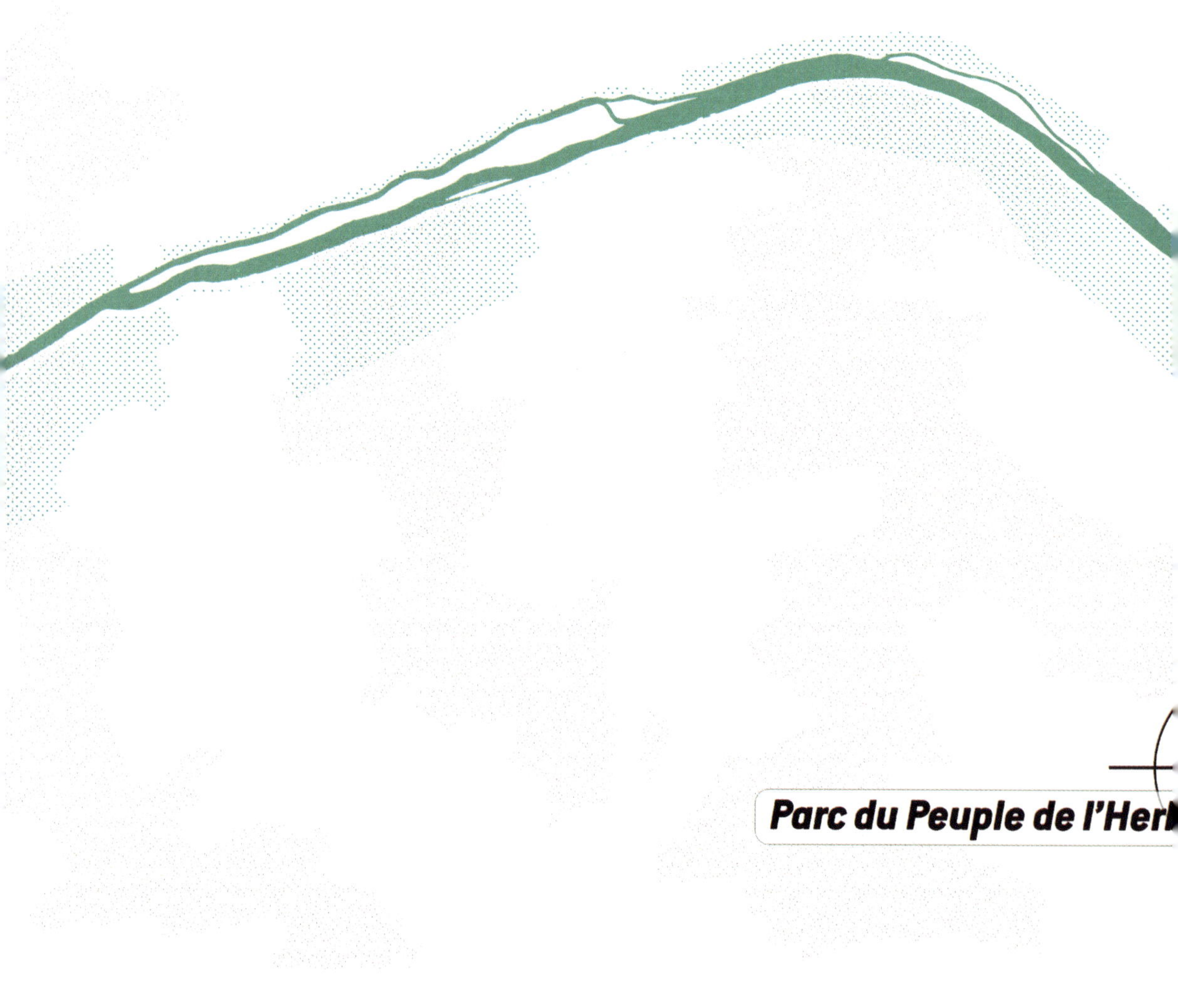

an-made, yet it
cosystems really are.

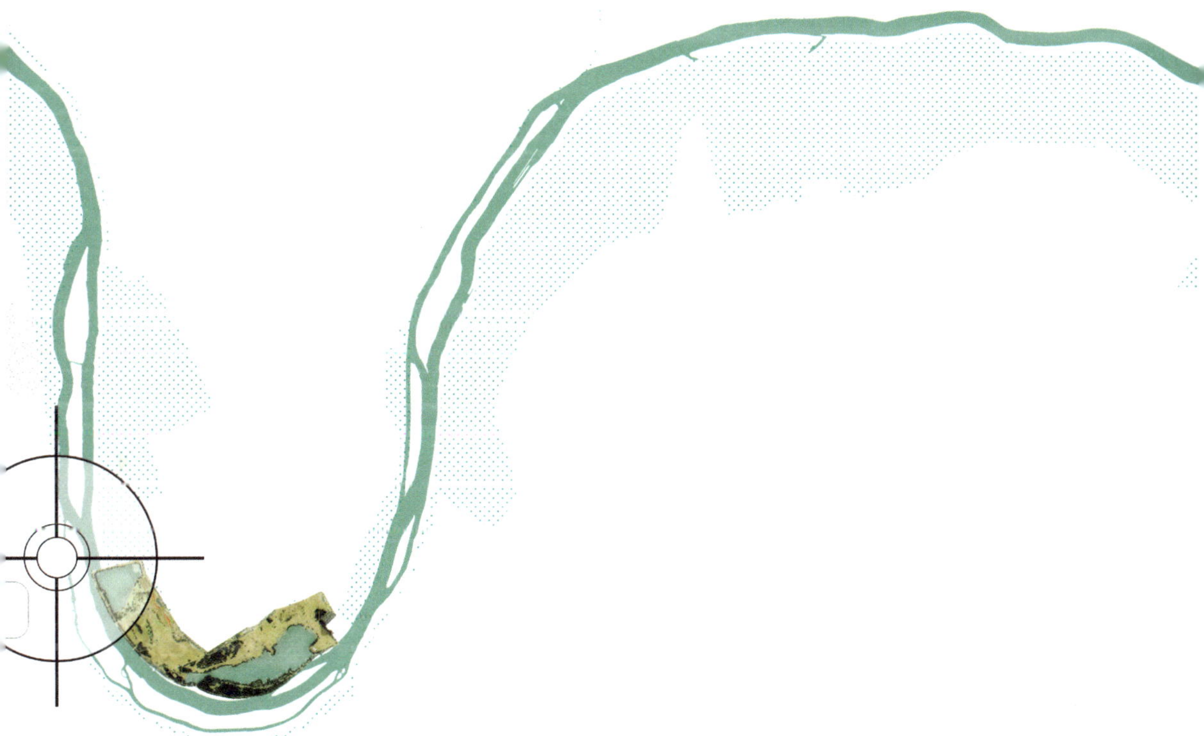

CRUE
1910
23.30
CRUE
1955
22.90
22.70
22.50
22.30
22.10
21.90
21.70
21.50
21.30
21.10
CRUES
20.30
20.10
19.90

3.M

The Parc du Peuple de l'herbe *comprises 113 hectares of reshaped floodplains*

This park covers more than a hundred hectares and is situated on former sand quarries along the Seine. By amplifying various natural environments, the project provides habitats for biodiversity. Located in a flood–prone area, it accommodates changes in the river levels and highlights them through the creation of an alluvial shore that follows the curve of the Seine, in keeping with phytoremediation processes.

Moreover, the Seine's potential flood levels are visualized using elegant, minimalist sculptural elements that serve as memorial markers.

Michel Hössler, Agence TER

3.1
Considering the landscape project as a negotiation platform

Starting in 2010, the Yvelines department, in collaboration with the Greater Paris Seine & Oise Urban Community and the municipality of Carrières–sous–Poissy, initiated the acquisition of the site as part of the sensitive natural areas policy. The development project led by these three institutions has enriched the reflections and visions of everyone involved. This fruitful collaboration resulted in an ambitious plan to reclaim an area prone to flooding and set on inhospitable soil, with the objective of providing a natural space open to the public. The negotiation platform was built on three goals: accommodating risk, preserving natural space, and welcoming the people.

To meet the challenge, we started by observing and analyzing the site together with geologist–naturalist Gilles Gallinet and the environmentalists from Écosphère. The goal of this teamwork between ecologists and landscapers was to restore and enhance living environments. This first phase of the project has led to the creation of new habitats. The attitude expressed by the experts and shared by the project management team highlighted the need to create a negotiation platform with the living beings that are often invisible in public parks. This is when the Grass People (le Peuple de l'herbe) came to the fore, and giving voice to the subsoil and the minuscule became a key concept, a way to address the challenge of negotiating space between humans and non–humans.

The park's early planning phase was a pivotal moment that united all stakeholders around the broad theme of the "Grass People."

3.2
Building community by gardening together

A metropolitan–scale natural park as a symbol of resilience

This was a new type of challenge for TER, as our studio was more used to working on smaller parks in densely populated urban areas. Here, we were faced with a 113–hectare site.

In January 2011, the Yvelines department issued a restricted tender for an infrastructure project to develop a landscape and recreational park in Carrières–sous–Poissy. We quickly realized that this project, involving earthworks, soil treatment, road building, various networks, ecological engineering, planting, and setting up outdoor furniture and wooden structures, would have to be done on a tight budget.

Out of 33 applicant teams led by landscape architects, five were shortlisted: Agence HYL, Ilex, Agence Laverne Paysagiste, Jacqueline Osty, and TER. The competitors were asked to submit a "memo outlining the project's challenges and the team's operational and qualitative approach," along with a panel of illustrative diagrams. The jury, composed of stakeholders and members of the CAUE 78 (the Council for Architecture, Urban Planning and the Environment of the Yvelines department), appreciated the original ideas of the shortlisted teams. The costs and the rationale presented in the Parc du Peuple de l'herbe proposal made this project a manifesto of resilience. It combined decontamination of soils, preservation of existing natural environments, and public accessibility – all within a very modest budget.

The plan suggested minimal interventions in certain areas – such as using a large central heliophilous wasteland to reinforce existing habitats, – and balanced them against more intensive work in other places, like pathways and park edges that would enable a connection with the city and the pedestrian flow.

↑ ©Agence TER

↑ ©Agence TER

3.3
Turning the project into a score that unfolds over time

Using the scientific expertise of naturalists for the benefit of the project

Open year-round and blending urban and natural environments, this ecological and recreational landscape park has become a new spot for getting away, learning, and having fun. Public engagement in environmental and ecological education is growing as the habitats expand.

Certain areas are kept free from human interference, allowing protected species to thrive. Two buildings designed by AWP architects are central to the landscape project:

— A thirteen-meter observatory provides a panoramic view of the new grand landscape of the Seine. Designated as an LPO (Bird Protection League) Refuge, the park has become an important part of the Seine's ecological corridor. Migratory, wintering, and nesting birds can be observed here, and various facilities for wildlife have been installed, such as a swallow tower, hibernacula (shelters for small animals like reptiles and amphibians), birdhouses, and vegetated rafts on the ponds.

— An insect house educates the public about the world of insects, focusing on these Grass People as one of the sources of biodiversity. This small museum allows visitors to observe the insects in vitro, and then conduct field investigations in vivo. The initiative combines education with scientific observation, offering a broad field of study for students and local residents.

3.4
Expressing care for the living world through aesthetic resolution

The river as one of the area's key assets

By working with the site's topography, digging out in some areas and filling in in others, we were able to enhance habitats ranging from dry to very wet zones. Michel de Certeau speaks about places as stories that can unfold; in this park, it's latent life that has unfolded and taken over the site. The banks have been completely redesigned to open the park to the river, creating a real connection with nature. This space extends for approximately 2.8 km and offers continuous walkways along the Seine. In a strategic study conducted in 2009, we identified this landscape entity as one of the "beaches" that form the territorial framework of the Seine Aval area. Large expanses of land between urbanized areas, these beaches stretch from the alluvial plain to the edges of the plateau; they are intended to evolve into high-value-added locations while remaining vast, open, agricultural landscapes, offering plenty of breathing space.

Like many rivers, in the 19th century, the Seine was canalized and deepened, its meanders straightened and adapted for transporting goods and merchandise. This has altered its natural cycle of movement between the minor and maximum beds according to rainfall. We became interested in the ebb and flow of flooding that had saved the site from being built on. Our aim was to enhance this natural but not easily visible phenomenon, letting people see it in action.

↑ ©Agence TER

Not everything can be *maintained* **and** *accessible.* **Landscapers need to make space for** *the living world,* **even in cities.**

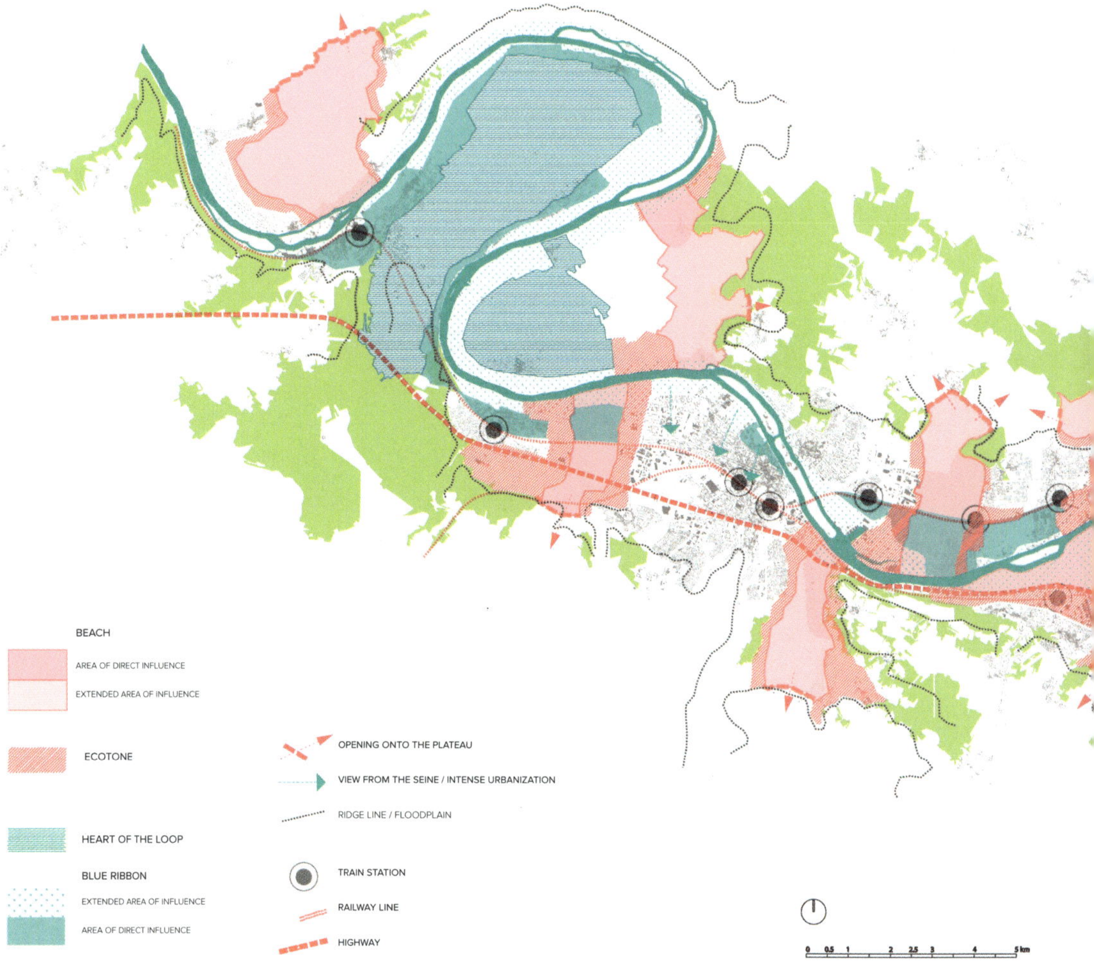

↑ Agence TER designed this park in parallel with working on a territorial strategy for the open spaces along the river Seine, developed for the Seine Aval National Interest Project.

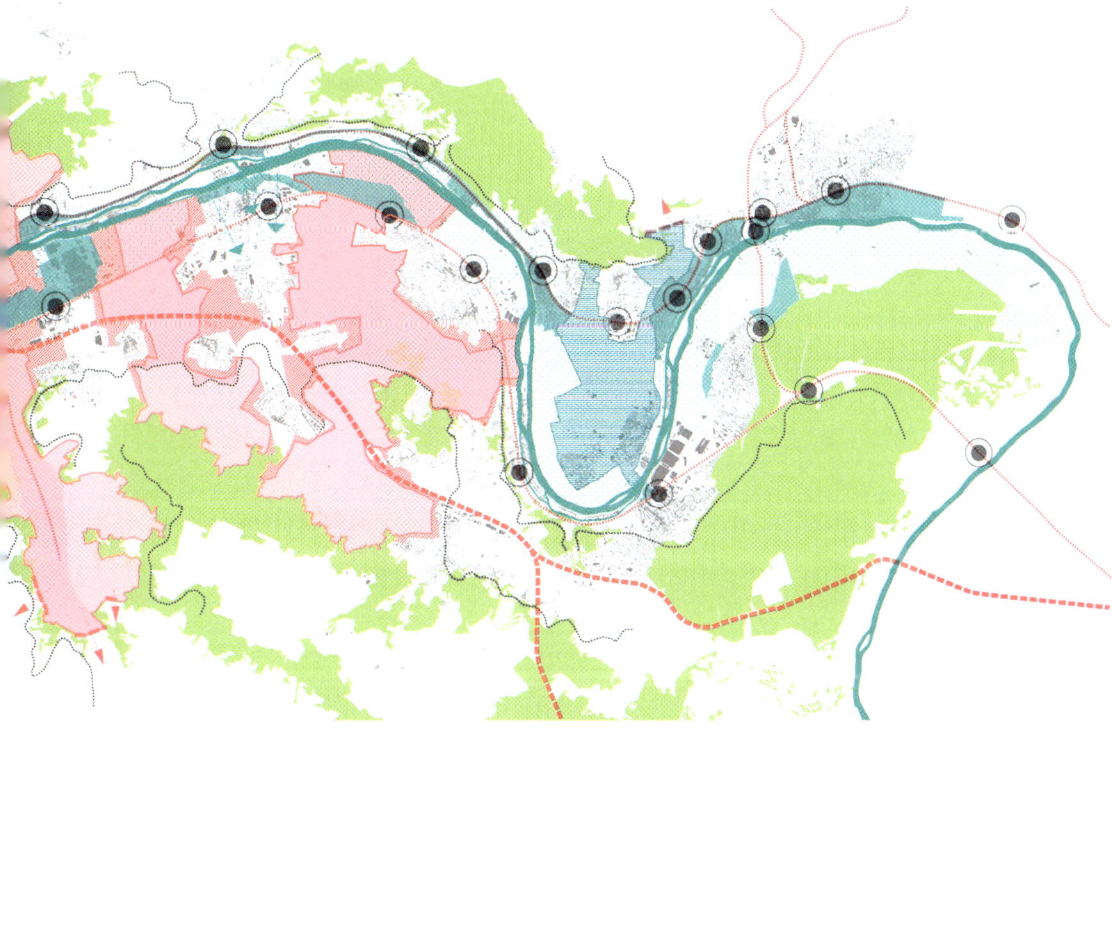

The transformation of a landscape shaped by its industrial past

Located within the Chanteloup loop and regularly enriched by the Seine's floods, the alluvial plain of Carrières–sous–Poissy was once used for market gardening. From 1890 to 2002, sewage sludge from the Achères treatment plant was spread here as fertilizer. However, the pollutants contained in the sludge eventually made cultivation impossible. Since the 1970s, gravel pits have been mined on this land, and the water holes have been gradually filled in.

The transformation of what had been an open–air landfill for about thirty years was an opportunity to look at living organisms as a factor of resilience and soil improvement, creating new habitats and relying on phytoremediation.

The soils, still showing traces of industrial activity, were decontaminated with the help of phytoremediation gardens, composed of plants known for absorbing heavy metals and hydrocarbons.

→ © Agence TER

Etang de la Vieille Ferme
Milieux humides
Aire de jeux
Ile pique-nique
Ile bosquet
Ile des mares
Maison du Parc
Parking
Jardins partagés
Grande prairie sèche
Jardins familiaux
Observatoire
Bosquets pique-nique
Phytorémédiation
Roselière
Cabanes de pêcheurs
Etang de la Galiotte
Prairie sauvage
Parking
Butte événementielle
Guinguette

The Office for insects and their environment

The Office for Insects and Their Environment (l'Office pour les insectes et leur environnement, Opie) has set up operations in the park. The 800 m² Insect House features a fun and educational exhibit about insects, complete with several vivariums and a butterfly aviary. The Opie organizes workshops, events, field trips, and screenings, while the Insect House serves as a meeting place and exchange hub for insect enthusiasts.

Surveys conducted by the Yvelines department have shown an increase in biodiversity. Often invisible and fragile, insects become noticeable mainly when they bite us or disrupt our activities. Despite this, they are a vital part of the food chain and a common good. The idea here was not to create a sanctuary park but to actively enhance biodiversity alongside recreational areas.

A sustained, long-term engagement from stakeholders helps in accumulating knowledge and studies. An agreement with the Opie and the Natural History Museum allows visitors to photograph plants and insects to contribute to databases. This is a good example of breaking down boundaries between disciplines: researchers become citizens, and citizens turn into researchers. This is an exciting prospect for the years to come, and the way in which we will be able to integrate our projects with the various forms of expert knowledge.

The pilot stages of the park sparked enthusiasm and gathered all parties around the broad theme of the "Grass People." Insect specialists, local residents, project managers, and architects are invited to contribute to the development of architectural facilities, habitats, and spaces dedicated to observing insects and providing sports activities for local residents. The park opened in June 2017, and attendance continues to grow, with many educational activities organized for the public.

→ © Agence TER

BIRDLIFE

Fringillidae
Cineraous finch
Serinus Serinus
Open areas, clearings and scrubland

Cettiidae
Cetti's warbler
Cettia cetti
Shrublands and wetlands

Emberizidae
Common reed bunting
Emberiza schoeniclus
Wetlands with reed beds, wasteland

Picidae
Black woodpecker
Dryocopus martius
Forested areas with spaced trees

Regulidae
Common firecrest
Regulus ignicapilla
Coniferous or deciduous woods, copses

AMPHIBIANS

Ranidae
Marsh frog
Pelophylax ridibundus
Sunny riverbanks and water bodies

REPTILES

ODONATA

Pelodytidae
Common parsley frog
Pelodytes punctatus
Dry or slightly damp environments

Natricidae
Barred grass snake
Natrix helvetica
Diverse environments with aquatic areas

Lacertidae
Common wall lizard
Podarcis muralis
Rocks, quarries, slag heaps

Corduliidae
Downy emerald
Cordulia aenea
Stagnant waters in wooded areas

Aeshnidae
Migrant hawker
Aeshna mixta
Wetlands, stagnant waters

Aeshnidae
Southern Migrant Hawker
Aeshna affinis
Temporary aquatic environments

Coenagrionidae
Small red–eyed damselfly
Erythromma viridulum
Stagnant, exposed wetlands

Libellulidae
Ruddy darter
Sympetrum sanguineum
Vegetation–rich wetlands

Aeshnidae
Southern hawker
Aeshna cyanea
Stagnant waters, rivers

Libellulidae
Red–veined darter
Sympetrum fonscolombii
Shallow, sunny stagnant waters

Coenagrionidae
Red–eyed damselfly
Erythromma najas
Wetland with hydrophytes

Libellulidae
Broad–bodied chaser
Libellula depressa
Wooded wetlands

Coenagrionidae
Goblet marked damselfly
Erythromma lindenii
Wetlands, stagnant waters

Lestidae
Common winter damselfly
Sympecma fusca
Wetlands, reedbeds

Coenagrionidae
Azure damselfly
Coenagrion puella
Stagnant wetlands with slowmoving water

Gryllidae
Common darter
Sympetrum striolatum
Stagnant waters in sunny areas

Gryllidae
Small pincertail
Onychogomphus forcipatus
Medium–sized streams

Libellulidae
Scarlet dragonfly
Crocothemis erythraea
Ponds, puddles, well–exposed sandpits

TERRESTRIAL MAMMALS

CHIROPTERA

ORTHOPTERA

Libellulidae
Four–spotted chaser
Libellula quadrimaculata
Around stagnant waters

Leporidae
European rabbit
Oryctolagus cuniculus
Extensive meadows

Mustelidae
Beech marten
Martes foina
Meadows near water, rocky hillsides

Vespertilionidae
Kuhl's pipistrelle
Pipistrellus kuhlii
Forested areas with water bodies

Vespertilionidae
Nathusius' pipistrelle
Pipistrellus nathusii
Forested areas with water bodies

Tettigoniidae
Speckled bush–cricket
Leptophyes punctatissima
Anthropized environments, sunny edges

Acrididae
Meadow grasshopper
Chorthippus parallelus
Wet grasslands

Tettigoniidae
Large conehead
Ruspolia nitidula
Herbaceous, sunny environments

Acrididae
Lesser marsh grasshopper
Chorthippus albomarginatus
Dense humid meadows

Acrididae
Chorthippus dorsatus
Chorthippus dorsatus
Meadows, forest edges, and forest paths

Acrididae
Rufous grasshopper
Gomphocerippus rufus
Dry grassy environments with tall vegetation

Gryllidae
Wood cricket
Nemobius sylvestris
Open woodland, clearings

RHOPHALOCERA

Tettigoniidae
Roesel's bush–cricket
Roeseliana roeselii
Wetlands with abundant vegetation

Tettigoniidae
Southern oak bush cricket
Meconema meridionale
Warm, shrubby environments

Acrididae
Aiolopus thalassinus grasshopper
Aiolopus thalassinus
Wetlands, meadows with a watering hole

Gryllidae
European field cricket
Gryllus campestris
Dry, sunny, sparsely vegetated environments

Nymphalidae
Peacock butterfly
Aglais io
Sunny meadows, wooded riverbanks

Pieridae
Orange tip
Anthocharis cardamines
Open woods, forest edges, wet meadows

Nymphalidae
Pearly heath
Coenonympha arcania
Grasslands, roadsides

Pieridae
Common brimstone
Gonepteryx rhamni
Clearings, scrubby wastelands

Lycaenidae
Holly blue
Celastrina argiolus
Shrubby wastelands, wet forests

Nymphalidae
Painted lady
Vanessa cardui
Open, dry environments, meadows, fields

Lycaenidae
Brown argus
Aricia agestis
Dry, sunny meadows

Pieridae
Pale clouded yellow
Colias hyale
Flowering meadows, clover fields

Hesperiidae
Meadowsweet skipper
Pyrgus malvae
Forest clearings, marsh meadows

Lycaenidae
Small copper
Lycaena phlaeas
Open, well–drained, exposed areas

Nymphalidae
Marbled white
Melanargia galathea
Flowering meadows, dry meadows, wastelands

Papilionidae
Old World swallowtail
Papilio machaon
Dry, sunny, flowering meadows

Nymphalidae
Meadow brown
Maniola jurtina
Open herbaceous areas

Pieridae
Clouded yellow
Colias crocea
Flowering meadows, open wastelands

Lycaenidae
Green–underside blue
Glaucopsyche alexis
Clearings, sunny and flowering wastelands

The management plan developed by Agence TER relies on differentiated management techniques, which have been passed on to the seven gardeners working in the park. The gardeners quickly learned the new practices that help with natural regeneration and the preservation of species while preventing the invasives. Waste collection is handled by an external service provider, and the habitats are monitored by departmental teams and various naturalist associations.

With this natural park project, we had the chance to explain how a river can function as a common good.

We worked on enhancing the different habitats. The existing ones – the banks of the Seine, ponds, man–made features, and large lawns – have been enhanced by subtly altering the terrain. The earth was repositioned to create drier, south–facing mounds.

We wanted to showcase the Seine. We created a bank that would increase wetland areas and allow for changes in the river's level, showing that the river is not just a place to watch barges or birds – it's a living organism, too.

While aiming to offer quality spaces for walking and exploration, we also make it a priority to develop these areas in a way that addresses the living environment. The steep banks with their poor vegetation have been reshaped – as a result, the reconstituted alluvial beach allows for the creation of habitats suitable for new species that can withstand the hazards and movements of the Seine.

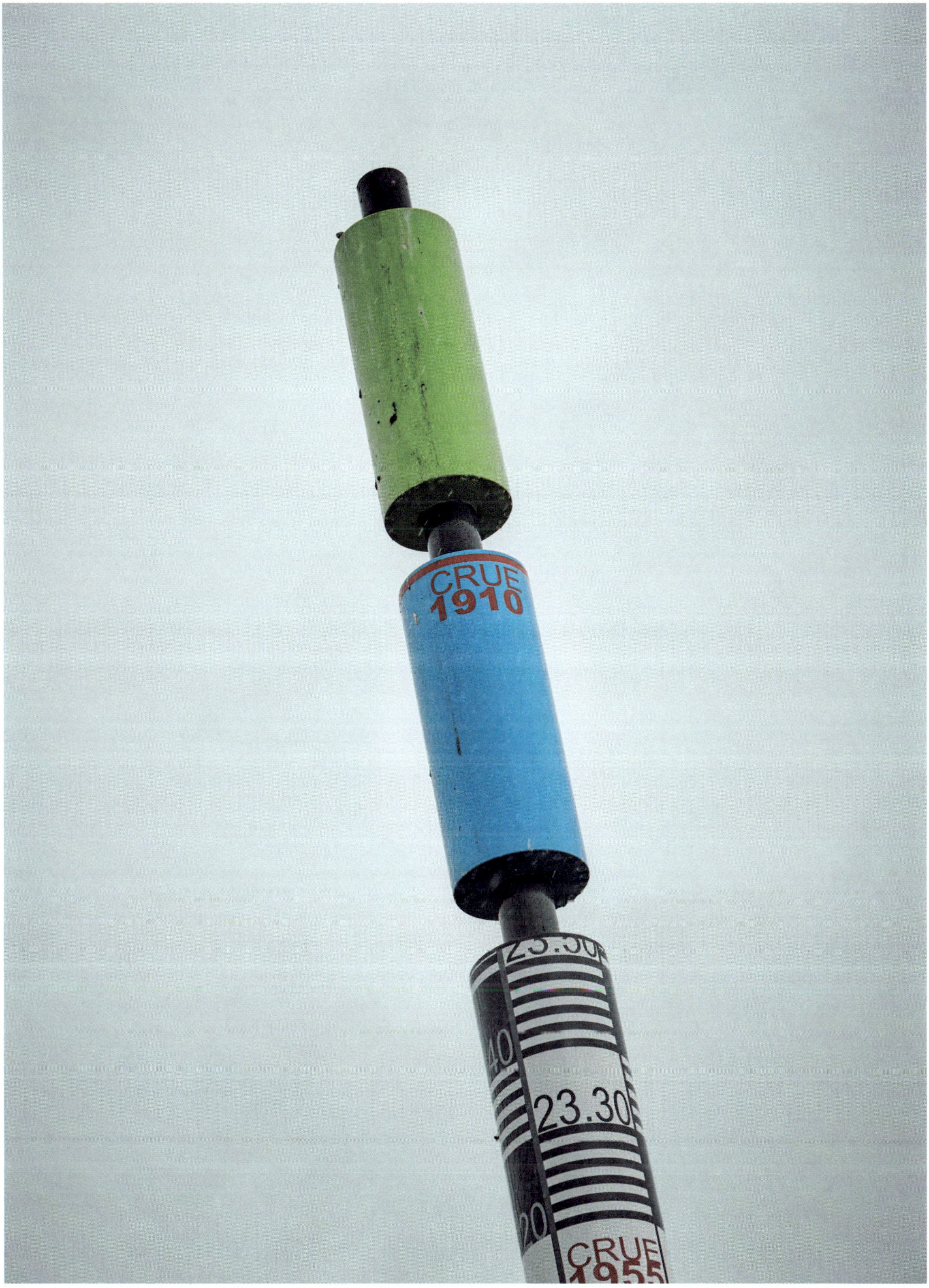
CRUE
1910
40
23.30
20
CRUE

↓ © Agence TER

crue 10 ans : 22.55m
crue 5 ans : 21.82m
crue 2 ans : 20.78m
non dépassé 11 mois/an : 19.79m
niveau moyen : 18.46m
non dépassé 3 mois/an : 17.90m

3.N The Aire, *the river and its double*

– Geneva

Getting into the flow of a landscape's long-term evolution

In dealing with the challenge of renaturation, this project raises a question about the role of the landscaper in setting up long–term dynamics of an area's geography. Here, the boundaries of control are disrupted by letting the force of erosion draw, and constantly transform, the lines. Instead of trying to copy life, we invite the unpredictable Third Landscape to participate in the design process.

Being involved in a project of this scale over a long period of time allows for the community's ongoing reflections on the site. A strong team working together for many years has been able to extend this reflection into more urban contexts. Current efforts are focused on establishing a watercourse as a foundation for territorial planning.

Mission River revitalization, public spaces
Location The plain of the river Aire, Geneva, Switzerland
Geographical coordinates 46°10'12.0"N, 6°05'23.0"E
Size 50 ha
Status Natural areas, public open spaces
Global budget 60 M €
Operating company Groupement Superpositions
Team Georges Descombes, ADR, B+C, Biotec, ZS

— Phasing
Design 2000 – 2020
— Implementation
2002-2006 Stage 1
2009-2011 Stage 2
2012-2016 Stage 3
2021-ongoing Stage 4

Photo credits Superpositions, Fabio Chironi, Jacques Berthet

Do and *let do.*

— Marielle Macé

This is a *paradox* **we**
the more *defined* **the i**
the river feels to crea
if the river is giving u
it shapes, over time, t
diagram that has serv
forms to come.

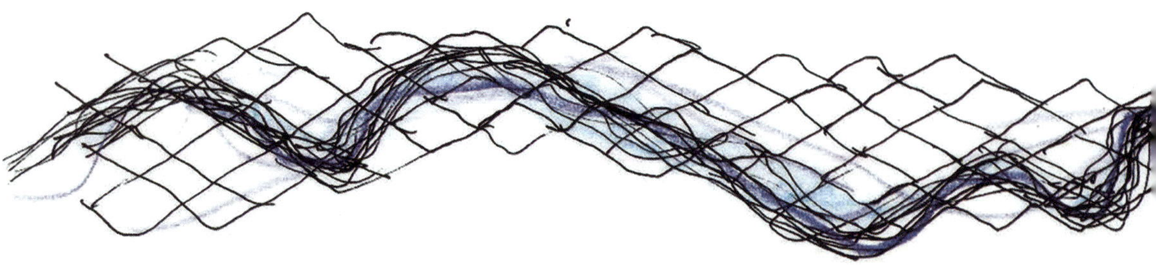

ave to admit:

itial grid, the *freer*

e its new bed. It's as

a lesson in the way

e evolution of the

ed as *a trigger for the*

3.N
The Aire, *the river and its double*

The Aire flows through a plain used for agricultural purposes. By the late 19th century, the river had been gradually canalized. In 2001, the State of Geneva organized a competition to restore its natural course by dismantling the canal – however, our proposal sought to transform the canal and combine it with the river. The project's complex layout brings together the new space of liberty given to the watercourse with a series of gardens set in the old canal. Together, they form a linear garden, highlighting different settings, views, and identities.

The river's outline is based on a diagram that has opened up a complex system of channels, providing a precursory, undetermined field for the water to flow through. This has served as a starting point for the new riverbed to form.

3.1
Considering the landscape project as a negotiation platform

The ecological drama in which the human planet is engaged has been the subject of systematic ignorance. That period is now over. Through the media that have become hypersensitive to the repetition of ecological "accidents," international opinion is increasingly mobilized. Today, everyone is talking about ecology: politicians, technocrats, industrialists (...), however, the ecological disturbances of the environment are only the visible part of a deeper and more significant malady, related to the ways of living and being in society on this planet. Environmental ecology should be thought of as a unified whole with social ecology and mental ecology, through an ecosophy of an ethico–political nature. (...) [It is a matter of] supporting each other in innovative practices that recompose individual and collective subjectivities within new techno–scientific contexts and new political coordinates. [1]

Thinking about the purpose of this project, we realize that, in order to truly improve the ecosystem of the river Aire, we have to take into account its entire watershed. This cannot be achieved without examining the current gaps in preserving this ecosystem and coming up with more realistic, effective, and legitimate solutions. We have to identify the conditions necessary for these efforts to be successful, looking into the legal framework, potential stakeholders, and the results of similar experiments conducted elsewhere. As Philippe Descola points out, this raises the issue of a political and legal organization that would ensure the real and effective protection of human and non–human collectives, such as watersheds. While there are known precedents, Descola highlights the challenge of granting legal status to such collectives due to the lack of symbolic recognition of a wider range of non–human elements in Western societies.

3.2
Building community by gardening together

One can wonder what's happening these days at the Aire site, this rural public space, an open–access river–garden. Could it be that a community is forming here, gradually reclaiming the area and imbuing it with a series of symbolic relationships? The site fills up with stories, desires, and a sense of joy from rediscovering the river and its beauty. Its emotional impact may create and intensify the need to reconnect with a wonderfully complex world. The world in which, according to Descola, people could take on the role of stewards, protecting a collective composed of humans and non–humans.

3.3
Turning the project into a score that unfolds over time

For us, the Aire project has been a major turning point. We were already convinced of the need to take into account "what's already there" – the geographical, historical, and social contexts into which we would introduce some meaningful moves to make hidden relationships visible. In this project, we took a serious look at living processes. Our ongoing research, conducted in collaboration with river geomorphologist Mathias Kondolf from the University of Berkeley, represents a shift in river restoration projects – from form-based designs to those based on the autonomous evolution of river morphology. Together with a team of researchers, Kondolf has established four criteria for assessing these process-based projects. The first criterion, the river space, relates to the new freedom given to the river, increasing the available space for fluvial processes and the connectivity lost due to human alterations. The second criterion, energy, evaluates the project's reliance on the natural energy of the system for restoration work, while minimizing external mechanical energy use. The third criterion, materials, examines how the project uses geomorphically suitable materials to support the evolution of the riverbed. The fourth criterion, time, considers the long-term goals.

The Aire project convincingly fits all four criteria, but also introduces innovative diamond-shaped earthworks that accelerate the new riverbed's self driven morphogenesis. This work is described in the text "Let the River Run" (presented in the pages that follow – t/n). The title is somewhat ambiguous: letting things happen doesn't mean doing nothing but rather finding the triggers to revive living processes.

3.4
Expressing care for the living world through aesthetic resolution

Facing the uniquely shaped mountains and the visible marks left by human activities, this long-stretching Rivergarden orchestrates views, encounters, identities, and materials within a precious and fragile territory, to evoke questions, concerns, and hopes.

The sense of calm and introspection, without which there can be no real garden, is sought throughout the different sites and paths, making sure visitors are never crowded.

The footprint of the canal is a crucial element for creating this sense of introspection. It provides a permanent mark that bounds and frames a series of settings, and introduces a complex sense of time, combining past and future, memory and desire. Working with traces and the memory of place is a delicate task that should not be seen as going back but rather as opening to all the possibilities suggested by such "encounters."

To achieve this, some shocking and rough situations have been introduced at certain points. Designed to refresh the visitors' attention, they offer new experiences through various sensations and emotional impacts, with an aim to trigger a process of involuntary memory – the only one that can create a collision of space and time.

Such provocations shake up one's expectations and revive buried, forgotten feelings. A concrete slab hanging over the river invites people to come closer and feel the water. It's an attempt to engage all the senses, and what a joy it is when a kid leans over, touches the water, and says "river!"

Let the river run

The Aire revitalization project in Geneva expands the space given to the watercourse, recognizing such expansion as crucial for the true restoration of the river. The project embodies a new relationship between the existing site and its transformation, between the old canal and the new river. The aim of this text is to present an original way of giving shape to the new riverbed: letting the river run. The artificial creation of a trench system, similar to the ravines that form during hydraulic erosion of soils, has been an effective way to speed up the riverbed's morphogenesis. What can we learn from the unfolding of these processes? Is this novel approach applicable to other contexts? To write about the history of this experiment, the reactions it has generated, and the questions that remain unanswered, is also to call for further exchanges with the authors of similar projects. After all, explaining "is seeking to connect with others and share an understanding of the world[2]".

The dynamic of waterways

The dynamic nature of river systems is crucial to their ecological vitality, with frequent disturbances such as minor floods generating great biological diversity and maintaining complex backwaters. The active erosion of riverbanks and the formation of sand and gravel bars produce a variety of habitats that native species rely on. All this spontaneous activity requires a big enough playground for the water and sediment flows to create a dynamic and constantly evolving river.

The deterioration of this dynamic, interest in its restoration, and wrong turns

In the 20th century, waterways underwent major changes for a number of reasons: ease of navigation, flood control, soil drainage, urban development, and, of course, climate change. In the planet's more urbanized areas, the resulting loss of ecological diversity sparked increasing interest in the regeneration of these waterways. Ironically, regeneration projects have too often sought to stabilize rivers by creating fixed banks with idealized shapes, following two different approaches.

The first, a "technical–scientific" approach, often associated with engineers, is based on quantitative data (water volume, speed of current, etc.) and calculable outputs such as the wavelength and amplitude of curves traced by the waterway; it uses rigid and heavy tools (riprapping, concrete, etc.).

The other, "cultural" approach is mostly associated with landscapers who design picturesque new rivers, often citing English models, and use "vegetation engineering" techniques. In effect, both these approaches to waterway restoration replace a rectilinear channel with a new sinuous one, and thus create an artificial river. One thing they have in common is that the sinuosity of the waterways thus restored is far more symmetrical and homogeneous than in natural rivers.

In many cases, and especially where the gradient is steep, the current powerful, and the sediment copious, the first more or less serious flooding causes the river to erode the structures that confine it, seeking to carve out new courses. Conversely, in areas where the water dwindles, the river becomes incapable of modifying its imposed course, which remains fixed without the slightest prospect of evolution.

Needless to say, this dichotomy between cultural and technical approaches is never so sharp, since in many cases, landscapers incorporate scientific touches in their projects, and engineers adapt their sites with more subtlety.

The space of freedom for waterways

In May 2006, we presented the Aire revitalization project at the "Spatial Recall" conference held by the University of Berkeley's Landscape Architecture Department – an event that had a major impact on our design. During the conference, Mathias Kondolf, a fluvial geomorphologist teaching at the University, exposed the inanity of the two earlier described ways of developing a new riverbed, and proposed a different approach, which consisted in "giving the new waterway a possibility to make its own bed by opening up a sufficiently wide playground where it could move, vary its width with changing flood levels, erode and deposit sediments".

This space, alternately called the "space of freedom", the "erodible corridor", and the "meandering space", is where the waterway, emerging from genuine autonomous morphogenetic processes, quickly attains the form that landscapers and engineers equally fail to achieve. Such types of spaces are usually created on less expensive land outside urban areas – yet, in the case of the Aire, the approach was tested in a heavily developed area on the outskirts of Geneva.

[2] Isabelle Stengers, *Réactiver le sens commun (Reactivating Common Sense)*, La Découverte, 2020.

01.

02.

03.

04.

A stroke of luck for the Aire?

Could we expect the "space of freedom" approach to be successful in the case of the Aire? To regenerate through an autonomous process, a river needs a sufficient volume of sediment in its catchment and enough energy to erode, move, and deposit those sediments. Most of the Aire's basin is relatively steep, providing favorable hydrography and sediment load for such evolution. With its torrential flow pattern, it carries a high average volume of sediments which, during major (centennial) floods, can see a tenfold increase. The Aire, therefore, seemed a good candidate for a project that would enable the river to restore its own course.

Aire comes from the Celtic "ar, al," which means "flowing water"

The Aire River flows from the slopes of Mount Salève, heading North over glacial moraines into a wide alluvial cone, and then through the plain until it joins the Arve River, just before the Arve merges with the Rhône in central Geneva. Nineteenth–century maps show that the Aire once had a braided, steep, and dynamic course with significant sediment deposits on its alluvial cone, and that it formed a series of meanders across the plain. After a major flood in 1878, studies were conducted to channel the river, leading to the first levee being built between the villages of Certoux and Lully.

In the 20th century, three kilometers of the Aire were "corrected" into a rectilinear canal to improve the lower valley's drainage and facilitate the growth of agricultural activities. Later, during the development of an industrial zone in the 1940s, more than a kilometer was channeled underground, to the point where the Aire meets the Arve. Finally, around 1980, to prevent the flooding of residential areas that had been imprudently built too close to the river, a tunnel was created to divert the Aire towards the Rhône.

The Aire revitalization project

At the end of the 20th century, due to changes in Geneva's water legislation, a new law was passed that established the principles of river restoration through seven articles. It included the creation of a special river fund to finance the works. In 2000, Switzerland's first river revitalization competition was held. The winning project by the Superpositions group proposed the development of a wide meandering space for the river by reclaiming agricultural and forest land, while transforming the straight canal into a series of public gardens. The project was planned in four stages; by 2020, the first three stages were completed, and work on the fourth stage began in 2021.

The first implementation phase

The first phase of the Aire's revitalization started in 2002, in parallel with the ongoing studies for the overall project. Focused on one pilot sector, this phase was limited to reshaping the banks, with no possibility to increase the space available to the river. The quick implementation of this experimental sector soon after announcing the competition results had a dual purpose: demonstrating the State's commitment to improving the waterways of the Canton of Geneva, and allowing the Superpositions team to fine–tune the collaborations across the various disciplines involved in the project.

Searching for an autonomous morphogenesis

Starting from the initial studies and sketches exploring the ways to develop the new riverbed, a cluster of coloured lines suggested a yet undefined shape to come, clearly manifesting the impossibility of determining this shape in advance. In further studies, the question remained open and without any satisfactory answer.

A first attempt

During the second implementation phase, a simple, broad, and uniform excavation was carried out, sufficient to hold the required volume of water. No other interventions were planned, allowing the new riverbed to form naturally, as the river was gradually carving out its new path in the space freed up for meandering.

Slow progress and limitations

In contrast to the projects where a river's new minor bed is defined right from the start, the success of autonomous morphogenesis strongly depends on high–flow periods, the only ones capable of providing the energy needed to initiate the process. Ironically, a wide meandering space, which is necessary for the river to freely establish its new course, becomes the very factor that slows the process down: spreading out over a larger surface, the water loses much of its erosive power.

05.

06.

07.

08.

The shapes to come

This is why, during the next stage of the project, we addressed the concerns about the length of the process by reviewing the behavior of fluids and materials that were crucial to the project. We explored an alternative approach using a preparatory design that could be able to both initiate and accelerate the natural formation of a new riverbed, without prematurely forcing the river into a shape. We found inspiration in the work of Pierre-Gilles de Gennes describing percolation, a phenomenon that can be roughly defined as the passage of a liquid through a porous material. Scientific diagrams representing percolation generally involve areas divided into polygons through which the liquid spreads randomly; they inspired us to look for a similar diagram tailored to our challenge.

Black squares

A first test of the model was improvised on a readily available "matrix": a slightly tilted chocolate bar, with milk poured over it.

Diamonds

This initial test has roughly confirmed the phenomenon, but the square shapes of the chocolate bar were not satisfactory, unlike the diamond shapes found on islands in alluvial plains, where they act as flow dividers.

Opening up possibilities

The diamond-patterned diagram creates a matrix that will trigger the process of morphogenesis without predetermining the shapes of the new riverbed. The diagonal configuration of the channels is intended to promote the bifurcation of water currents while rapidly generating the complexity sought for the new riverbed. In his essay on Francis Bacon's paintings, Gilles Deleuze revisits the term "diagram." According to Deleuze, at times Bacon would put on the canvas what he himself called a diagram, "something, a trace, a stain that counters the ever-threatening cliché, a shape emerging too quickly." This arbitrary gesture opened up a field of possibilities.

Sizing and implementing the grid. Hydraulics and construction

The search for a balance between the resistance of the riverbanks and the intensity of the water flow determined the dimensions of the diamond pattern, the thickness of soil stripping layers, the width and depth of the channels. To these decisive elements was added a correlation between the dimensions of the two kinds of curves: those of the meanders of the old river and those of the diagram.

The nature of the materials

The dimensions of the diamonds and the width of the channels were not influenced by the nature of the materials present on site, even though it was expected that the gravelly ones, present in certain segments, would be rapidly carried away by the river, creating more space to accommodate larger floods.

Beneath the layer of topsoil varying between 20 and 50 cm, there is a layer of sandy silt, whose thickness ranges from a meter at some points to two meters at others, and which covers a slightly sandy layer of gravel. Upstream of the new riverbed, the first diamonds were dug out in a highly silty environment, while further downstream, the diamonds' side walls revealed layers of gravelly material.

Anticipated erosion

Knowing that it was essential to give the river enough space for accommodating major floods, could we rely on the accelerated erosion of the diamond shapes to quickly create that space? This was the hypothesis put forward, assuming that the centennial flood could, once the work was completed, flow without spilling over, and estimating that, within a reasonable timeframe, the river would carve out a bed capable of containing larger floods. This approach had a double benefit of significantly reducing the volume of earthworks and preserving valuable sediment in the remaining islands.

The diagram covers the ground

Once the topsoil was removed, the diamond pattern was mapped onto the entire meandering area, in preparation for digging the furrows.

Precautions

To avoid compacting the new riverbed, a tracked scraper was used. This machine not only dug the trench but also transported the excavated material to the toe of the bank, where it was loaded onto trucks. Achieving the four-meter width of the channels required two passes with the scraper. This technique prevented the trucks from driving on the future riverbed, which would have caused compaction and created channels that could artificially direct the water flow.

09.

10.

11.

12.

June 13, 2014: The water flows in

The diamond-shaped furrows were evenly filled with water, and erosion started with surprising speed, triggering the desired process of self-driven morphogenesis.

Floodplain

This diagram sets the process in motion, opening up a corridor where the river continuously shapes and changes its own minor bed, but also leading to the formation of a vast floodplain where small increases in flow bring about similar transformations. The river's playground is thus significantly expanded, while remaining within the defined limits of the project's meandering area.

Differentiated erosion

As expected, the highly gravelly diamonds were quickly eroded, and their materials formed bars across the entire width of the river, resulting in a general leveling of the bed. The diamonds carved from more compact, silty materials resisted erosion for a longer time; in these areas, the river deepened its bed by creating small canyons instead of eroding the diamonds.

Acceleration of the process

The surprisingly fast pace of self-driven morphogenesis can be explained by the fact that the water currents face lateral resistance, which maintains their strength and pressure on the banks. However, this pressure sufficiently weakens the banks to let the destruction/construction process happen quickly.

The overall loosening of the site creates a network of gullies. This is one of the most feared phenomena in soil conservation, as it leads to accelerated hydraulic erosion.

Gully erosion is one of the most common forms of soil loss on land insufficiently protected by vegetation. In other words, one could say that, from the initial clearing of the site to the digging of diamond-pattern channels, the project has been intentionally designed to cause hydraulic erosion, in a kind of reverse application of all soil conservation principles.

Metamorphoses

The diamond-shaped pattern triggers continuous upheavals that promote the development of rich biodiversity. We observe erosion and deposition processes similar to those seen in alluvial plains. Various environments form across the space allocated to the new river: sand and gravel bars, temporary ponds, terraces of different heights that are either wet or dry. During successive high-flow periods, these features change, disappear, and reappear in new places, causing significant alterations to the riverbed, including shallow sections and deep pools that serve as safe havens for fish when the river is low.

The width of the riverbed varies significantly, causing variations in flow speed, which leads to a high diversity of sediment grain sizes. The more diverse the substrates, with different levels of moisture, sand, gravel, and pebbles, the more diverse the resulting plant life, which attracts a wide range of animal species: butterflies, dragonflies, amphibians, reptiles, birds, and small mammals. These complex habitats also benefit from the events like floods or strong winds that cause trees to fall into the river or create logjams from deadwood. To promote vegetation growth and limit invasive plants, the banks and diamond-shaped areas were promptly seeded with wildflower meadows and riparian species; additionally, a large number of planted trees and shrubs helped restore a continuous canopy, essential for the survival and mobility of wildlife.

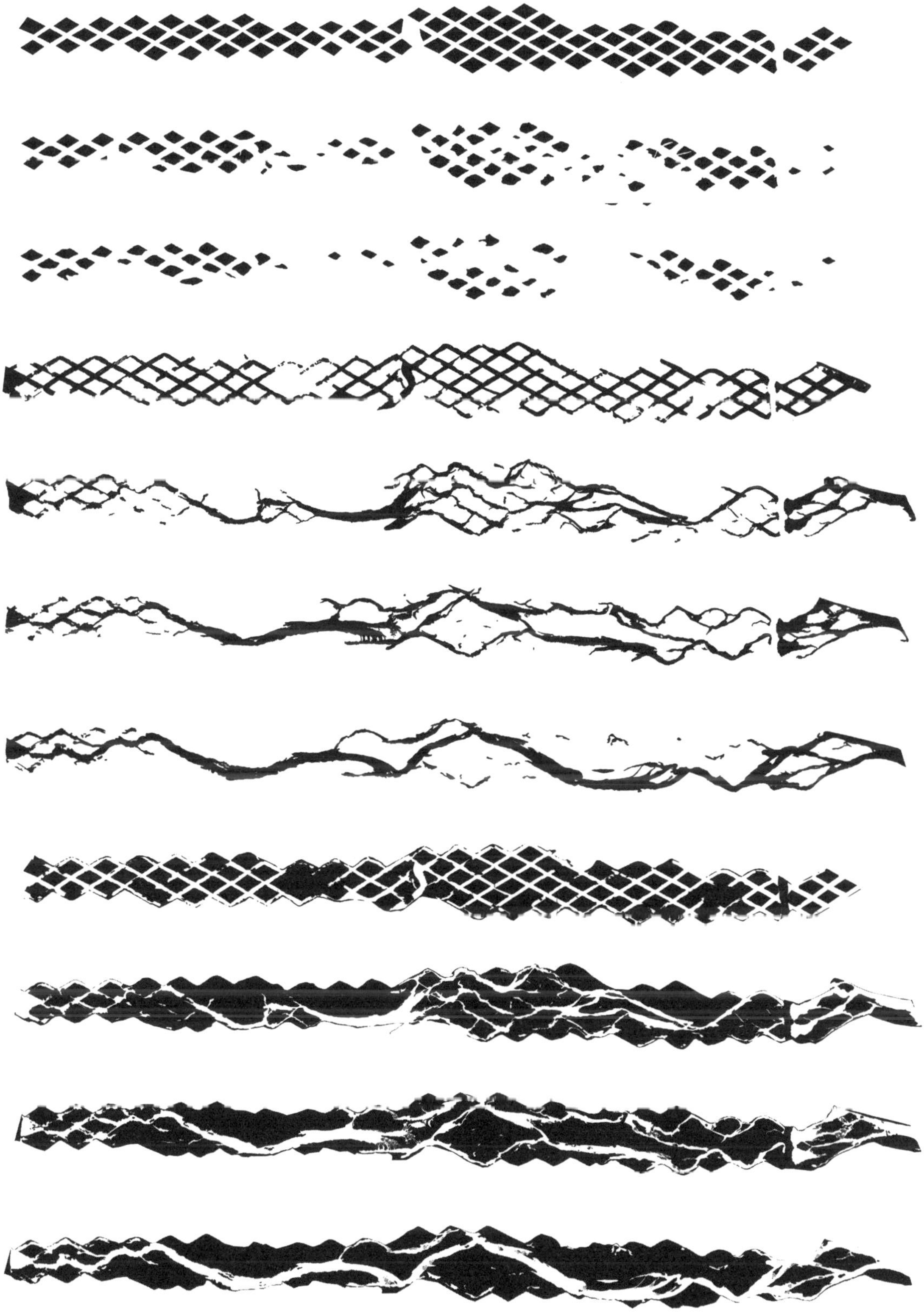

The Aire, an open-air laboratory

The transdisciplinary composition of the research group introduced an element of experimentation right from the outset. Biologists, environmental scientists, hydraulic engineers, architects and landscapers who have come together in Superpositions to work on the project brought with them a wealth of experiences and achievements. During the almost twenty-year-long process of research and implementation, a new shared expertise has gradually developed to meet increasingly ambitious demands. By drawing on their specialist knowledge and stepping outside traditional boundaries, all of these disciplines were able to collaborate on the project's hypotheses and find ways to test them.

This approach was encouraged through the team's connections with the Architecture and Landscape research group at the University of Geneva. It's impossible not to mention André Corboz, the Geneva-born historian of architecture and urban planning. His expert, compelling reminders of the need to consider the historical depth of territories and understand the reasons and conditions for their continuous renewal have profoundly influenced the working methods of many participants of this research.

The exploratory nature of the project, which involved questioning existing laws and regulations, has been consistently supported by the State of Geneva's River Restoration Service as part of its river revitalization program. This supportive attitude was crucial to the project's success; it is probably this experimental aspect, along with the exceptional conditions provided for it, that explains the project's wide recognition. Legal reform is a complex and slow process, which is why it's essential that exemptions, as advocated by Dominique Bourg, be used to open fields for experimentation. These exemptions are the only way to test new proposals for organizing our territories.

An ongoing experiment

It's too early to assess the long-term impacts of this experiment. The hypothesis that excavation can be minimized and that the river can be allowed to shape its own bed bed has been validated. A walk along the Aire shows that the river has quickly carved out its bed, although it has not yet experienced significant morphogenetic floods. However, the risks of starting this process without setting strong, permanent limits on the river's movement had to be considered, since we are observing that, in certain segments, the Aire is trying to reclaim the entire area of its old meanders. Therefore, it will be necessary to rethink the current boundaries of the river, consulting with all involved parties, especially farmers, and to plan for any subsequent interventions required in the short or medium term to either reinforce the current banks or allow for a broader river space.

3.0 Aldeia Maracanã

– Rio de Janeiro

Rexiste !

Combining "We Exist!" and "We Resist!," Aldeia Marakanã's slogan boldly proclaims its fight against the invisibilization of Indigenous peoples. "We were here long before the Bible was written," they remind us. As Brazil's first urban Aldeia (Indigenous village), it was founded on an abandoned heritage site that had long been designated for the Museum of Indigenous Cultures, a project that never happened. Claiming the right to live on their ancestral lands, in 2006, several dozen families from different tribes settled in this sacred place, which for millennia served as a major burial ground for the region's tribes and is now part of the northern districts of Rio de Janeiro.

Creating a garden, both for subsistence and medicinal purposes, was a vital necessity here: with no sewage or electricity, the residents live in precarious conditions. Despite these challenges, one of the twelve Indigenous universities on the American continent – a network dedicated to recovering and passing down ancestral knowledge – has been established in the Aldeia Marakanã. Students and supporters from around the world come to learn from Indigenous wisdom, while the Indigenous community is learning to use social networks to their advantage.

Mission Occupation by indigenous people
Location Rua Mata Machado 126, Marakanã, Rio de Janeiro, Brazil
Geographical coordinates 22°54'48"S, 43°13'38"W
Project leader Teko Haw Maraká'nà (Aldeia Marakanã)
Size 14,300 m²
Duration ongoing

← ↓ ©Kaue Maciel

Team Potyra Guajajara, Urutau Guajajara, Mayra Guajajara, Julia Xavante, Maria Enia Guajajara, Galvino Guajajara, Lisi Potyguara, Sandro Akroá, Ricardo Ajuricaba, Lucas Munducuru, Dário Jurema, Esther Pataxó, Ana Lúcia Guajajara, Kael Guajajara, Vinícius Guajajara, Vanessa, Kathelen Puri, Mônica Lima Mura, Joana Guajajara, Regina Guajajara, Milena Guajajara, Cajanã Tupiniquim, Winona Evelyn
Facilitator Pierre-André Martin
Photo credits Kaue Maciel, George Magaraia

Research has confirm
20,000 years, we've b
tubers, fruit trees, and
plants. The European
our gold; they also too
and knowledge, even
They seized our lands a
forests. **But they could**
Now, the seeds of our
starting to sprout agai
land itself.

— José Urutau Guajajara

ed that for over
een domesticating
medicinal
didn't just steal
k our plants
esorting to torture.
nd cut down our
n't wipe out *our roots.*
civilization are
n, because *we are this*

3.0
Aldeia Maracanã, *being part of the living world*

Stepping into the world of Indigenous cultures requires extra care, as Indigenous time is different: it dances to the rhythms of the living environment. Backed by our convictions about the way the world works, our willingness to act and be effective can sometimes offend subtle sensitivities, but it's nevertheless important to our efforts.

This is an invitation to pause and turn to silence, observation, and active listening so that we could simply become part of, before trying to become part of the change.

However, it's not about keeping these cultures unchanged forever, nor about reinforcing our myths of the noble savage and lost paradise by fighting against time. Today, dancing, singing, and praying to the living world also means making use of our digital worlds, blending city and forest cultures to protect and restore life.

Pierre-André Martin

← ©George Magaraia

3.1
Considering the landscape project as a negotiation platform

This is not a "project" but a vital struggle for the recognition and respect of the rights enshrined in the country's constitution. The demarcation of Indigenous lands does protect some areas, but they are constantly being worn away by logging, mining, and agriculture. Deforestation is recorded daily, and its impact on global climate dynamics is well-known.

Land demarcation is as much a revolution as it is a negotiation. Many of the 305 Indigenous peoples, speaking a total of 274 languages, are being forced to settle and reinvent their way of life around agroforestry, a practice that has been in place for millennia. At the Aldeia, a kind of "reclaim" is happening. Violent police evictions, the return of families to ancestral lands, and legal actions by both Indigenous people and the state show the power struggle happening on physical, legal, and symbolic levels.

Initiatives are welcomed, and many collectives independently run various activities. Although the Cacique holds moral and spiritual authority, the organization is not hierarchical. Everything here is about negotiation, resourcefulness, and self-organization, as the public authorities, despite recognizing the area as ancestral land, don't offer any help or services.

During yet another turbulent eviction, marked by police violence and illegal detentions, Cacique Urutau chained himself to a tree for 26 hours. Epitomizing the contempt for Indigenous people, this "occupation" triggered harsh political reactions, with one deputy even saying, "those who love the Indians should go to Bolivia, where the President is not only Indian but also a communist." Evo Morales then responded against this intolerance and racism, causing an uproar that reached the United Nations.

3.2
Building community by gardening together

The community here is being built on multiple levels at the same time:

— Locally, in connection with the Aldeia Marakanã site,

— Nationally, in relation to the recognition of the rights and cultures of Brazil's Indigenous peoples,

— Internationally, through the network of Indigenous Universities open to all.

This multidimensional aspect of the community makes the Aldeia a true, albeit informal and unrecognized, embassy for the political and cultural existence of Indigenous peoples.

This struggle brings together Indigenous families from different tribes and students from various fields and backgrounds, including some French and other Europeans "following in the footsteps of Lévi-Strauss," jokes Cacique Urutau, who holds a master's degree in Linguistics, with a big laugh. The University is known for teaching around fifteen languages, as well as songs, prayers, stories, and traditional medicine that uses more than 2,000 plants.

There is a real challenge in making the Aldeia visible and recognized internationally. The community is active on social media and hosts many visiting Indigenous people, including artists and artisans (if we can even categorize their social role in these cultures). The audience was deeply moved when MCs from Brazil's economic capital São Paulo came to the Aldeia to rap in their ancestral languages. Many young Indigenous people don't reject schooling or digital tools, but they strongly assert their identity and resistance.

↑ ©George Magaraia

↑ ©Coloco

↑ ©Coloco

3.3
Turning the project into a score that unfolds over time

The priority here is to improve living conditions, as there are no sewers, running water, or electricity – only two solar batteries that are enough for charging phones, but not for a fridge. It's a daily struggle where every day is a challenge, and anything can happen, like the fire that destroyed the Museum's valuable archives of now-extinct cultures. "Everything suggests that they want to erase every trace of our existence," comments the Cacique.

Time doesn't flow like a smooth river where everything goes according to plan. The outcome is one of conflict, uncertainty and controversy. "We could imagine a cultural site open to everyone, welcoming tourists from around the world," Urutau says when asked about a brighter future. In the meantime, the residents become plumbers, masons, electricians, and gardeners to handle emergencies and rebuild the Aldeia with their own hands. They'll be happy to manage their village on their own, but wouldn't mind getting some help from the authorities, just like any other cultural or heritage project.

Archaeological digs are expected to start soon to uncover traces of the ancestral cemetery, proving the sacred nature of the site. "In our language, there is no word for progress. Instead, the core of our communities is the harmony and well-being of everyone," explains the Pagé (spiritual leader) Kixtin. Bimi, his daughter and apprentice in the art of plant healing, adds, "We want a well and electricity so we can continue working on our craft after dark. Far from the folklore to which we are sometimes reduced, we young people want to build our world with the best of both."

↑ ©George Magarai

3.4
Expressing care for the living world through aesthetic resolution

In the Aldeia, it all started amidst ruins and trash. Everything was abandoned, and some buildings even had their roofs torn off to make them uninhabitable. The first residents built their homes using wood and whatever materials they could find. The botanical garden provided them with palm leaves and bamboo at first, but that supply stopped when things got tense. The Indigenous people also built communal homes and spaces. Finally, they began planting fruits, vegetables, and medicinal plants, letting wild plants grow around them to protect the crops from prying eyes and thieves.

Photos of the Aldeia bear witness to its reality: sad ruins on an abandoned parking lot where life persists – children playing, plants breaking through the asphalt, and groups organizing to continue the struggle. Indigenous art has taken over the walls on which spray-painted banners are displayed. There's a lot of singing, praying, and storytelling. Monthly programs offer plenty of opportunities for learning and sharing, and the international convention of Indigenous languages, also hosted by the Aldeia, is attended by tribes from all over the Americas.

The Aldeia has a well-designed website that posts news; it also features the Manifesto, which is reproduced on the pages that follow and is the result of many collaborations. Urutau explains: "Our young people post a lot on Instagram, sometimes even frenetically. This is how we communicate – no editing, no moderator, no spokesperson."

Here we stand, *taking*
story. **We don't want t**
memories.

We demand recogniti
done for this country.
the Whites, the immig
invaders, a lot.
We demand respect.

— **Ash Ashaninka**, one of the Aldeia Marakanã's leaders of re *charge of our own*

be just living

n for what we have
We have helped
rants, and even the

stance

↓ ©Kaue Maciel

TEKO HAW
MARAKANÃ

Tekohaw Maraká'nà: a multiethnic Indigenous village in the heart of Rio de Janeiro

In Aldeia Marakanã, we exist and resist to ensure that the connection between Native cultures and Western culture allows for a beneficial coexistence for both sides while preserving the nature to which we belong. Based on this nature-respecting system, we have created the Aldeia Marakanã Multiethnic Indigenous University.

The people who lived on our lands before the arrival of the first colonizers 520 years ago were not considered as Cariocas, Fluminense, or Brazilians. The area now known as Rio de Janeiro was inhabited by various peoples with different customs, languages, and physical traits. We understand that we are part of the land and that we must fit into a unified system without ever exploiting, let alone destroying it, – this is how we see nature in its cycles of birth and death. The colonizers, who saw us merely as an obstacle to their exploitation of metals and precious resources, deceived us through indoctrination, enslavement, violation and killing under the guise of a "civilizing" mission.

At the end of the 18th century, the area along the River Marakanã (named after a native bird) was occupied by sugar plantations owned by the Jesuits.

In the 19th century, the former Fazenda de São Cristóvão, a 14,300 m² property [where the Aldeia Marakanã is now located], was donated by the Prince of Saxony, husband of Princess Leopoldina, to be reserved in perpetuity for the research on tubers and seeds, and for their cultivators – that is, the Indigenous populations.

At the beginning of the 20th century, the site hosted a research center focused on the cultivation of native plants, based above all on Indigenous knowledge. The Indian Protection Service (SPI) was established here with the aim of protecting the original peoples, but it ended up being used to arrest leaders and repress the Indigenous movement.

In 1953, controversies over Indigenous territories led to the creation of a Section for the Protection of Indians within the National Council. The same year saw the establishment of the first Latin American Indian Museum in the Aldeia, which remained active until 1978. After that, the building was abandoned for nearly thirty years.

→ ©Kaue Maciel

In 2006, the Indigenous movement in Rio de Janeiro decided to settle on the site to honor the memory of the ancestral inhabitants, and because they viewed occupying a sacred and traditional place for preserving original culture as a just cause. It also became a place to welcome the Indigenous people passing through the city, and the descendants of former local residents who were at risk or socially excluded and unable to find decent housing.

Since then, we, the Indigenous people who live here, have been facing constant attacks from the forces of repression linked to real estate speculation. Despite this, the awareness of our mission in this symbolic place has led to the creation of the first multi–ethnic and intercultural space for exchanging practices and original knowledge – a space that would reflect the diversity of the Indigenous societies of over 300 peoples and nations currently present in the country. The Aldeia Marakanã Multi–Ethnic Indigenous University has been established.

Today, in the heart of Rio, our gardens produce corn, manioc, beans, pumpkins, passion fruits, sweet potatoes, and other crops that we grow. We also teach about the rich cultural heritage of the country's first inhabitants, including languages, cosmologies, arts, and sacred medicine.

(Here are just a few examples of the events taking place at the Aldeia: the Sacred Feminine Cycle debates; the First National Conference on the Mental Health of Indigenous Peoples; the Intercultural Congress of Resistance of Indigenous and Traditional Peoples of Marakanã; the 19th Conference of Indigenous Languages – as well as theatrical productions, music and dance performances, and the teaching of indigenous crafts and techniques.)

These initiatives could have been considered emblematic of the city's cultural offerings, but instead they are perceived as challenges to the official authorities who are aligned with the interests of major capitalist corporations. Located next to the Marakanã Stadium, the Aldeia was an obstacle to the construction of a shopping center planned by then governor Sérgio Cabral (currently in prison) and the construction company Odebrecht. In addition to the cowardly demolition of the buildings where LANAGRO (National Agricultural Laboratory) operated, a walkway was built on part of the sacred Indigenous land to facilitate the passage of sports fans. After the sporting events were over, the area was once again abandoned before we decided to reclaim our property.

The universities of th
knowledge **for their da**
it to the pharmaceuti
we have our own univ
databases. They are
who *genuinely wishes*
interested in making

— **Ash Ashaninka**, one of the Aldeia Marakanã's leaders of r

e Whites *collect our*
:abases and then sell
al industry. But
ersity and our own
pen to anyone
to heal, **not to those**
n profit.

istance

Katu ahy!

According to the Citizen Constitution of 1988, Indigenous lands include those used for Indigenous people's productive activities, those essential for preserving the environmental resources that are vital to their well-being, and those necessary for their cultural reproduction. Therefore, the land and the building that once housed O Museu do Índio (The Museum of the Indigenous Populations) – the first place to collect and preserve some of our artifacts and instruments and to showcase our customs and practices – belong to us.

This heritage must be protected and officially guaranteed as an irreplaceable value of Brazilian culture, acknowledging the cultural contributions of the original peoples who were present here long before the pre-colonial period. It must be preserved and maintained so that the people living there can protect and defend it. Our presence in the Aldeia affirms our identity and the need for autonomous management that characterizes all Indigenous peoples.

We offer the society a space not just for socializing but for exchanging knowledge, practices, values, and ideas with the local culture. We have people trained in Western laws and knowledge. Therefore, we are part of this urban society, and we demand respect and recognition of the value of this exchange.

As the Native people whose blood has for millennia nourished this land with knowledge and courage, we are deeply committed to having our culture and dignity recognized. Every time we express ourselves through our stories, our sacred fire, and the veneration of our Encantados, we are creating a new reality based on respect and knowledge, moving beyond mere survival on this Earth, and overcoming the tortures, racism, and genocides that have affected our peoples. This place was once used to show the 20th-century traditional society what Indigenous people were. Today, it is where Indigenous people themselves show their value to contemporary society – to anyone who is willing to see it.

Far from being an "urban dump," as the enemies of nature and life call it, the Aldeia Marakanã is a vibrant movement, a community that has survived centuries of cultural and physical oppression. Regardless of how often Indigenous peoples are stripped of their possessions, discriminated against, silenced, and ignored, they will find ways to resist, survive, and reemerge. And this space will be part of the city too.

The complete text of the Manifesto is available at www.aldeiamarakana.com

↗ ©George Magaraia
→ ©Kaue Maciel

FORA PM

The Amazon...

Recent research on the functioning of the biosphere shows just how important the planet's largest tropical rainforest, the Amazon, is for regulating the global climate. Pilot and eco-explorer Gérard Moss has described a phenomenon that he calls "flying rivers": "large volumes of water in the form of humid air that move with the winds" and exist due to the water evaporation from the millions of hectares of Amazonian trees (source: GEO). This makes the areas south of the Amazon – regions that would normally be desert at this latitude – one of the most fertile places in the world.

If these flying rivers were to disappear, it would have a serious impact on the climate. With the current pace of deforestation, tracked by a Brazilian government mission with radar-equipped planes flying daily over the Amazon, the need for ecological restoration is urgent. According to Brazil's National Water Agency, even under the most optimistic scenario of a 1.5°C temperature rise, most Brazilian rivers will see their flow decrease. There is indeed a possibility of reaching a point of no return.

However, in an ecosystem that took 60 million years to become what it is today, restoration is both very complex and very difficult. There are chains of co-dependencies where some species rely on specific bees for reproduction, while these bees depend on a certain orchid, and so on. We have to admit that, despite all our scientific knowledge, we do not know how to recreate the richness of these unique ecosystems. Therefore, let's protect what remains and continue to deepen our understanding of and our experiences in regeneration to learn more. Let's finally listen to those who have lived in these areas for millennia and know how to communicate with other living beings.

In the Amazon, heavy rains make the soil very poor, pushing the region's biodiversity up into the trees. When the trees are gone, the rain washes everything away, exposing poor subsoil, which makes regeneration extremely difficult. Still, there are initiatives like those in the Xingu region, where networks of women collect seeds, replant, and restore on a large scale. Let's not forget that the Amazon rainforest is actually an agroforest, where human influence has been present for more than 20,000 years. Many fruit trees found there, such as the cupuaçu, result from Indigenous cultivation.

Besides deforestation, there is also the settlement of nomadic peoples who are "confined" to Indigenous lands – the darker side of protective strategies. The territories are protected, but this forces nomadic peoples to become sedentary, even in the forest, – which is a major challenge as it requires them to create completely new infrastructures that are alien to their cultures.

In this context, a new approach to landscape is emerging, right at the edge between the world's largest forest and Latin America's largest cities.

↓ ©Kaue Maciel

↗ ©Jhwhverdonk | Dreamstime.com
→ ©Operação_Hymenaea, Ibama from Brasil, CC BY 2.0, via Wikimedia Commons

3.P Ingenious Landscapes

– around the *Planetary Garden*

The ingenious connection between farmers and their environment as an inspiration for the future

Amid the challenge of feeding humanity, we encounter the people who cultivate, garden, and harvest while nurturing a harmonious relationship with nature that rewards them. These encounters inspire and give hope. The precision of these gardeners' actions, their keen observation of the landscape show a consideration for other living beings, those with whom they interact.

Here, respect for life is a primary condition. The illustrations presented in this chapter capture the complex relationships with the Earth that keep us alive. Through these encounters, we find reasons to continue the work of our ancestors and learn to be better at providing fertile solutions for tomorrow.

Mission Illustrated report
Locations visited in 2021 CANARY ISLANDS Lanzarote, MAROC The argan groves of the Anti-Atlas, TUNISIA The Gafsa Oases and the Ghar El Melh lagoon
Locations planned for 2022 CHILE Chiloé Island, PERU Andes, ECUADOR Province of Napo, MEXICO Xochimilco, TANZANIA Mount Usambara, BALI Karangasem, SPAIN Huerta Valenciana, Valle Salado

Team Atelier Pareto — Héloïse Bouju & Simon Gabillard
Partners The GIAHS Secretariat of the FAO, The Municipal Council of Lanzarote, ANDZOA Maroc, FAO Tunisie, ASM Gafsa

Photo credits Simon Gabillard
Image credits Atelier Pareto

Is a *positive Anthropo*
This is an investig
agricultural landscape
balance **between hu**
and the dynamics o

cene **even possible?**
ion into unique
that embody the
an activities
living systems.

3.P

Ingenious Landscapes, *telling the story of agricultural heritage*

"Ingenious Landscapes" is an immersive investigation into the resourcefulness behind unique agricultural territories. It uses landscape as a springboard for decoding, analyzing, and showcasing the various actors involved in shaping these territories, their motivations and interrelations.

Driven by its authors' curiosity, this report becomes an opportunity to reconsider the role of human interference in maintaining the resilience of living systems – and pave the way for a positive Anthropocene, one in which humans are neither central nor intrusive. By highlighting the stories of local actors, our report offers an alternative to an agriculture increasingly driven by productivity.

Atelier Pareto — Héloïse Bouju and Simon Gabillard

3.1
Considering the landscape project as a negotiation platform

A territory is shaped by many various factors (climate, geology, fauna, flora, humans...), acting together or independently, each with their own timing and reasons for transforming this shared foundation.

Sometimes these forces clash, while other times they align and agree on a fair balance that ensures a place for all and allows the greatest number to thrive. This is what we call negotiation.

"Ingenious Landscapes" is a journey exploring agricultural landscapes that embody this negotiation, finding a balance between human activities and ecological dynamics. It tells stories co-woven by different living beings, where humans are not necessarily placed at the center (to borrow the words of Anna L. Tsing), and never act as intruders or harmful disruptors.

These landscapes serve as prototypes of a possible positive Anthropocene, where humans, somewhat like beavers, assume their role as builder species, significantly transforming their environment but benefiting a broader food chain than the initial balance allowed.

"Ingenious Landscapes" takes an iterative approach, exploring agricultural sites that exemplify successful negotiations between living communities, revealing the ties between different actors and showing how a shared understanding of landscapes can form the basis of future negotiations.

3.2
Building community by gardening together

In these farming areas, community starts right at the level of a plot and involves the farmer, their tools, the wind, the soil, but also the stones left by the farmer to trap sand, the mulberry tree keeping birds away from apricots, the argan tree roots holding onto rainwater, the tide bringing in nutrient-rich sand, the female palm tree needing careful hand-pollination, ... and that patch of wild herbs kept for the pollinators, and that pair of hoopoes nesting in the old fig tree... Here, farming involves both living and nonliving things – a whole community that gathers around it.

Beyond this farmer-environment connection, the community extends on a larger scale among the farmers in an agro-ecosystem. From Lanzarote to southern Tunisian oases and Ghar El Melh's lagoons, everyone has a link with this "shared garden" because almost everyone is a farmer! Taxi drivers, public officials, teachers, retirees, workers, healthcare professionals, construction entrepreneurs – each owns a plot of land, a piece of ground to cultivate their food or keep friendships alive.

In these places, two things stand out: smaller plot sizes, averaging less than one hectare, and a tendency to juggle multiple jobs. This makes farming a shared practice, common to all, rather than being left to a small part of the population like in France. How do we feed the world? Maybe the answer is in each of us being a little bit of a farmer?

3.3
Turning the project into a score that unfolds over time

How can we pass on these agricultural landscapes? How can we ensure their dynamic preservation, keeping them alive rather than static? This is the challenge for many territories: to update practices and organizations so that they continue being meaningful and effective.

Each territory shows examples of reinventing the idea of the commons, working to build new forms of solidarity around agricultural landscapes. After all, a landscape is not a one-man business! These commons are built around the multiple roles of agriculture. For instance, in Lanzarote, workers in social reintegration are taking over from elderly vintners and preparing the way for the younger generation; in the argan groves, the practice of the *agdal* is reinterpreted through agreements between local associations and foresters; in the oases, cooperatives are reorganizing the sharing of resources (water rotation, compost, drains, seeds).

But this creative updating is nothing new; it's inherent to these territories, for the rural environment is a laboratory, especially in the context of extremely limited resources – or, worse, climate instability. Innovation and near-constant adjustment are essential for the survival of the system as a whole. This traditional agriculture has always been experimental, evolving day by day and year by year: adjusting to winds and tides, selecting seeds, inventing tools, creating substrates...

From this ongoing action-research (trial-error / trial-success) emerges collective humility and great inventiveness: one person's project is always inspired by another, in a manner that is more cooperative than competitive.

3.4
Expressing care for the living world through aesthetic resolution

The farmers we have met impressed us with their profound attachment to their land and, even more so, with their almost daily engagement with the landscape. Their work goes far beyond productive, food-related, or economic concerns. Aesthetic appreciation, perfecting their craft through repetition, and the joy of being outdoors are all driving forces behind their work, with an aesthetic aspiration that is both visual and experiential.

This creates landscapes with a strong, omnipresent aesthetic, born from the constant care and attention of those who shape them.

Maybe this is what makes a beautiful landscape: the sum of careful, small acts of attention towards all living things, including humans.

Many of these farmers are retired, working part-time, or farming alongside other, remunerative jobs. They farm without aiming for economic profitability. At a loss, then? No, they gain emotionally, in a way that is outside the commercial logic.

It's hard work, for sure! Digging up the *rofe* (a local term for volcanic pyroclasts, the lava powder ejected during eruptions and used as mineral mulch), rebuilding dry-stone walls, or redesigning canals and *mesqas* are all exhausting tasks, but they are done with a philosophical approach: "When you feel tired, you stop. You take a nap under a fig tree, or you look up at the landscape and remember why you're doing this."

It's as if, once the economic aspect is removed from the picture, farming takes on a different meaning: an invitation to create, to participate, to interact with other living beings.

"Ingenious Landscapes" is first of all an investigative journey into our relationships with living things, into the shape of rural life and the link between nature and culture that farming represents. It is an ongoing project that, after exploring four sites in the Mediterranean and Macaronesia, now continues in South America's Andean and Amazonian regions.

Faced with the challenges of changing French agricultural models, we decided to look for alternative stories and examples that are already working elsewhere. We were interested in the farming practices that persist without relying on heavy technology or pushing productivity too far.

The main goal of this report is to showcase and document the remarkable network of the GIAHS (Globally Important Agricultural Heritage Systems) sites and to answer two questions: "What does a productive agro–ecological landscape look like? How does one live there?"

The focus on landscape is intentional; it represents a non–specialized, broad perspective that emphasizes the connections between the various components of a territory rather than the specifics of each individual element. It's about seeing what's in between.

The report positions us as observers, interpreters, and synthesizers. To tell the story of these ingenious landscapes, one must step back, stay alert, observe and listen, write and draw. In the end, you realize that the technical aspects of these agro–systems are remarkable precisely because they complement other fields of expertise. The solutions for sustaining these systems stem as much from the philosophical relationships between humans and living beings and among the living beings themselves (like the way the argan tree is treated in Morocco's Anti–Atlas), as from the techniques used in harsh geo–climatic conditions (like the ones adopted by the farmers in Lanzarote who work with the soil, rofe, and wind), or from reimagined governance (restructuring the commons, creating landscape intervention brigades, and so on).

These landscapes serve as examples of a unified world, breaking away from the nature/culture divide and its extractivist and protectionist tendencies: a world in which humans are living beings among other living beings, sustaining life together. What sets them apart from more "conventional" models is the individual connection, the relationship each person has with the land. It's as if they have a stronger awareness of the link between the world you live in and the world you live from.

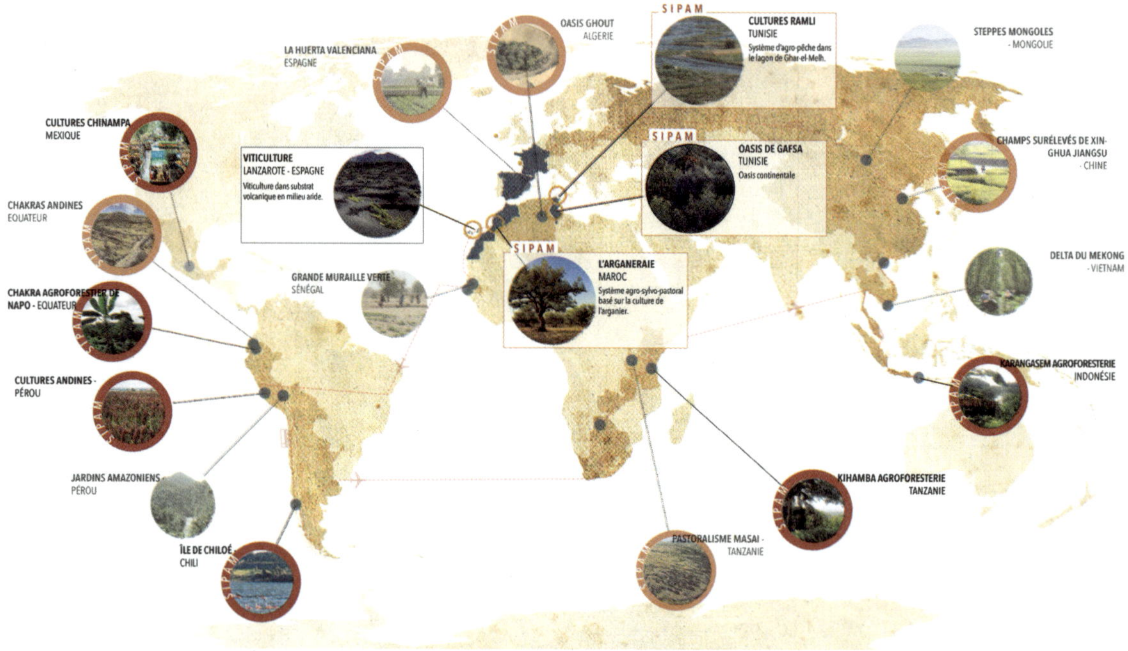

Globally Important Agricultural Heritage Systems (GIAHS)

Agriculture and its practices are now at the heart of concerns about landscape evolution: deforestation and monoculture pressures on major tropical forests, more frequent droughts and expanding deserts, rising sea levels, salinization and submersion of large fertile deltas... With more than 75% of the world's population expected to be urban by 2050, what will the rural areas that feed us look like? Will they be intensively and exclusively productive, or will they take on new aesthetic, cultural, ecological, and technical dimensions?

If an agricultural landscape is shaped by human transformation, is it doomed to be detrimental to the ecosystem and its inhabitants? Can't there be mutualistic relationships that benefit both humans and non-humans?

In this context, the GIAHS sites stand out for their exemplary ability to combine production, resilience, and experimentation, serving as laboratories for old and new agricultural practices. The GIAHS program, created in 2011 by the FAO (United Nations Food and Agriculture Organization), recognizes regions for the ingenuity of their agricultural practices "that create livelihoods in rural areas while combining biodiversity, resilient ecosystems and tradition and innovation in a unique way."

"Ingenious Landscapes" is an inquiry into virtuous agricultural negotiations between humans and the living world, seeking out a new vision for farming. Atelier Pareto, a young firm led by two landscapers, wished to engage with these sites to better understand and narrate them: how do they function? How does one live there? To go places where one can learn about the different approaches that blend agriculture, ecology, and society; to discover other kinds of relationships with the living world and other ways to manage shared resources, adapt to risks and to climate instability.

For this two-year-long project, a dozen sites have been identified in collaboration with the FAO's GIAHS Secretariat and local stakeholders who are committed to preserving, reinventing, and passing on these sites. In 2021, the first series of site visits focused on different agricultural practices in arid climates (150mm annual rainfall), including mineral mulching in Lanzarote, agro-sylvo-pastoral systems in Morocco's Anti-Atlas, the historic oasis of Gafsa, and lagoon farming in Ghar El Melh, Tunisia.

Immersing yourself

This is a field project. Each site is the subject of a several–week immersion, allowing us to explore it from all perspectives and engage with a wide range of stakeholders (farmers, residents, local government officials, GIAHS project leaders, FAO experts, scientists, or researchers). Their testimonies are essential to our understanding of the territory and how they perceive it.

Whenever possible, we volunteer with local residents. This is driven by our desire to be in close contact, to share daily routines, to contribute directly, and to experience the effort involved in these landscapes – in short: to participate! It's an opportunity to apply local skills and gain insights into the pleasures and challenges of this type of farming. We had remarkable encounters with people returning to the land, either as a reaction to a world losing its direction or simply due to a love of agriculture: seeking a return to a "simple" – or rather, meaningful – life.

Each session is organized in cooperation with local partners and institutions responsible for the GIAHS label. It's a two–way exchange: they offer their knowledge of the area, and we provide them with graphic material for their communication purposes. Sometimes our work helped support ongoing initiatives or revive stalled projects... There is no monetary exchange, unless there are mutual interests or a collaborative project arises from our meeting.

Among all the agricultural areas you will see, *none are as radical* **as Lanzarote.**

Harsh climate conditions

With only 140 mm of rain per year, Lanzarote has one of the lowest rainfall rates in Europe. Unlike other Canary Islands, Lanzarote's low–lying terrain does not capture the moisture from clouds carried by the trade winds. Worse still, almost 90% of the rainfall evaporates before it can seep into the ground and irrigate the soil. The island has no underground water reserves: springs are scarce, and wells provide only brackish water. On the other hand, coastal air keeps atmospheric humidity high and fairly steady, and there is significant dew.

Another characteristic of the island is its high volcanic activity. The last major eruptions occurred from 1730 to 1736 and then in 1826, forming the Timanfaya volcanic chain and covering a quarter of the island's surface with lava and ash.

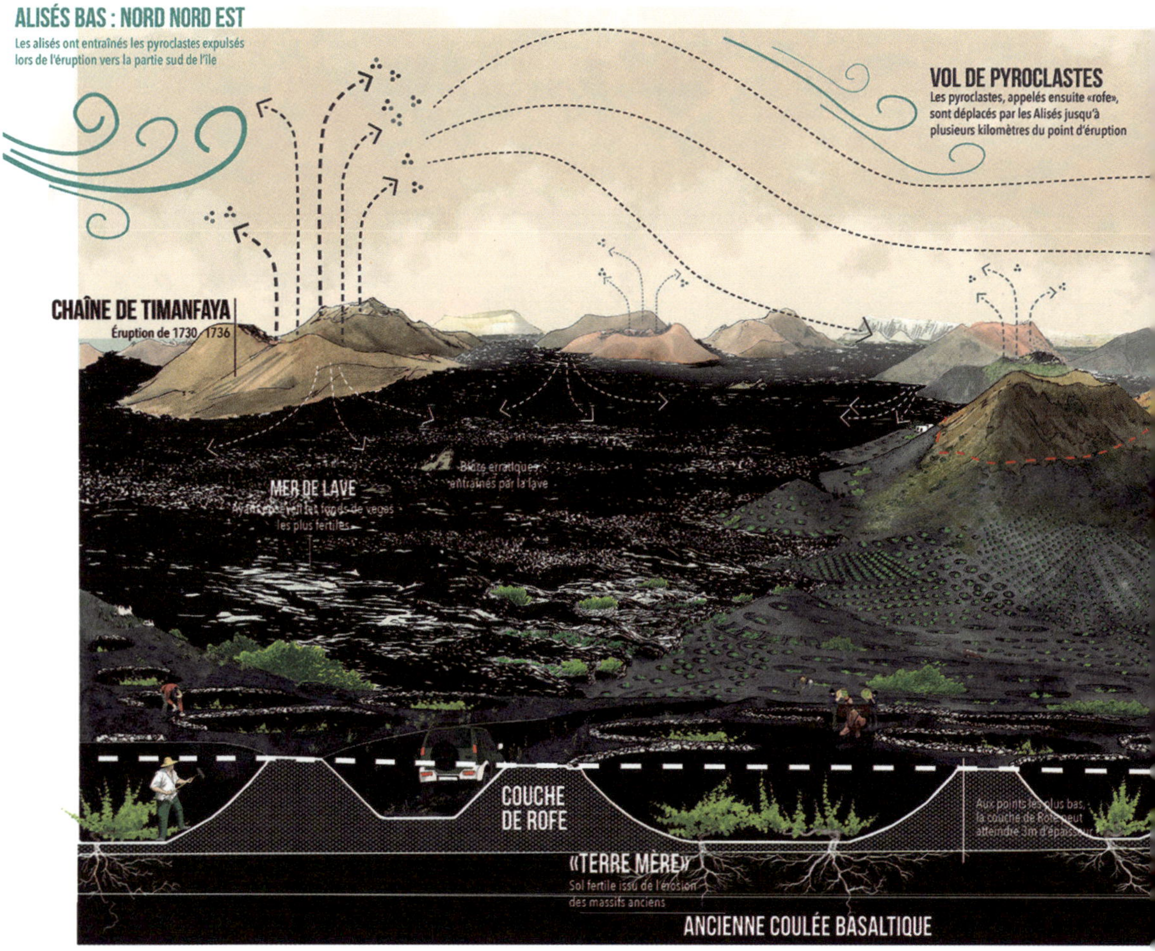

Negotiating with the volcano — recovering fertile soils

The vineyard of La Geria is one of Lanzarote's most striking and iconic agricultural landscapes. The region, literally buried under six years of eruptions from the Timanfaya volcanic chain (1730–1736), now hosts a unique agrarian practice that takes advantage of this volcanic event.

Farmers have managed to uncover the fertile soil from before the eruption beneath the layer of volcanic sands and lava dust (known as rofe). Manual excavations in the rofe create circular craters in which grapevines are planted, allowing their roots to reach the fertile soil buried by the eruption. The rofe layer, ranging from about thirty centimeters to several meters thick, acts as a mineral mulch that retains soil moisture for months, captures dew, maintains temperature, and protects plants from the wind.

It takes tough and persistent negotiation to continue farming these lands, replanting vines and fruit trees, and turning the rofe burial into an asset. The result is a landscape with a unique geometry, its gray and black hues dotted with the green of the vines in spring, creating a dialogue with the peaks of the volcanoes.

Attention to each plant

In La Geria, plants are not cultivated in large groups, like in a wheat or barley field; what stands out here is the meticulous attention given to each individual plant. Each vine or fruit tree is treated as a unique entity; the vines may be several decades old and are a living record of the farmers and their families before them.

While these practices are agricultural in nature due to their productive outcomes, their implementation resembles the practices of gardening. Each vine has its own *hoyo* and *soco* (crater and stone wall); every morning, farmers use their *sacho* (a variant of the hoe) to weed the rofe, making sure not to mix it with the soil. It's crucial that the rofe stays separate from the soil (barro): if mixed, the rofe becomes clogged and loses its effectiveness in retaining moisture. Everything is done by hand; mechanization is not an option! The only exception is a winding path between the vines that allows vehicle access and facilitates handling.

According to the winemakers, a plot is considered beautiful when it is *bien atendida*: much appreciated, the care and attention are reflected in the regularity of the socos and the clear black rofe.

Salvar la Geria: a project combining social integration and landscape restoration

Salvar la Geria (Saving la Geria) is a project that, over the past three years, has successfully restored around one hundred hectares of abandoned vineyards. An agronomist coordinator and three teams of workers involved in socio-professional integration work full-time in La Geria's vineyard. Their job involves clearing abandoned plots, restoring hoyos, rebuilding socos, and pruning fruit trees. The *cuadrillas* (teams) work on plots of farmers who request this, and who commit to maintain these plots for at least five years or transfer the vines to another vintner through the Banco de Tierras (Land Bank) system.

The initiative primarily targets traditional hoyos and the most visible plots, located along roadsides or on slopes, as these have the greatest impact on the landscpe. It also serves as a social tool, prioritizing support for elderly farmers, women, and young vintners, and providing motivation for the extensive work involved in managing La Geria's vineyard.

By combining heritage and social goals, the project's funding is not tied to vineyard profitability or the wine market. Salvar la Geria highlights the significance of this agricultural landscape as a common good beyond productivity and economic gain: it seeks new ways to sustain this landscape by fostering partnerships between public entities and private agricultural actors.

Landscapes that provide sustenance and have been *heavily altered by humans*, **yet do not deplete the natural environment.**

Alliances with the dynamics of life

The ingenuity of these agro–systems comes from the alliances they have built with natural dynamics, allowing them to adapt to severe natural conditions like lack of soil, water scarcity, extreme temperatures, and more. The productive and nourishing landscapes that result have been heavily altered by humans, yet without depleting the natural environment; on the contrary, these ecosystems grow richer and more complex.

Sometimes the transformations are significant and clearly noticeable, like the circular vineyards of La Geria in the black fields of Lanzarote, while at other times, they are more subtle, like in the sparse argan forests.

Each territory shows a different type of this mutualism, each developing its own practices, and often seeking for ways to pass them on, evolve, and update.

The areas explored so far reveal two ways to balance production and ecosystems:

— Highly specialized skills (for reconstructing substrates like in Lanzarote or Ghar El Melh, or maximizing the irrigation from a natural source like in the oases),

— Collective negotiation mechanisms (such as the agdal, a practice that supports mutualism between agro–pastoralism and the argan forest).

Creating microclimates

In La Geria, everything revolves around creating a microclimate that supports plant growth. Naturally, few plants thrive on thick layers of rofe, as the lack of soil and scarce rainfall make it a harsh environment for life to develop – at the very least, they slow the colonization process.

Human alterations to this volcanic ecosystem benefit both the people who farm it (agro–ecosystem) and a wider range of animals and plants that find shelter and resources from the planted vegetation. Human intervention speeds up the return of life to these mineral areas, allowing a larger community to flourish.

Expanding this agro–system to the *campos enarenados* has helped cover other fertile valleys, protecting their soil from erosion, leaching, and the loss of the little organic matter present.

The convergence of a volcanic event and the agricultural aspirations of Lanzarote's inhabitants has created an agro–ecosystem that not only stabilizes the human population in this resource–poor territory but also supports a unique and specific biodiversity native to the island.

The vineyard of La Geria also fosters a distinct social microclimate: relationships among winemakers, camel drivers, oenologists, historic bodegas and new micro–wineries, moments of relaxation in the *cuartos de apero*, the traditional harvest festival, workers involved in Salvar la Geria, and athletes participating in the annual half–marathon... There is a whole community developing around the vineyard and its incredible landscapes.

The voices of the landscape: transmission and evolution

On the heroic vineyard and the difficulty of passing it on.

Giving a voice to the people met across La Geria: allowing their joys, doubts, and aspirations to be heard. There is a mix of different profiles, and multiple activities are the norm: retirees who keep up family plots or reinvest in La Geria with savings from other jobs (tourism, construction, transport...) – often more for the love of the vineyard than for profit! There are also younger vintners, men and women, taking over plots to develop new and eco-friendly wineries. However, the vineyard's size is gradually shrinking, with small plots disappearing and estates growing larger.

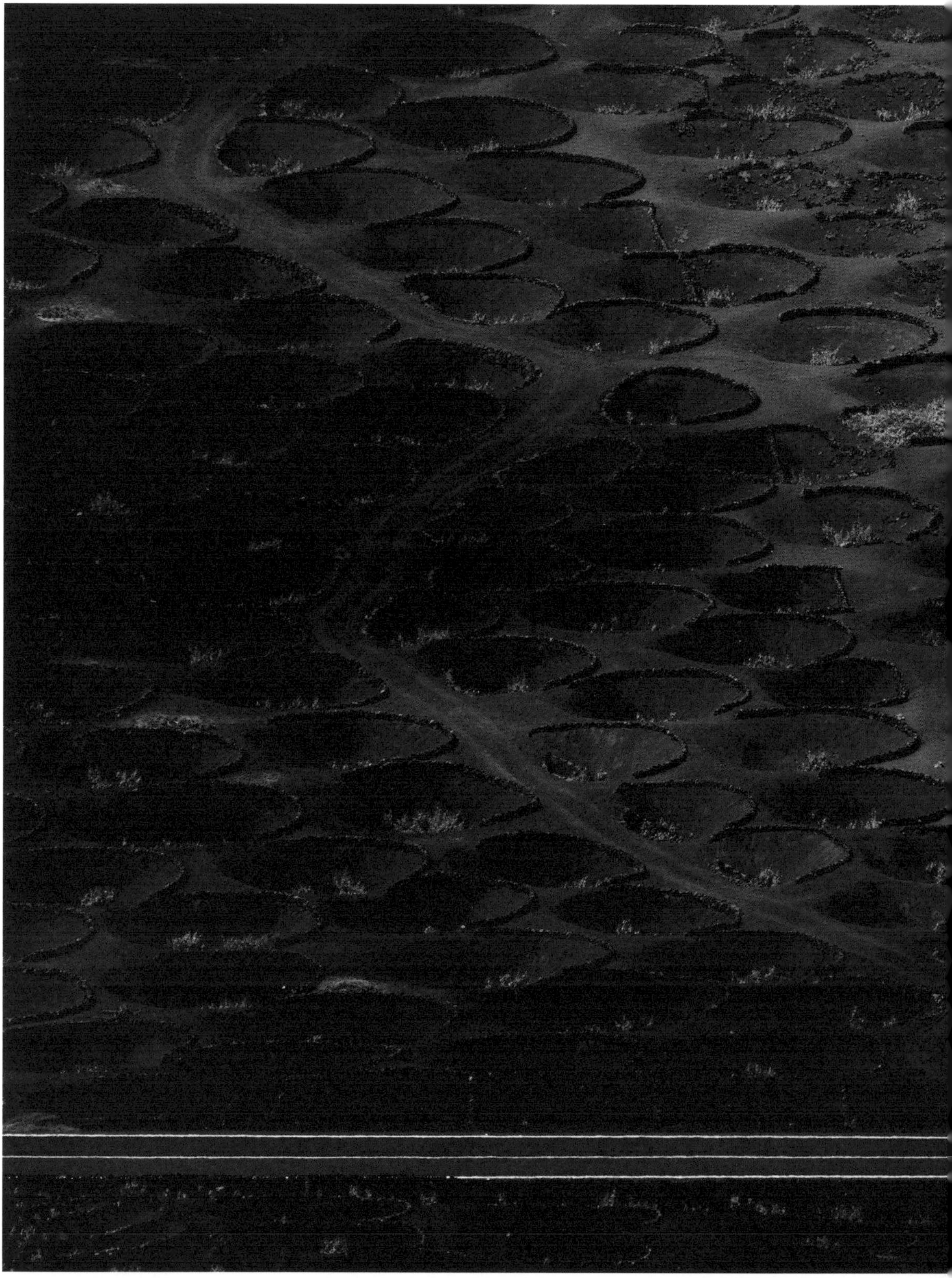

3.Q
Cerros Isla

– Santiago de Chile

Connecting abandoned areas as a metropolitan political project

A group of academics and activists has discovered a gem hidden in plain sight: a series of 26 hills (cerros) emerging from the continuous urban fabric of Santiago, a city of five million inhabitants. Hosting diverse species and activities, these spaces without a plan behind them have caught the eye of developers and sparked the imagination of naturalists who saw them as a unique opportunity to rethink our relationship with nature in the city. Years of advocacy have brought this issue into Santiago's urban planning debate.

As a network of *Third Landscapes*, the Cerros Isla are now recognized as a collective project. The need for recreational spaces during the Covid pandemic has accelerated this process, with several projects emerging from nearby neighborhoods, potentially tripling the amount of the city's accessible natural areas.

Location Santiago de Chile, Chile
Geographical coordinates 29°56'22.06"S, 71°13'29.86"O
Size Several locations over 641,4 km^2
Status Open natural public space
Research Francisco Vásquez, Fernanda Ruiz
Designer Ana Shiaku
Funding Fondart, Convocatoria 2019

Collaborators Fundación Cerros Isla; Museo Benjamín Vicuña Mackenna; Omaira Catherine Arboleda Velásquez (academic advisor)
Development Since 2010

Photo credits Marcos Zegers, Guy Wenborne

The Cerros Isla proje
Santiago's 26 insula
spaces for public use.
Mediterranean climat
and desertification i
landscape is not gree
This calls for a *shift i*
many years to put the
of the hills into natur
the political agenda.

ct aims to *recover*
hills as *natural*
n Santiago, with its
e, scarce water,
sues, the natural
n but yellow.
n perception. It took
transformation
l parks on

RENCA LA LLEVA

3.Q

Cerros Isla, *turning abandoned spaces into natural urban parks*

The Cerros Isla Foundation is a nonprofit organization focused on promoting and protecting Santiago's hills as urban natural parks. In the face of the city's particularly acute environmental, social, and economic challenges of the past three years, the Foundation engages with public and private stakeholders and the community to develop strategies for enhancing these natural entities.

In this context, Cerros Isla works locally with associations and municipal services to foster the reclamation of previously overlooked natural spaces through respectful use. Several projects are underway, each with its own approach and outcomes, all aiming to strengthen and enforce regulatory protection.

Cerros Isla — Catalina Picon, Fernanda Ruiz

3.1
Considering the landscape project as a negotiation platform

The Cerros Isla project began when I was living next to one of Santiago's hills. I used to go up there with my dog. One day, I noticed that they were starting to build on these natural areas. I decided to look into it and met other researchers and architects studying the hills' status. This was back in 2010.

We then conducted a survey of these freestanding insular hills, and, with some university funding, carried out research that led to the first publication on the subject in 2012. We identified the hills' potential, both ecologically and socially. Nobody knew about them. They were completely off the radar for the municipalities. Due to weaknesses in urban regulations, these hills, some of the few remaining open spaces in Santiago, were starting to get developed.

In 2013, we decided to create a foundation. The Cerros Isla Foundation became a platform that brought together academics, local and regional governments, the state, businesses, and people with money. The Foundation managed to influence the public agenda, emphasizing the urgency and importance of turning attention to these hills. This was the Foundation's key initial goal: we relied on public recognition as a prerequisite for integrating the hills into the metropolitan network of public spaces.

3.2
Building community by gardening together

This initiative raised a lot of questions at different levels of responsibility, making it hard to secure funding. People would ask us: why do I have to finance a public park project that should be managed by the state? The importance of natural spaces in the city was a concept that had very little resonance. Citizens had no idea about the value of such spaces for their physical and mental health.

After completing our research, we put together a book to share all the information we had collected. We wanted to highlight the value of the hills from social, economic, and ecological perspectives – a subject that didn't exist in the first place. Today, it's easier to explain our intention: we succeeded in showing people the great importance of these hills.

We have never seen ourselves as activists. We approached the issue from a theoretical, academic, and practical standpoint. We have engaged with multiple communities and recently discovered still other small communities and organizations located close to the hills and also working to restore them. We are trying to bring all these people together to cooperate as a network named Red, Amigos de los Cerros (Network, Friends of the Cerros).

3.3
Turning the project into a score that unfolds over time

In 2010, we started an informal group, and by 2013, the Foundation was created. Since then, we have carried out several research projects and published a number of books. We established the core issue and built a community.

In 2021, we launched a wonderful project called "The Day of the Hills." The Foundation coordinated with different communities and had the support of the municipalities to invite citizens to render the hills more visible and valuable. The idea is for this Day to become an annual event, spreading from Santiago throughout Chile. We are also working on a major project to conduct a nationwide survey of all the hills in the country. We wrote a public letter and shared it on social media, inviting people to sign it, learn about the project, and offer their support. There's still a long road ahead, and the hills serve as the spearhead of a broader message advocating for the value of natural areas in the city.

3.4
Expressing care for the living world through aesthetic resolution

In central Chile, the natural landscape is yellow. Despite our collective image of a green park, the ecological capacity, unfortunately, doesn't align. Amidst climate change, there is no longer enough water to irrigate a lawn. With this model of an urban natural park, we seek to alter perceptions. Instead of being artificially green with planned and maintained vegetation, the hills are meant to retain their natural state.

There is also the matter of accessibility versus preservation. During the pandemic, people were not allowed in public spaces like squares. Tired of being cooped up, they started venturing into the hills. This prompted us to think of how access to the hills could be made easier without causing them damage. Trails are at the heart of this reflection: how do we design them in a way that minimizes impact on the land, simplifies governance, and cuts down on maintenance? The aim is to improve accessibility, transforming these natural spaces into social hubs and meeting spots. Imagine a (limited) green space where uses vary depending on the character of the slope: gentler slopes would be open to a wider audience, while steeper parts would be for the more agile. By tailoring programs to the topography, we can control and guide uses to protect the hills.

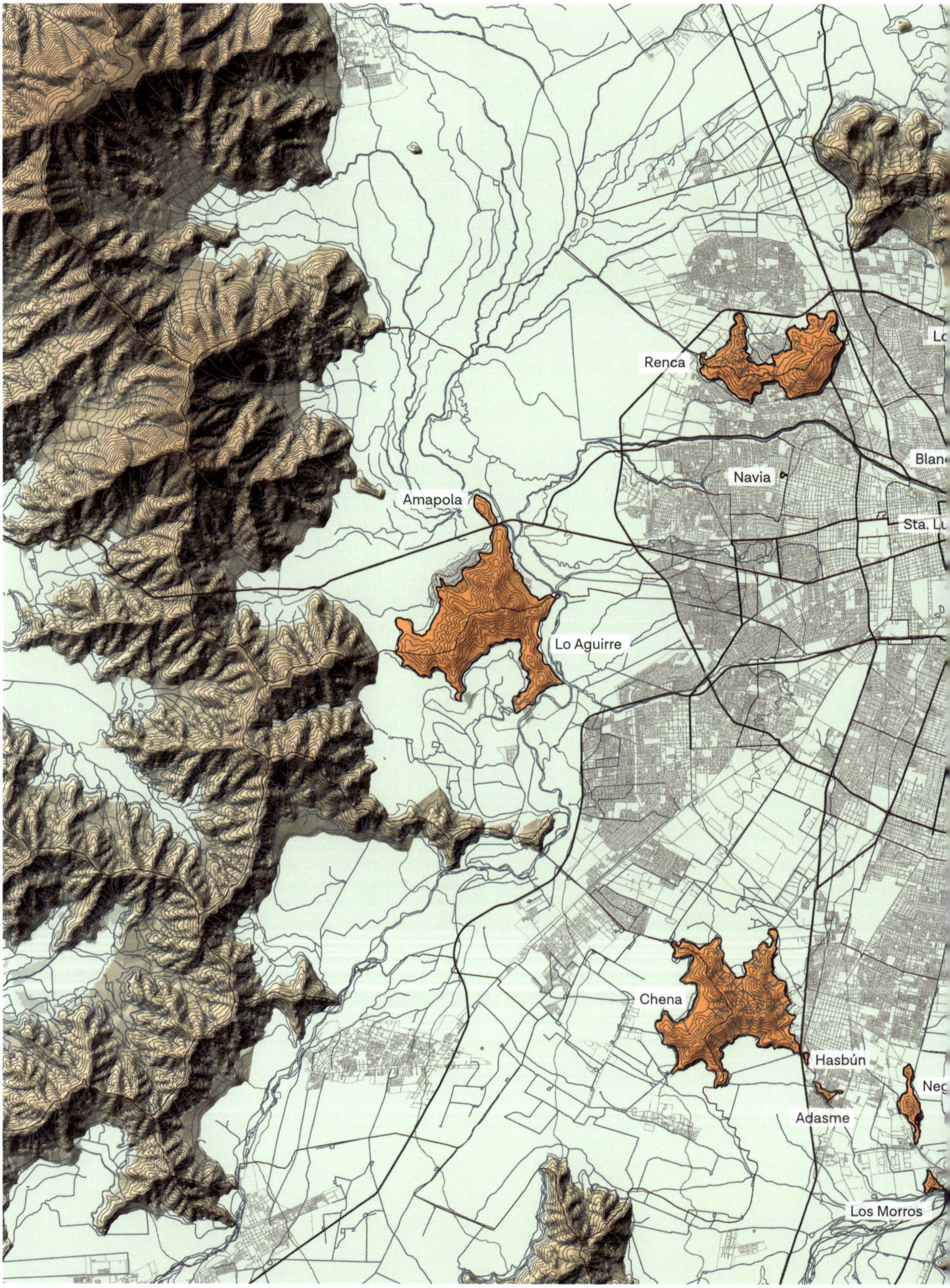
Renca
Navia
Amapola
Sta. Lu
Lo Aguirre
Chena
Hasbún
Adasme
Los Morros

Loma Larga
El Manzano
Dieciocho
Del Medio
endros
Alvarado
Los Piques
Calán
Apoquindo
San Luis
San Cristóbal
Jardín Alto
Chequén
La Ballena
Las Cabras

Inventing new management models

We have identified 26 sites in Santiago and 62 in the region. Although these lands are designated for public use by law, about 80% of them are already privately owned. We have successfully encouraged local governments to take responsibility for the hills already classified as public spaces. Municipalities started investing in these areas, figuring out how to reclaim them as parks. But there's still the issue of privatized land. We have developed a public–private management model for the consulting and transformation of these hills into natural urban parks.

Today, the Foundation is a point of contact for the Cerros. We try to reach out directly to landowners and involve them in this public–private management model. The Foundation provides advice to those who don't know what to do with their land, guiding them through the transformation process. We are working with them on a comprehensive master plan, so they have a complete vision of the hill, even if they are only intervening on part of it.

To set up this comprehensive plan, we conduct a detailed study of the hill, covering environmental, geological, and soil aspects. This helps us create a management and investment model. What's fascinating about these studies is that they transform the hill from a dump site into a valuable source of information. Our goal is to restore the ecological state of these hills, but, in order to do this, we need to know what their initial condition was. Moreover, we carry out legal studies, and also conduct a historical analysis, talking to nearby communities and residents. Each hill has a unique identity: one is linked to Catholicism, another to indigenous Mapuche peoples, or to an adjacent cemetery.

These studies are part of a participatory program. Once the survey is completed, we develop a master plan for the hill. We then engage directly with the local people, discussing the plan and gathering their input. We are well-received. The people who visit the cerros are often the most vulnerable part of the population and can't imagine that these hills might be private property. It's something completely beyond their reality.

Compensation

In Chile, there is a law stipulating that if you undertake a project that generates air pollution, you must compensate for it; similarly, if you remove native vegetation, compensation is required. However, this compensation is often highly inadequate, and the government is unable to properly monitor or enforce it.

We are therefore developing a plan that would allow us to request regional funding and create a "compensation platform" for consolidating Cerros Isla as a system of natural urban parks. This digital platform would facilitate the process, connecting those who have to provide compensation with hill owners and public institutions. Often, there is a lack of suitable land for compensation, so our project aims to direct funds towards comprehensive rewilding of the hills. Many compensation efforts are not supported by a long–term perspective, and tree plantations often fail due to poor maintenance. A company may cut down a native forest and plant a monoculture to compensate for it, but their plantation will die after a few years because no one tends to it. Hence, we are working to steer these efforts into a more effective, long–term project.

Cerros Isla began as
backed by any *physic*
something that wasn
then manifested itsel
The landscape is a c
reflecting conflicts, d
tensions. It's also an
doesn't happen on its
make yourself availab

a project not
al reality. **We saw**
t there, and which
in the society.
ollective product,
verse interests, and
intentional act. **It**
own; you have to
e **to appreciate it.**

“Instruct the spirit of *non–doing* **as one instructs the spirit of doing.** *Elevate indecision to a political level.*”

— **Gilles Clément** *Manifeste du Tiers paysage (Manifesto of the Third Landscape)*, ©Sens & Tonka & Cie, 2004

Education

In this Foundation, we also have an educational component. Some people use the hills without care, which raises an educational issue. As more people want to visit these hills, we tell them: "Great, use them, but, as responsible users, take your trash with you, stick to one path, and be mindful of preserving this natural space in good condition." This is an issue we bring to public attention, an issue we are frequently asked about, given our position between private landowners and public users.

We give university courses and lectures, and are working on developing educational visits to turn the hills into outdoor classrooms where schools can offer environmental education. We have also mapped out trails that schools can use for teaching science or subjects related to Chilean history right there in the hills.

In central Chile, the *yellow.* **Despite our co** **of a** *green park*, **the e** **unfortunately, doesn'** **Amidst climate chan** **longer enough water** **With this model of an** **park, represented by** **whole, we seek to** *al*

atural landscape is
llective image
cological capacity,
align.
ge, there is no
to irrigate a lawn.
urban natural
the Cerros Isla as a
er perceptions.

3.R Underwater Landscape Plan

– The Calanques National Park

Revealing a landscape through dialog

The Calanques National Park has adopted an action plan that views the terrestrial and marine landscapes as interconnected and takes into consideration their proximity to the metropolis of Marseille. The plan involves the reduction of infrastructure in the park's core area while managing access, boundaries, and transitions – and prioritizing, in all actions, the preservation of natural dynamics.

This unique multidisciplinary study expands the concept of landscape to new, unexplored territories and introduces a new dimension to the landscaper's role, setting relationships with the living world as a priority. It underscores the essential function of the landscaper as a mediator among various stakeholders. The issues raised by this approach, as well as the mutual contributions of complementary visions, practices, and representation models, provide opportunities to reduce human impact and allow environments to evolve more freely.

Mission Underwater Landscape Plan for the Calanques National Park
Location Department of Bouches-du-Rhône, France
Geographical coordinates 43°12'34"N, 5°26'57"E
Size 43,500 ha of Marine Park core area, 97,700 ha of adjacent maritime area along the 80 km of coastline

← ©Parc national des Calanques

Project duration 2017–2019, followed by the validation by the partners in 2021

— Team
Client Parc national des Calanques
Project managers Atelier Coloco landscapers (group representative) with Pierre David, Gilles Clément, and Andromède Océanologie
Photo credits Coloco (unless otherwise specified)

When the *horizon disa*
drifting without a visu
senses become engage
It’s no longer about a
between your eyes an
on dry land; *here, you*

→ ©Fabien David, Coloco

ppears **and you're**
al anchor, *all of your*
through immersion.
direct relationship
d a vast expansion, like
navigate as you feel...

3.R

Underwater Landscape Plan of *the Calanques*

The challenge of studying such a vast marine territory suggested a new approach to building a shared culture among different maritime stakeholders. By treating the underwater landscape as both a subject of study and a tool, we could bring together the experiences of scientists, fishermen, divers, boaters, ecologists, and managers. Will they be able to move beyond their individual perspectives, recognizing the common value of these landscapes?

The unifying power of landscape as a notion is used here to foster a culture and practices harmonized with the sea. The stakes are huge, both now and in the long run.

Miguel Georgieff, Coloco

← © Parc national des Calanques

3.1
Considering the landscape project as a negotiation platform

The experimental nature of the Underwater Landscape Plan became clear from the outset. Unlike terrestrial landscapes, the concept of an "underwater landscape" is not intuitive. First, it had to be explained and coordinated in order to develop a vision of what an "underwater landscape plan" could even be. This shared initial work helped participants reveal their perspectives. Diverse experiences – those of a biologist, an oceanographer, a fisherman, a diver, a club manager, and a park ranger – came together, each bringing a different approach. The intersection of these distinct viewpoints has set the stage for collaborative work.

Each participant walked in with a bit of a defensive attitude towards their own predefined views. The underwater landscape revealed itself as the studies progressed. Everyone agreed that the purpose of this landscape plan had to be the preservation of the sea, otherwise all parties would lose. The underwater landscape has thus become a platform for negotiating and even reconciling their sometimes conflicting interests.

This initial phase highlighted that, as a term, "underwater landscape" did not require a single definition but offered an opportunity to merge these two notions in a novel way, opening new areas of thought. Using it allows both underwater and landscape tools to be applied together, broadening the definition of landscape. It's a step toward incorporating the landscapers' contributions into areas where they haven't been involved before.

3.2
Building community by gardening together

In this garden–territory, the community involved are those who engage with the sea as a space for experience rather than leisure. Over two years, through a series of workshops, a cohesive group of about a hundred participants was formed.

We stepped in where people, although everyone knew one another, only spoke to each other when issues arose. The landscape approach allowed us to bring them together outside of their usual interactions. The workshops helped to ease the tension that had already arisen or was anticipated, for example, during the mooring plan negotiations that took place at the same time.

By employing unconventional tools such as drawings or sound recordings to capture the noises of propellers and fish, the workshops allowed everyone to share their experiences and feelings, making more tangible the underwater landscapes that we couldn't physically explore.

We sought original representation methods based on immersion, combining them with more traditional cartography and block diagrams. These tools were used in a new way for an extraordinary case: the underwater landscapes ranging from 0 to 2,000 meters deep.

↓ ©Parc national des Calanques

3.3
Turning the project into a score that unfolds over time

Ideally, all our projects unfold over the long term. The client asks questions, and the landscaper proposes increasingly coordinated directions for intervention, or sometimes for non-intervention. With this Underwater Landscape Plan, the Calanques Park has shown a clear intent to improve the ecosystem's quality.

When creating an underwater landscape plan, the goal is not to outline specific actions or physical projects, but to make the landscape tangible, facilitating dialogue with the stakeholder community.

As landscapers, we contribute to composing the score but must then leave the interpretation to the client. The responsibility rests with the client, who will implement the landscape plan over approximately ten years, based on current needs and community priorities.

The landscape plan is not a binding document but a guide toward best practices. For the plan to succeed, the Park's team must be as active in its implementation as it was in its creation.

The underwater landscape plan also highlights the long-term actions undertaken in the Calanques Park, such as the cessation of harvesting in certain areas, which has led to a tenfold increase in biomass within just a decade.

3.4
Expressing care for the living world through aesthetic resolution

In French, we don't have an exact equivalent of the English term "seascape," and "underwater landscape" somewhat lacks clarity. Thus, many of the scientists involved in the project pointed out that "a landscape is made up of several ecosystems" and that "an ecosystem contains multiple landscapes." The graphic tools in this Underwater Landscape Plan are designed to show what an underwater landscape is and to reveal what is usually invisible. Beyond traditional maps, we explored drawing, particularly digital painting. The beautiful images created by interpreting or extrapolating from photo sequences aren't "real," but they give an idea of what a person might encounter underwater in terms of landscape. It's an aesthetic exercise that fuels the imagination.

Drawing allowed us to shift our perspective. We combined multiple views from divers or robots to depict these landscapes, moving away from the usual underwater photo cliché that focuses on a fish or algae in close-up. With drawings, we could visualize specific rocks, mosaics, and the opacity of the water.

The feelings created by this imaginative work – that's the landscape! We no longer perceive the landscape in a segmented manner based on the species that inhabit it; instead, we approach it through ecosystems.

These representations and the action proposals from the Underwater Landscape Plan were presented to the public alongside a photo exhibition on canyons and the work of artist Nicolas Floc'h. This entire process has created a space for discussing the park and the measures needed to reduce human impact.

↑ ©Olivier Borde, Malvina, underwater painting

↑ ©Margaux Bidat

The main objective he *very existence* **of these** *means of experience.* **I** **landscapes through in** *the traditional bounda* *and marine environm* *feel the continuity of th* **across the entire surf**

re is to *reveal the* **landscapes** *by* **xploring underwater mersion** *eliminates ries between terrestrial nts,* **letting us** *e landscape* **and Life ce of the Earth.**

← Transect between terrestrial and underwater landscapes in the Calanques National Park. The elevation difference between the terrestrial peaks and the canyons exceeds two thousand meters. ©Fabien David, Coloco

The Third Landscape underwater

The Calanques National Park has a unique geological and landscape configuration. It is the only terrestrial and marine national park adjacent to a metropolitan urban area. Moreover, due to its varied environments, this territory contains a wide range of landscapes: coastal limestone reliefs with the 676-meter-high Mount Carpiagne, cliff areas where the coastline juts out over the sea, and beaches nestled in coves carved by streams. At sea, the mostly sandy seabeds on the continental shelf are dotted with shallow areas emerging as single islands or archipelagos. Offshore, the depth plunges over 3,000 meters into canyons carved by rivers millions of years ago, when sea levels were more than 100 meters lower.

Due to its diversity, the underwater coastal geomorphology of the Calanques includes different landscape types with diverse morphological features, water dynamics, and species suited to each habitat. Geographically, the park is located in the northernmost part of the western Mediterranean. Here, cold-temperate biodiversity intersects with southern tropical biodiversity, enhancing the variety of structuring species and underwater landscapes. On-site, underwater, nothing compares to these extremely varied, ever-changing seabeds, constantly reshaped by currents and winds, forming one of the most beautiful landscape mosaics in the Mediterranean.

"The Calanques National Park is home to underwater landscapes that are unique in many respects: here, the blue of the water is more intense and often clearer than elsewhere; the verticality of the gorgonian sea walls creates a very distinctive atmosphere, and the richness of the fauna that inhabits this relatively small area is remarkable."

Frederic di Meglio,
photographer and diver

Steering the study by adapting the methodology to how the meetings evolve

This study offers a new approach to creating a shared culture among various stakeholders. To achieve it, we approached the landscape both as a theme for exploration and as a tool. The unifying power of the landscape concept was invoked here to foster a more harmonized culture of the sea.

Between 2019 and 2021, we organized dives at iconic sites, along with a dozen thematic workshops, some conducted at sea. Coordination meetings aimed to incorporate the perspectives of all participants, from biologists to fishermen. Through dialogue between public and private practices, we sought complementary insights from these marine experts. The process brought together about a hundred individuals who shared their experiences and knowledge of the sea. The partnership between landscapers and oceanographers helped integrate the sometimes conflicting view-points without losing sight of the common goal – that of keeping the underwater landscapes alive.

Beyond the diversity of skills and perspectives, the shared experience of diving had unexpected effects. By blending distinct land-based experiences into an unusual community with blurred contours, this underwater experience has gradually built a shared foundation among participants. Their precise and detailed descriptions of the landscape, as perceived during the dive, revealed an intimate dimension that enhanced the evocative power of the captured images.

Through this shared marine experience, we collectively created a sense of territory.

↗ ©Fabien David, Coloco
→ A three-dimensional view of the marine and terrestrial base of the Calanques National Park territory. This visualization allows for an instant grasp of the topography and the continuity of the terrain.

Cap de l'Aigle
L'Esquine
Banc
des
155
87
93
112
100
84
127
109
118
122
70

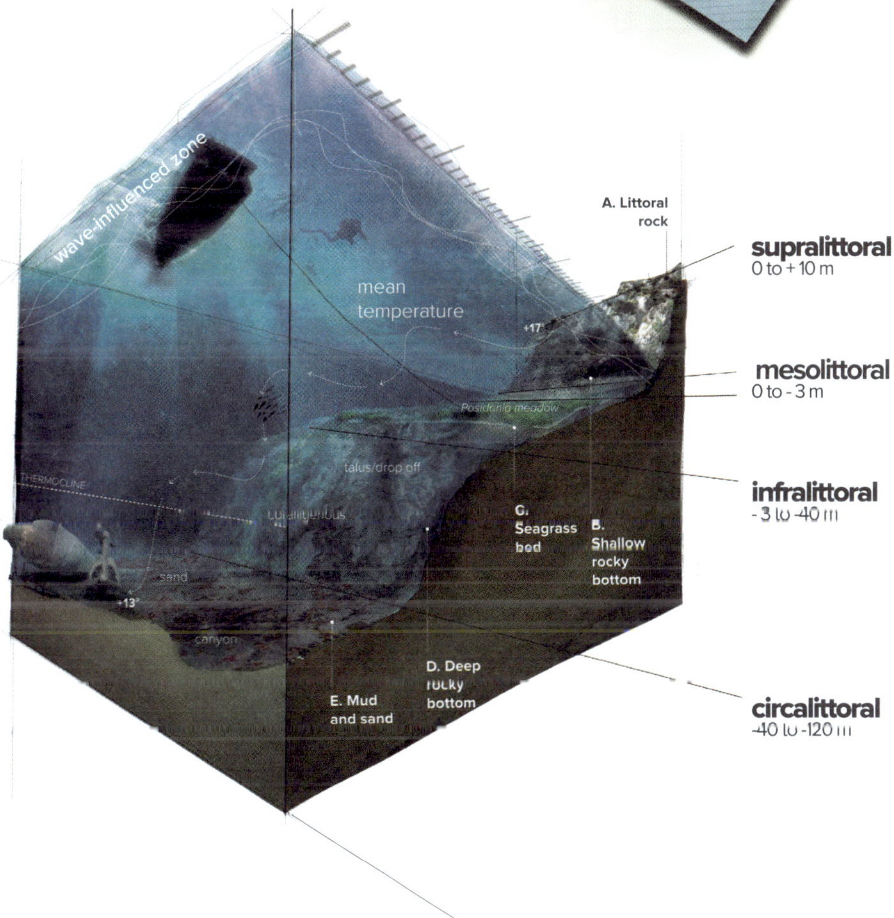
wave-influenced zone
mean
temperature
+17°
Posidonia meadow
talus/drop off
THERMOCLINE
sand
+13°
canyon
A. Littoral
rock
supralittoral
0 to + 10 m
mesolittoral
0 to - 3 m
infralittoral
- 3 to -40 m
C.
Seagrass
bed
B.
Shallow
rocky
bottom
D. Deep
rocky
bottom
E. Mud
and sand
circalittoral
-40 to -120 m
bathyal
below -120 m

Recognizing the existence of unknown landscapes

For the first time, underwater landscapes were to be studied in their territorial dimension by combining spatial, biological, and use aspects. We proposed that participants discover these landscapes through diving. Could the concept of landscape, derived from an almost entirely visual terrestrial perspective, be applied to this unique underwater environment?

During the workshops, emphasis was placed on what makes the experience of underwater landscapes different from terrestrial ones. Central to a terrestrial landscape experience, the sense of distance to the horizon and unfolding panoramic views are either missing or entirely different here. The body is horizontal and drifting constantly; the eye struggles to find a point of reference as there is no anchoring structure. The movements of a floating body are slowed by the density of water. Breathing becomes a conscious, noisy effort. Immersed in an element that isn't our natural environment, we hover in a kind of amniotic space that we have forgotten entirely. Constrained by this condition, which requires constant and multifaceted adaptation, we are engulfed in a kind of ecstatic torpor leading to a powerful contemplative experience.

Through numerous workshop discussions, landscapes became an experience that we learned to describe. Sound travels four times faster in water than in air. When diving, the soundscape is very present, especially since vision is no longer the dominant sense. This auditory dimension combines with proprioceptive signals from a body slowed by the density of water. Movement requires conscious effort. On land, multisensory perception, including touch and taste, is often secondary to our visual and aesthetic culture of experiencing a space. Here, sensory functioning and perceptual synthesis are entirely disrupted.

The special equipment needed for diving is a constraint. Beyond forty meters, deep underwater landscapes are inaccessible. On land, we can't go everywhere, but over time, one starts to develop a sense of territory through using and visiting places, relying on maps, on the things others have seen and shared, and on certain narratives. There was no map of the Calanques' underwater landscapes, so we made one. Creating narratives was key to building a shared view and reaching a common understanding of these landscapes.

The configuration of the seabed was known to a few experts because of studies and reports on monitoring particular species in a particular site. Beyond these isolated approaches, pooling information based on our diving experiences was a key step in bringing our perspectives together. As we were producing the graphic representations of these experiences, there was a pivotal moment when we realized that we were finally on the same page, working together to protect a piece of the Planetary Garden.

→ An attempt to transcribe the sensations of underwater landscapes. Perception modes are completely different underwater, changing the ways we analyze, appreciate, and evaluate landscapes. Often, words are not enough.

Debating the landscape: between perceptions and scientific data

Starting with the personal experiences and knowledge of each participant, we developed our study using the landscape plan method: drafting a landscape assessment at the territorial scale, defining key future directions, setting landscape quality objectives, and creating an action plan for the coming years.

The assessment compiled a large amount of data that had never been gathered before. A single map was able to reveal the complexity of the territory. The diving experiences, which brought back many memories, transformed a map into something to be viewed – a map of landscapes, not just a map packed with information. The challenge here was not to showcase the beauty or the typicality of these landscapes, as we do when working on land, but to show that, through experience and perception, and thanks to the insights gained from exploration, these environments can become landscapes in their own right.

↗ Map of the Submarine Landscape Units of the Calanques National Park — © Fabien David, Coloco
→ Annotated diagram of the submarine continental shelf. The illustration reveals the invisible and stimulates discussion.
→ Working map, used in workshops and annotated by various participants. It combines scientific information, place names, and aspects of local culture.

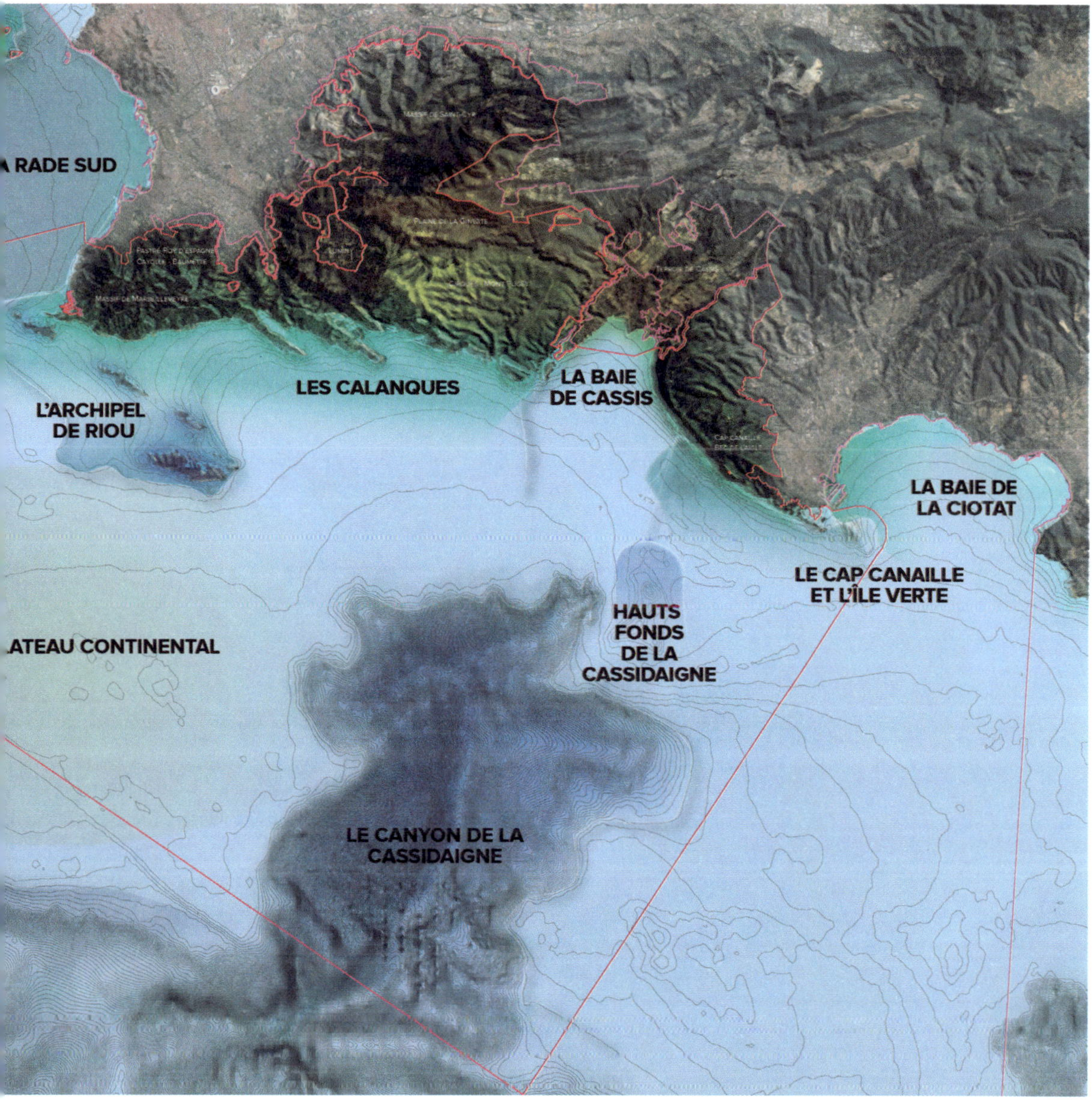
RADE SUD
L'ARCHIPEL DE RIOU
LES CALANQUES
LA BAIE DE CASSIS
LA BAIE DE LA CIOTAT
LE CAP CANAILLE ET L'ÎLE VERTE
HAUTS FONDS DE LA CASSIDAIGNE
PLATEAU CONTINENTAL
LE CANYON DE LA CASSIDAIGNE

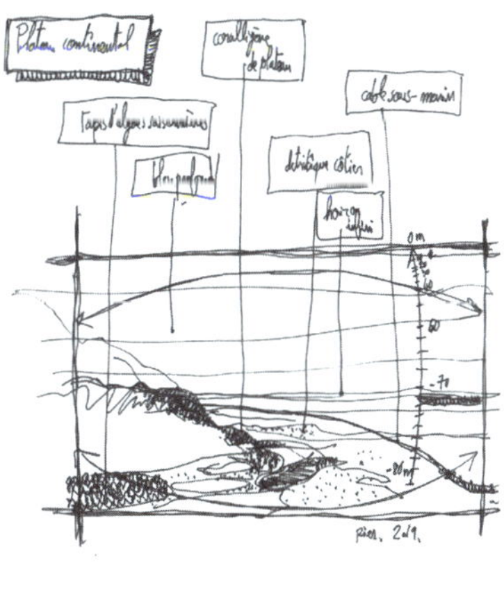

Sketching evolutionary paths for these landscapes while reducing human impact

The Underwater Landscape Plan highlighted an essential aspect of the landscaper's work: the capacity to bring together different stakeholders of a territory around the same table, map, or boat. The study and debate on the underwater landscapes of the Calanques have shown the global need for collective thinking about the future of territories.

"Thanks to the sea, we are connected to everything else. The planet is in the water, life is in the water. It's obvious everywhere, but we feel it even more here, better than in any other environment. It becomes clear that, although everything is connected, humans, who are responsible for destruction and degradation, are mostly on land. It's their actions that have an influence, and that's where change needs to happen. My dream is to have transparent water, free of plastic."

Gilles Clément
Extract from The Calanques Landscape Plan

In light of the current ecological crisis, protecting marine environments is becoming a major priority. Our landscape project aimed to make the case that maintaining this environment's ecological health is a goal in which humans have a role. How do we communicate, to both the public and the policymakers, the questioning, the research, and the solutions needed to safeguard our source of oxygen, food, and our incredible dreams?

Metropolitan impact is the primary factor disrupting the Calanques National Park. Directly or indirectly, it weakens environments and degrades underwater landscapes. Across different landscape areas, the threats to marine biodiversity are varied, but some causes of ecosystem damage are consistent along the entire coastline, mainly due to human activity and, more broadly, climate disruption.

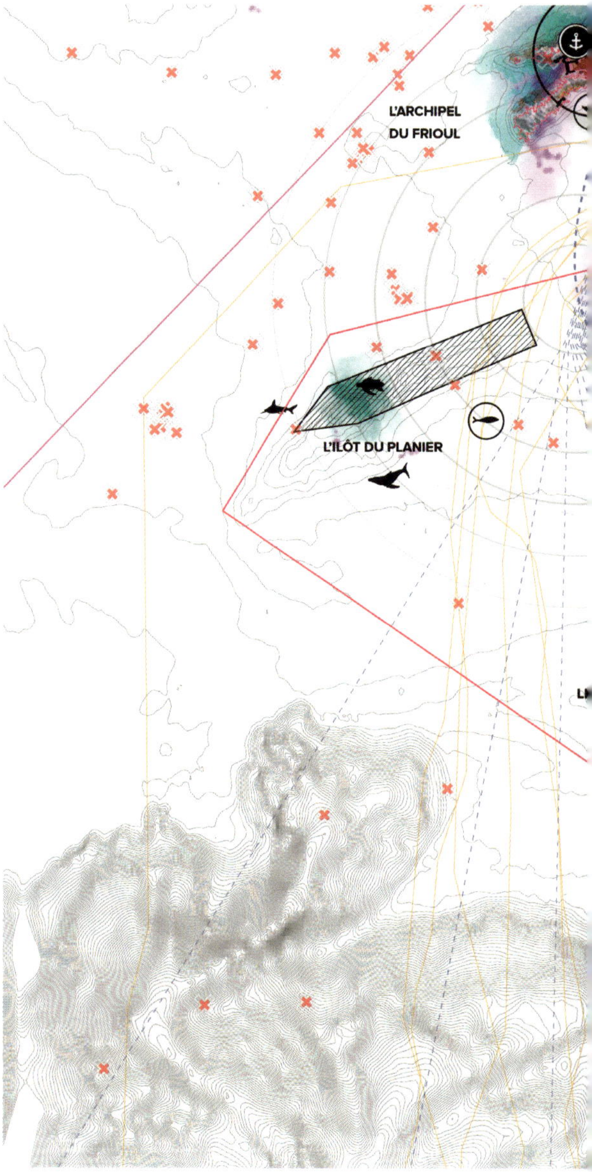

↗ Map of underwater landscape issues. Identifying zones with ecological and landscape richness, plus the locations of wrecks and underwater remains. Highlighting different types of human impact. © Fabien David, Coloco
→ Underwater views showing the effects of human activity. © Fabien David, Coloco

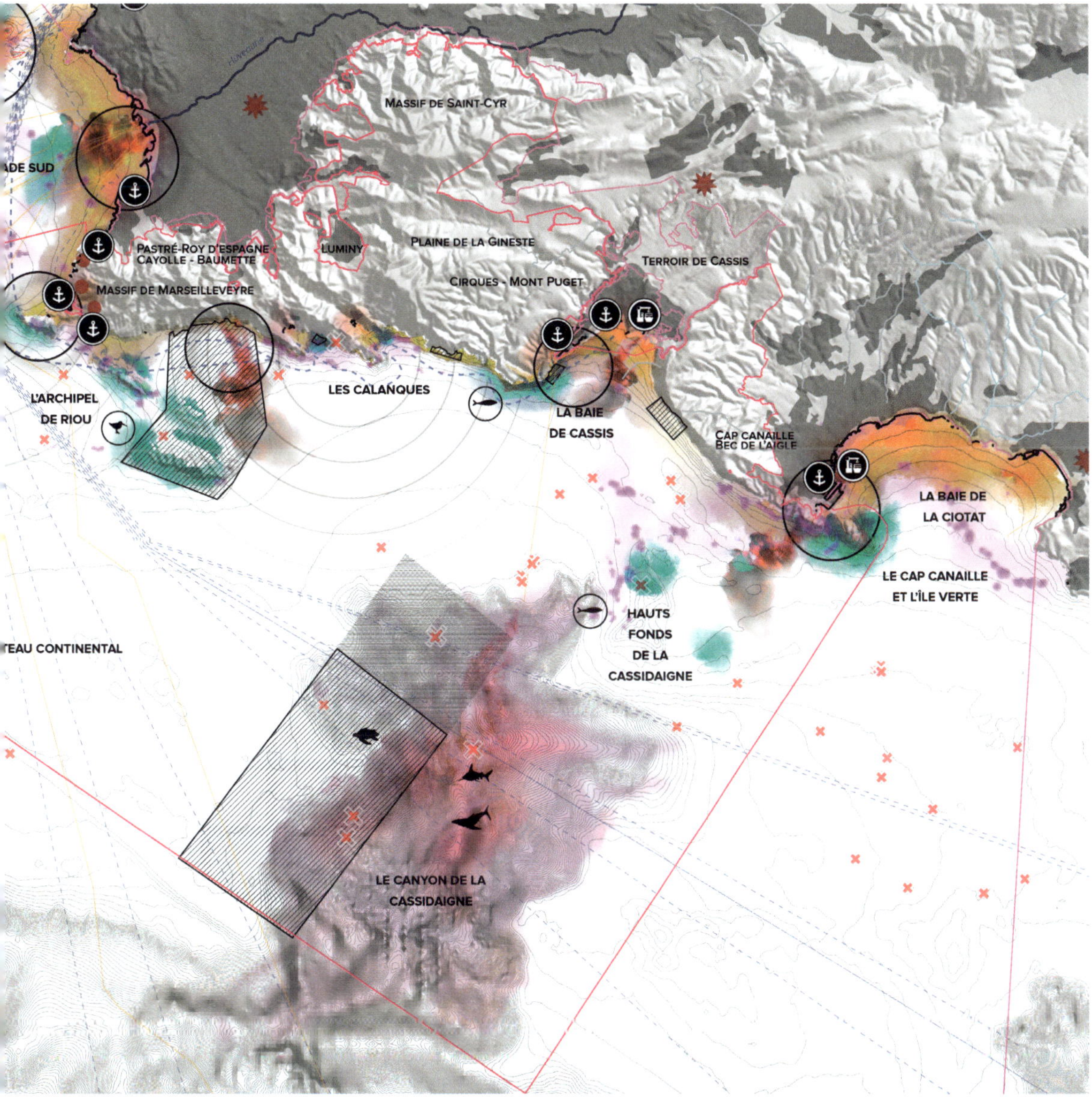
ADE SUD
MASSIF DE SAINT-CYR
PASTRÉ-ROY D'ESPAGNE
CAYOLLE - BAUMETTE
LUMINY
PLAINE DE LA GINESTE
TERROIR DE CASSIS
CIRQUES - MONT PUGET
MASSIF DE MARSEILLEVEYRE
L'ARCHIPEL DE RIOU
LES CALANQUES
LA BAIE DE CASSIS
CAP CANAILLE
BEC DE L'AIGLE
LA BAIE DE LA CIOTAT
LE CAP CANAILLE ET L'ÎLE VERTE
HAUTS FONDS DE LA CASSIDAIGNE
TEAU CONTINENTAL
LE CANYON DE LA CASSIDAIGNE

Engaging with a territory that has no formal project

The underwater landscapes of the Calanques are not the kind of places where a landscape plan can prescribe developments or operations. How can one engage with a territory that lacks a formal project and isn't designed under terrestrial planning conditions?

We have learned to view this area as a Third Landscape whose richness is vital to our collective future. However, a Third Landscape can't be governed by a plan that designates areas for development or de–development. At this point, the action plan for protecting and enhancing the underwater landscapes could only operate through indirect influence, by setting up protective measures or limiting certain practices. Sometimes, the most constructive action is to stop intervening.

Here, the goal is not to find suitable project sites for applying development principles that illustrate a sound strategy, as we would do on land. It's about collectively choosing areas where we should not intervene, and thus allow for natural regeneration processes. Instead of accumulating isolated decisions that inadvertently lead to disruptions, ceasing to act becomes a project in itself.

Since human–induced disruptions often cause landscape and environmental degradation, reducing the intrusion of toxic substances like chemical compounds or fertilizers serves as a lever for guiding transformation on land. Similarly, at sea, we can set up exclusion buoys to prevent anchoring, limit boat speeds to reduce noise, or expand no–fishing zones to protect breeding areas. Thus, it has been decided to propose a territorial project that reduces impacts, marking a change in practices.

Towards a shared culture

Ranging from an operational vision for concrete and immediate actions to long–term research goals, a combination of thinking and doing has shaped the overall discourse. The landscape plan encourages an attitude of "care," which means paying attention, noticing details, and embracing a sense of wonder that naturally leads to protecting and preserving shared spaces – in which, by reducing or eliminating human impacts, the natural dynamics of life can be restored.

An important complement to the measures outlined in the Landscape Plan is education for all local school children, but also for visitors. Collective education is needed to raise awareness about the environments, landscapes, and the impact of current coastal practices. The sea endures, tolerates, and often repairs the ignorance and unconscious behaviors of those who harm it. In partnership with the Metropolitan Government of Marseille, the Calanques National Park has set up an ambitious program to provide tools and resources for protecting and showcasing its landscapes. The water surface is no longer seen as a boundary beyond which the landscape ends.

"It's not about us showing off the underwater landscapes of the Calanques – it's about these landscapes shaping our attitudes and behaviors... What we can do is try to understand them better, and gain more clarity about what has created and continues to create them."
Jacques Collina Girard, marine geologist

In 2023, The Calanques Underwater Landscape Plan won the FFP (French Landscape Federation) Landscape Award.

Online document

Video presentation: Landscape Experience(s)

↗ ↓ ©Margaux Bidat

3.S A Primary Forest for the Future

— Western Europe

Rising to the challenge of a Life-centered project that pushes the boundaries of our imagination

This current utopia is a necessary exercise in optimism. A project that is urgent and that challenges our ability to collaborate across geographic scales. It calls for patience and trust to create an irrevocable force for the benefit of others – one that would last far beyond any individual ambition.

It tests our capacity to think long-term, at least 700 years ahead, and to consider vast areas: a minimum of 70,000 hectares. This effort must inspire political forces to collectively recognize the ecological wealth that underpins the concept of Putting Life First.

Stepping back from the final outcome allows us to focus on the various kinds of coexistences needed to maintain these treasures. Can we rise above individual interests to implement such a vast and essential project?

Mission Letting a primary forest recover in Western Europe
Project leader Association Francis Hallé pour la forêt primaire (the Francis Hallé Association for Primary Forests)
Perimeter 70,000 ha in Western Europe
Location Cross-border with a base in France
Timing From 7 to 8 centuries

← ©Arnaud Hiltzer

Objectives Maximizing biodiversity, carbon storage, climate regulation, soil fertility
Functioning Free evolution of a forest ecosystem
Vocation Research, contemplative tourism, territorial development
Credits Where "©Actes Sud 2021" is mentioned, the text is taken from the publication *Pour une forêt primaire en Europe de l'Ouest: Manifeste (Towards a primary forest in Western Europe: a Manifesto)*, Francis Hallé, Éditions Actes Sud (2021)

The primary forest –
to as "ancient" or "v
a *tall forest* **where the**
species grow to their
basal trunk diameter,

— Francis Hallé *Pour une forêt primaire en Europe de l'Oue*
Manifesto), © Éditions Actes Sud (2021)

ometimes referred
rgin" forest – is
oldest trees of each
maximum **height,**
and root spread.

: Manifeste (Towards a Primary Forest in Western Europe: a

3.S

A primary forest in Western Europe: *for a revival spanning seven to eight centuries*

Regardless of latitude, a healthy forest is objectively beautiful, but it is also highly complex, which can sometimes be intimidating. To appreciate the beauty of a forest, one must first become acquainted with a landscape far more complex than our own: in my view, anthropization means simplification. Forest landscapes have different levels of aesthetic appeal; intact forests, known as "primary," are the most beautiful because, in addition to their exceptional dimensions, they harbor the highest diversity of plant and animal life that can exist at a given latitude. We should also get used to the unique features of primary forests like rotting wood covered with a carpet of mosses and flowers, and occasionally, large animals. These elements all contribute to the beauty of the forest. Despite its complexity, we should not fear the forest; it is serene, beautiful, fascinating, and, especially in tough times, it makes those who love it feel good.

Francis Hallé

← ↓ ©Pierre Chatagnon

3.1
Considering the landscape project as a negotiation platform

Francis Hallé's unique scientific experience and his foundational proposal were at the origin of this project. It has brought together nature experts, as well as citizens from diverse backgrounds, who are eager to take concrete steps to protect our planet and pass on an enriched natural heritage to future generations. By joining forces, they wanted to bring this idea to life, explore its concrete implications, and fulfill its promises. Our Association's work aims to create the best possible conditions for this idea to become a practical contribution, relevant to societal debates and to collective actions in France and Europe concerning climate change, biodiversity collapse, our ethical and aesthetic relations with forests and living beings, and new ways of collaboratively building our living environments.

3.2
Building community by gardening together

Such a project makes little sense on its own, separate from the broader issues related to the role of trees and forests in our societies, and from the specific concerns of the areas where it might be implemented. Although innovative, it fits in with existing European or national initiatives and policies. It's not about creating something ex nihilo in the middle of a desert. This project is driven by a collective intelligence, which is necessary in order to share all its aspects thoughtfully and accurately. It aims to contribute to territorial development by bringing real potential to the table. It requires collaborative work between citizens coming up with proposals, stakeholders and institutions. It also requires new forms of governance implied by this shared approach.

We wish to integrate our proposal into a broader reflection that connects the idea of this vast, freely evolving space with a real territorial project around it – a reflection that encompasses not only forest-related activities, but also education, culture, tourism, etc.

It could actually be a Unesco Man and the Biosphere (MAB)-type super-reserve or experimental super-IBR (integral biological reserve), with our project placed at its heart and serving as a lever of intelligent territorial development.

3.3
Turning the project into a score that unfolds over time

This is clearly a transgenerational project whose duration – only determinable after selecting the site – will span seven to eight centuries, starting from an existing forest aged, for instance, 200 to 300 years. This timeframe, which no one can shorten, is dictated by the growth of trees, limited to four months a year at 45–50° latitudes, due to cold winters. These seven to eight centuries will allow three phases of forest development: first, the pioneer trees, then the post-pioneer species, and finally the primary forest trees.

The management approach chosen will be "free evolution"; nothing should be removed from or added to the original site, with the forest self-managing over the long term, evolving towards maximum naturalness. Fallen trees will be left on the ground, and, as the dead wood decomposes, it will restore soil fertility and start food chains that will eventually support large wildlife. No trees will be planted, and the forest processes will occur naturally: seed dispersal by wind or animals; establishment of root symbioses with soil fungi; spontaneous regeneration of the tree cover; thinning out of excess trees via natural selection, and the closure of the canopy. No intervention will be made on the growing trees.

3.4
Expressing care for the living world through aesthetic resolution

It has been so long since we last had a forest of this quality in France that it's probably worth explaining what it actually is:

A primary forest is a forest that, in theory, has never been cleared or exploited since its origin. If it has been, which is almost always the case, enough time must have passed for it to regain its primary characteristics. This is not a quick process – it takes centuries. It's a tall forest where the trees have reached their maximum height and diameter; it has a closed canopy and a complete range of fauna.

The primary forest is the ecological optimum for the region in which it is located and the best antidote one can imagine against climate disruption and the degradation of our natural environments: it maximizes carbon dioxide absorption, stores the most carbon in both wood and soil, minimizes pollution, and ensures maximum fertility, soil stability, and protection of water resources. It also supports maximum biodiversity, including large animals, and has the best resilience against climatic challenges and biotic attacks. Finally, as an optimal ecological system, the primary forest perfectly embodies the beauty of Life. Whether animal or plant, visible or invisible, it is the sign of the free development of Life's own dynamics.

The difference betwee
a young one is immed
when you are on-site.
even *hear* **the beauty.**
explanation; it is *preci*

— **James Balog** *American ecologist,* © Actes Sud 2021

n an old forest and
ately obvious
You can *see, feel,* **and**
It requires no
e, direct, and tangible.

↓ ©Jessica Buczek

Francis Hallé

Born in 1938, Francis Hallé is a biologist, botanist, and professor at several universities.

Hallé's fascination with the ecology of tropical forests and the architecture of their trees has taken him across continents to study these ecosystems. It was also his unwavering commitment to drawing that has steered his research towards the humid tropics.

Starting in 1985, he led the Radeau des Cimes (Canopy Raft) missions, overseeing the scientific aspects of research on tropical forest canopies for 30 years.

Between 1960 and 2004, he published numerous scientific papers and authored several popular books, translated into multiple languages.

In 2019, he founded the Francis Hallé Association for Primary Forests, dedicated to realizing his dream of restoring an ecologically pristine forest in Western Europe, undamaged by human intervention and left to evolve freely. This vision encompasses the maximum accumulation of carbon, biodiversity, soil fertility, and natural beauty.

→ ©Francis Hallé

A definition of the primary forest

Extract from Pour une forêt primaire en Europe de l'Ouest: Manifeste (Towards a primary forest in Western Europe: a Manifesto), ©Actes Sud 2021

A brief description to begin with: the primary forest – sometimes referred to as "ancient" or "virgin" forest – is a tall forest where the oldest trees of each species grow to their maximum height, basal trunk diameter, and root spread. Thanks to both living and dead trees, the soil here is particularly fertile, and biological diversity is at its peak, giving the primary forest an unexpected role as both a cradle and a museum of living forms.

It is a dark forest because its canopy is completely closed, except, of course, in temperate latitudes during winter when the trees stand leafless. However, the primary forest is not monotonous; windthrows caused by falling dead trees and the clearings maintained by large herbivores create a pleasantly varied landscape. I hope you'll excuse this subjective stance, which for me is essential: of all forests, the primary ones are the most beautiful. In scientific literature on forests, beauty has not, until now, been given the place it deserves, and this manifesto aims to fill the gap.

In contrast, the secondary forest – sometimes referred to as "forest regrowth" – is low, with young, excessively numerous trees that have slender trunks. The canopy is riddled with gaping holes, which are reminders of the crowns of major trees that were cut down. The biological diversity is reduced, particularly due to hunting and the harvesting of dead wood. While I may understand the people who admire a secondary forest and find it beautiful, I fear that they just haven't had the opportunity to compare it with the gold standard: the primary forest.

The comparison made by American ecologist James Balog is striking: "The primary forest is to the secondary forest what the Grand Canyon is to a sewer." Balog goes on: "Old–growth forests have character; the imprint of time has given them biological complexity and an eloquent architecture, all of which young regrowth forests lack. The difference between an ancient forest and a young one is immediately obvious when you are on–site. You can see, feel, and even hear the beauty. It requires no explanation; it is precise, direct, and tangible. A healthy society should be guided by aesthetics, and its response to the question of beauty should never come as an afterthought. It is difficult to live in a society which forgets to see and celebrate beauty because that society is dried up to the bone."

← ©Pierre Chatagnon

Restoring high biolog
us to embrace the *lon*
of the forest itself. Ou
paced by a frenetic rh
this forest project, we
rediscover the value o
and *intergenerational*

Let's learn the art **of d**

cal diversity requires
g cycles of nature **and**
lives today are often
ythm, but through
can beneficially
f long-term thinking
transmission.

oing nothing.

Reviving a primary forest means...

1 — Combating global warming
Forests are a major response to global warming due to their natural ability to reduce carbon dioxide, both through the life processes of trees and by storing carbon in the soil.

2 — Restoring a large biodiversity reservoir
Forests ensure the restoration of biodiversity reservoirs accommodating large and small mammals, as well as insects, fungi, cavity-nesting species, and an immense variety of plants.

3 — Protecting human life
Forests contribute to protecting human life against pandemics by maintaining and developing ecosystems that are large and varied enough to ensure a good balance of life overall.

4 — Ensuring the abundance and quality of water resources
Forests contribute to regulating climate, to precipitation, and to the storage and filtration of water.

5 — Advancing research
Beyond monitoring and evaluation, plant and animal biologists, botanists, or pharmacologists will have much to discover in natural environments left free from human intervention. In this regenerating forest, local stations and observatories, such as flux towers, will allow scientists to observe, analyze, and evaluate processes, generating new knowledge.

6 — Supporting territorial development, citizenship, and artistic practices
We imagine using this natural space for educational activities and discovery experiences aimed at the wider public, notably for teaching sustainable practices regarding soil, natural areas, wildlife and plants. The goal is also to promote small-scale, highly regulated tourism.

There could even be a center for conferences and exhibitions about nature, focusing especially on wild forests.

→ ©Pierre Chatagnon

The history of forests **did not start with the history of humans. It's actually** *the other way around.*

→ ©Pierre Chatagnon

3.T Le potager des Autres (The Others' Kitchen Garden)

— Potager du Roi (The King's Kitchen Garden), Versailles

A year of Putting Life First

A garden is defined by its enclosure; it's a part of the world where we keep the living things that we value most. The idea of what is "best" changes over time and across cultures. The methods of creating a garden, its forms, and the types of management are a reflection of their era. In today's world, marked by globalization and cascading ecological crises, what kind of garden should we cultivate to explore our relationship with living things?

The Potager des Autres (the Others' Kitchen Garden) is a relational experience, not just among humans, but with all living things – plants, animals, fungi, microbes... Showing concrete and visible applications of diverse experiments from around the world, this garden has breathed life into the exhibition *Putting Life First*, because direct encounters with living beings are irreplaceable, and because they perfectly complement a more intellectual and visual approach to our landscapes and the challenges they face.

The different collectives working on–site offered guided tours, each shedding new light on this composite garden. The multiple initiatives were not cataloged in neatly identified squares but woven together into a vast, multi handed tapestry of Life. Each story added a new layer of interpretation, enriched by previous contributions.

Mission Exhibition/garden for the biennale Bap! 2022
Geographical coordinates 48°47'55.4"N, 2°07'08.9"E
Location Versailles, France
Size 3,000 m²
Status Temporary artwork, temporary and traveling exhibition
Client Île-de-France Region, École Nationale Supérieure de Paysage (ENSP, the Versailles National School of Landscape Architecture)

Concept Coloco (exhibition design: integral designers∫)
Implementation Barbier Noémie, Baticle Murielle, Bonnenfant Nicolas, Borrelli Fransceca, Brenier Selma, Cochet Anne–Laure, Depondt Marie, Farou Paul, Georgieff Miguel, Georgieff Pablo, Goncalves Alexis, Lefort Lorraine, Michels Kevin, Pardon Estelle, Siegel Isabelle, Tourneboeuf Cécile, Wambergue Tiphaine, the gardeners of the Potager du Roi + SPORA + Object Growing + the ENSP students + integral designers∫ + Tinctoria...

This is a garden culti *Calls to Create*, **highli** *with and for living thi* **primarily through** *obs* **and** *sharing* **multidisc**

rated through
hting collective work
gs, **and managed**
rving, staying curious,
plinary practices.

↑ Sketch — © Coloco & Co

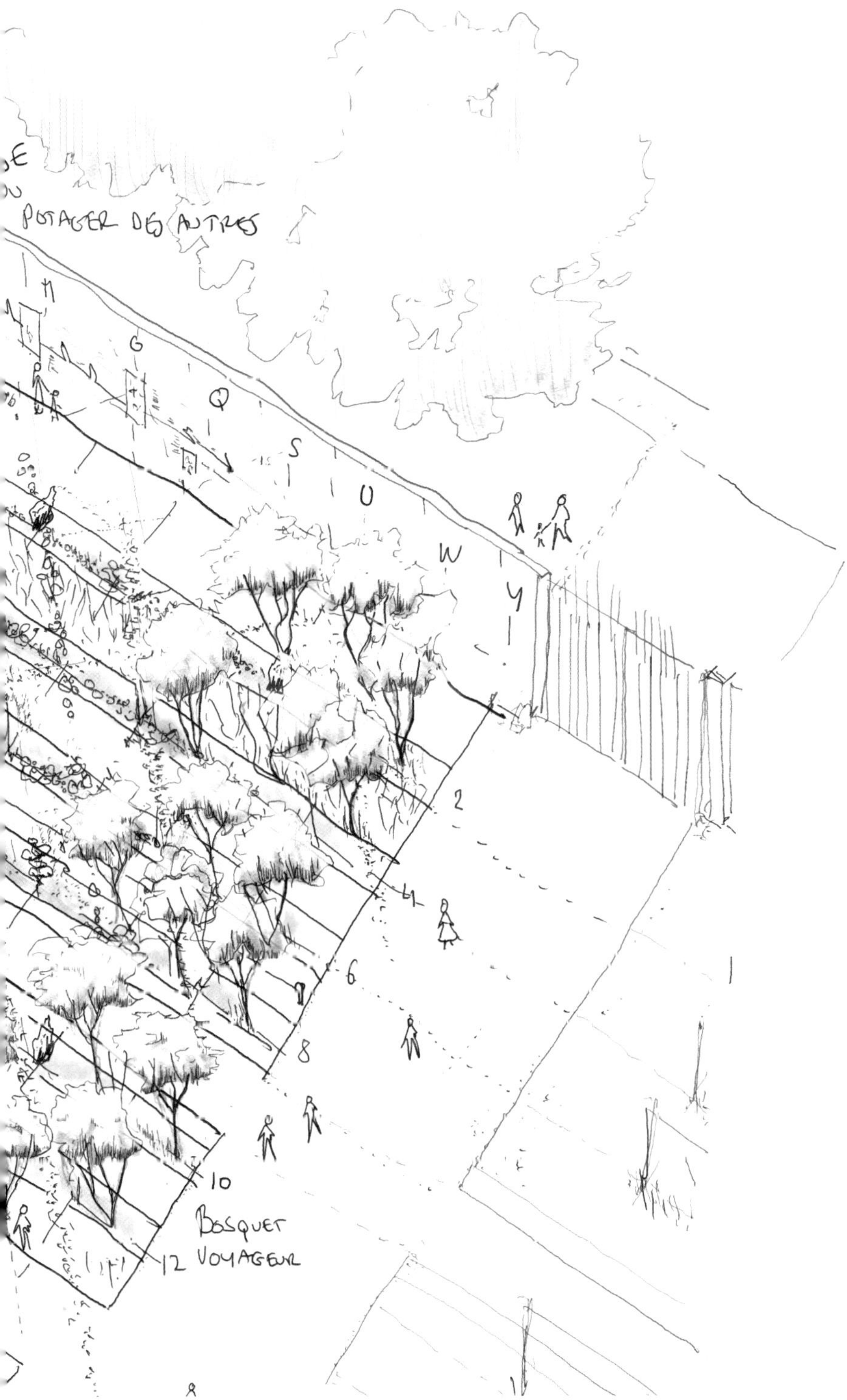
POTAGER DES AUTRES
BOSQUET
VOYAGEUR

3.T

The Potager des Autres, *Putting Life First*

The Potager des Autres was a call to create a garden, launched during the 2022 Biennale of Architecture and Landscape at the Potager du Roi (the King's Kitchen Garden) in Versailles.

Starting in October 2021, we set up a grid to host various gardening projects, the nature and scope of which were unknown at the time due to a flexible process adopted by the curators. We wanted to be ready to embrace the diversity of contributions, with minimal effort and maximum adaptability to all initiatives that would emerge.

The Potager des Autres provided everyone with the opportunity to collectively create a garden, merging all sensibilities and practices. The aim was to unite energies and bring together different fields, from mycology to gastronomy, and from phytosociology to free jazz. Over the three months when the garden was open to the public, before and after visiting the exhibition, people were offered an initiatory stroll, together with an invitation to get into action. Life is the art of encounter!

← ©Emmanuel Gabily

3.1
Considering the landscape project as a negotiation platform

Since 1678, the Potager du Roi has been a place of excellence for agronomic research, initiated by Louis XIV. The Potager des Autres sought to revive a long-unused section of the garden.

When we first visited the building that would host the exhibition, the three thousand square meters in front of it were covered with a black plastic garden tarp. The idea of extending the exhibition with a garden quickly became evident, though it would take eighteen months of hard work to formalize it as a temporary art project. This is the first time the ENSP has taken on such a commission within a site classified as a historic monument. Moreover, the open-ended nature of the project made it impossible to predict the final outcome, which complicated administrative handling. Defining it as a temporary artwork resolved concerns about its future, allowing us to keep the options open.

Respecting all forms of life that emerged as the garden grew, the primary task was to "arbitrate" throughout the maintenance period, adjusting our practices based on discoveries and curiosities. This required careful observation, patient exchanges of opinions, and the ability to make collective decisions by an ensemble of actors that intermingled and complemented each other.

In the fall of 2022, as planned, the garden lost its status as an artwork. Visitors loved it so much that the idea of keeping it was considered, but this would have required gardeners to maintain it, a resource which the Potager du Roi lacked. The Potager des Autres will therefore continue to spread into the different other gardens we are creating, where new opportunities for collaboration will carry this adventure forward.

3.2
Building community by gardening together

It all starts with a framework grid, a spatial and temporal scenography of the living environment. We have to earn the trust of the site's gardeners and then the faculty at the ENSP, whose curriculum is being altered by the Biennale. After that, we'll have to address the needs and dynamics of each initiative. This kind of work is a daily exercise in diplomacy. The geometric grid serves as the physical support for everyone's coexistence. Once these relationships take on a concrete form, it becomes possible to bring together very different visions, and even to discover unexpected resonances. This is where unpredictable encounters, sympathies, and friendships occur.

This collective creative process, whose form is not predetermined, goes beyond any individual intent. Constantly making compromises between geometry and Life that kept overflowing this geometry, the gardeners had to decide, one step at a time, how to coexist with the plants that grow and spread, sometimes in spectacular ways.

What does it mean to build a community with non-human entities? This question is at the core of our discussions. Building a community means that we have to pay attention to the quality of all our relationships with them, from exploitation to admiration. It also involves caring about them, respecting them, and, perhaps, finding ways to show them our sympathy.

For this to happen, we should start by learning their names. We carried out several labeling campaigns, botanical and mycological tours, and a Botanical Dub event where each plant has been introduced. Personally introduced, we might say – because, as with all living beings, representing one's species is by no means defining it. All of us, humans and non-humans alike, are unique individuals living together in communities.

↑ Workshop n°1 — October 2021 — © Alexis Goncalves

↑ Workshop n°3 — April 2022 — © Emmanuel Gabily

↑ May 2022 — © Alexis Goncalves

3.3
Turning the project into a score that unfolds over time

The temporary nature of the Potager des Autres called for a specific approach. From seeing the black tarp to dismantling the garden, the entire process spanned just one year. In the fall, the grid was laid out with stakes and strings, and mulch was added to mark the first diagonal paths. This created an initial pattern of textures on the ground, which was then complemented by the first plantings of seeds and bulbs.

Alongside this spatial plan, there was also a timeline to follow. To manage the timeline, we used a linear spreadsheet that helped us coordinate the participation of gardeners, scientists, musicians, DJs, and even mixologists who responded to the Call to Create. On a large wall, the timeline displayed photos, drawings, and slogans, serving as a record of gardening efforts and exchanges. Visitors could see the process as it happened, and even join an activity, get into action, put their hands in the dirt. The score guided the garden's composition, anticipated how things would be carried out, and legitimized the notation of improvisations. It served as a map to help navigate the garden while narrating its history. Everyone could interpret it from their point of view and according to their sensibility, thus telling their own version of the story. Within an overarching vision, countless micro-decisions were made every day: how tall to let the plants grow, when and how to reshape the paths, whether to densify or thin out the areas that are too sparse or too crowded...

After the Biennale ended, we gradually stepped back from managing the garden. This allowed us, as landscapers, along with students and visitors, to observe the natural evolution of the ecosystem and the flourishing of Life, which, in turn, imposed its own forms upon human-designed geometry.

The Potager des Autres is going to spread to several gardens in Île-de-France, where the plants will be permanently planted. We have collected a lot of seeds, which now rest in their neatly labeled envelopes, waiting for the next garden where they would thrive as part of future scores yet to be written.

↑ June 2022 — © Yann Monel

3.4
Expressing care for the living world through aesthetic resolution

A garden, shaped by human hands, follows certain compositional rules. Since ancient times, geometric design has been the way humans show their control over the living world and impart meaning to the garden as a work of intellect. Plants also carry symbolic meanings, associated with deities, spirits, or virtues. Gardeners are known for using plants like painters use their palette, skillfully blending forms and colors into artful compositions.

The Potager des Autres did not deviate from these rules but made them both explicit and negotiable, giving credit to plants as genuine creators within the collective of gardeners. Sometimes, if a plant grew beyond the designated lines, it was the lines that were redefined, following the principle of Putting Life First. In other places, a clean trimming of edges would highlight the deliberate choice to let a seemingly chaotic mix of plants grow freely.

The Potager des Autres honored diversity. It followed in the footsteps of the horticultural excellence project initiated by Jean-Baptiste de La Quintinie. Admittedly, our work was much less challenging, as sourcing plants from around the world is far easier today than it was in his time. We took this opportunity to grow over 120 varieties of plants. These were not arranged by geographic origin, family, or color. Instead, it was the sequence of interventions that created a continually evolving aesthetic, much like how Life itself works.

It felt refreshing to see the plants typically associated with certain aesthetic references – a parson's garden, grandma's vegetable patch, or an herb garden – reimagined in a sort of grand remix. From what visitors have told us, the garden was definitely surprising. It sparked curiosity about living things and how they were cultivated here. "It's not me, it's the Other," we might say, acknowledging shared authorship.

↓ © Estelle Pardon

Working together allo
more value to the pro
with living things, an
to *coexist with other fo*
through the Call to Cr
values such as auton
solidarity, and mutua
inspired by the living

ws us to give
fessions that interact
d to re-learn how
rms of life. **Here,**
eate, we promote
omy, generosity,
support, often
world.

Fertilizing the soil

July 2021 – March 2022

Started on a compact and infertile soil, the Potager des Autres was eventually able to support a diverse range of life forms.

To recreate a living soil, several steps were undertaken:

— species such as sorghum and dock were planted by the Potager du Roi gardeners to decompact the soil with the root systems;

— once the plants reached the end of their growth cycle, shallow tillage of about 10 cm was used to mix in the organic matter;

— in October 2021, the grid defined by Coloco was marked out, followed by mulching the crop areas;

— planting in Call to Create mode took place from October 2021 to June 2022;

— hibernacula were created using trimmed plants;

— the soil was mulched with garden pruning debris.

With soil being a key element in the living dynamics of ecosystems, these activities have stimulated the organic matter cycle and ecosystem vitality.

The composition of the Potager des Autres began with addition by planting, and continued with an approach focused on subtraction to create and maintain pathways through the vegetation.

↗ Covered soil — Summer 2021 — © Alexis Goncalves
↗ The first workshop, marking out the grid — October 2021 – © Alexis Goncalves
↗ The first workshop, marking out the grid — October 2021 – © Nicolas Bonnenfant
↗ A planting session — April 2022 — © Emmanuel Gabily
→ Pruning — © Emmanuel Gabily
↓ Mulching layout

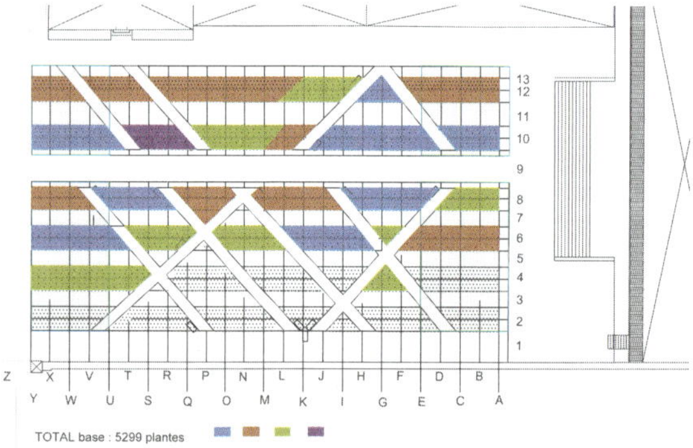

F
G
Janvier —
Février
2022

Timeline — the garden score

September 2021 – July 2022

Tracing the month-by-month evolution of the Potager des Autres, this 60-plus-meter timeline unfolded along the wall that separates the Potager du Roi from the Pièce d'Eau des Suisses (the Lake of the Swiss Guards). Exiting the exhibition rooms, visitors could literally walk through the garden's history in chronological order.

Each month, a blank sheet was made available for recording new interventions, with part of it reserved for adding photos, drawings, and writings.

Everyone was welcome to express themselves, choose a plant to draw, jot down a thought, or paste a photo. The wall became an expression of the various initiatives and a key to understanding how they were coming together.

Just like the garden itself, the timeline was also a call to create – in this case, to create a true garden score.

↗ Composing a score for the garden
↗ The timeline in the making © Emmanuel Gabily
↓ © Yann Monel

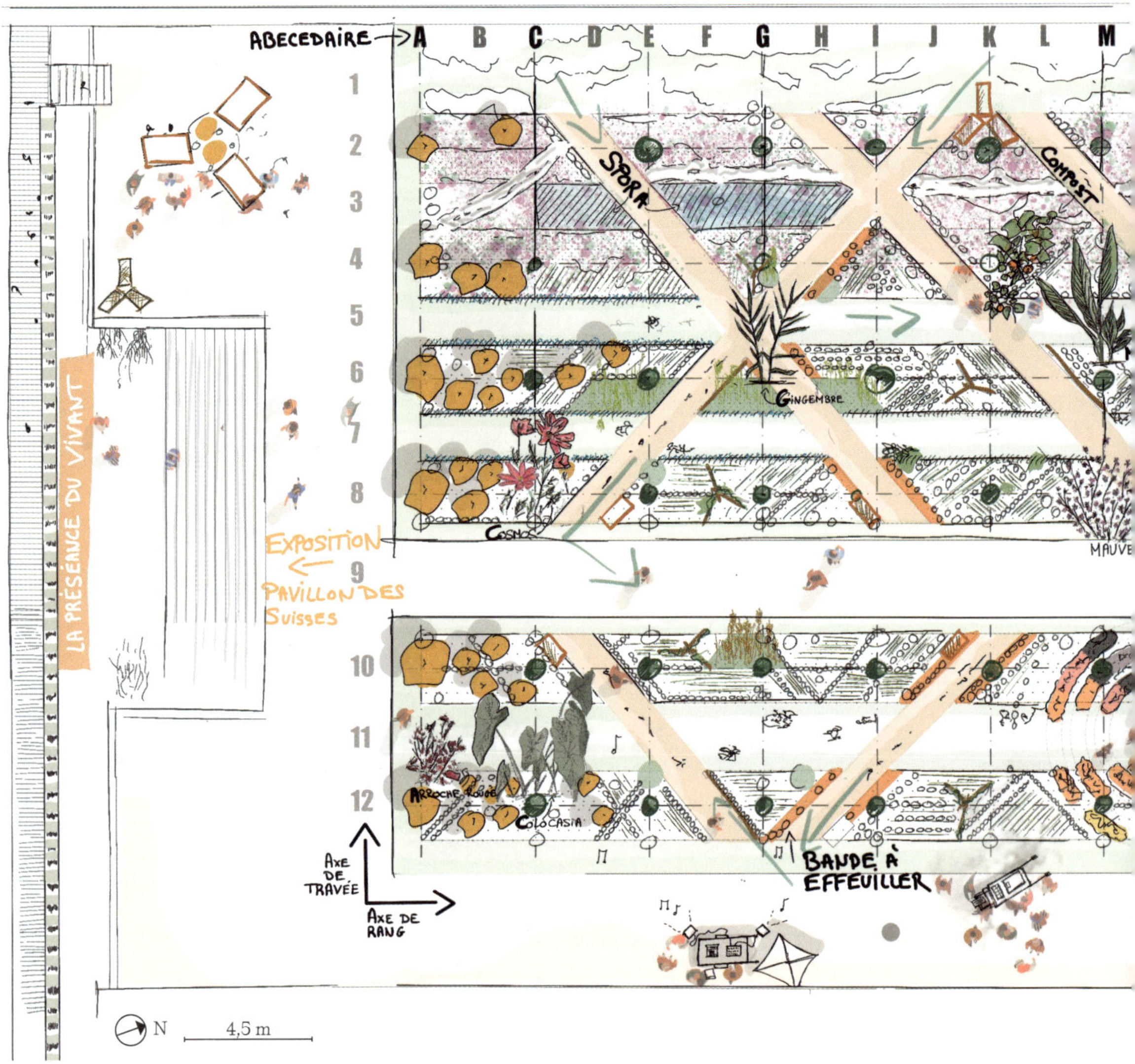

The Potager des Autres — the layout of initiatives

October 2021 – August 2022

Invitation à l'oeuvre / Call to Create: Projects led by associations, artists, students from the ENSP, and Coloco.

Abécédaire / Alphabetical Guide: Classification and planting of certain species according to the garden's pathway axes to facilitate plant recognition for visitors.

Bande à effeuiller / Pick-Off Strip: Planting a diagonal strip of aromatic herbs to be picked off.

Tinctoriales / Tinctorials: Planting a chromatic circle of plants used for dyeing. A dyeing and botanical painting workshop with Emmanuelle Bouffé (July 2022).

Object Growing: Making furniture from mycelium; creating three furniture modules in the soil of the Potager des Autres.

Bosquets voyageurs / Traveling Groves: These trees and shrubs have spent six months in the Potager des Autres before being permanently relocated to other projects throughout Île-de-France.

Compost: A compost bin made from pallets and planted with cucurbits, beans, potatoes, etc.

Epi collector: Experimental plantings of heritage wheat in partnership with the producers advocating for its conservation.

Légumes perpétuels / Perennial Vegetables: Planting perennial vegetables, a continuous food source.

SPORA: Mycorrhization of a plot in the Potager des Autres to observe the benefits of fungi on surface crops. Highlighting the role of fungi in agricultural and forest ecosystems.

+9 activities during the BAP biennale: Painting with plant-based inks, manual mowing, vibraphone performances, electronic naps, Botanical Dub, construction and installation of birdhouses by high school students, harvesting for cooking, distillation, a 24-hour "Vivants d'abord" (Life First) event, seed collection, and other activities.

5 Call to Create workshops: Open workshops to mark out the grid and plant the Potager des Autres.

+150 days of "landscape duty": A small full-time team was in charge of observation and maintenance from October 2021 to July 2022.

4 planting sessions for children: Preschool and primary school children from Île-de-France came to plant their produce in the garden.

9 projects: Projects by associations, students, and Coloco; turning the garden into an experimental space.

Epi-collector — Murielle Baticle, Tiphaine Wambergue

April 2022

Epi-collector was an occasion to lead a project differently, allowing us, the landscapers at Coloco, to freely experiment with a theme. As our team explored the use of green manure in agriculture, the conversation has gradually led us to cereals. Do they belong in this garden? Aesthetic, political, and educational considerations were brought together to find an answer.

Epi-collector, a collection of cereals planted at the heart of the garden, invited visitors to appreciate the visual appeal and diversity of these nourishing grasses, to listen to the sound of their awns in the wind or rain, and to closely admire the anatomy of their ears. From sowing to harvest, we observed the rapid growth of the cereals. They captivated the visitors and brilliantly won their place in the garden.

Putting together a varied palette to represent a plant family that is not very familiar to gardeners, we faced the challenge of sourcing. With limited seeds available from conventional agriculture, we had to turn to organic farming and traditional practices that embrace diversity.

Cereals are typically known from large-scale farming operations. Peasant seeds, on the other hand, are exchanged among farmers and cannot be sold commercially. These farmers cultivate heirloom varieties, harvest and multiply them, thus helping to preserve a valuable genetic heritage. They can sell their harvest once it has been processed. Over the past several years, various associations, networks, and collectives have been formed to promote the sharing and exchange of seeds, fostering alternative cultivation practices.

The farm at the Domaine Les Bruyères (located in the department of Loiret) entrusted us with about twenty samples of peasant seeds, or landrace wheat varieties, which we planted sporadically in the garden: Gros Bleu, Rouge de Bordeaux, Rouge du Roc, Hérisson, Blé de Saint Priest, Poulard, Pongho, Mélange des Bruyères... These regular plantings, sown in winter (marked on the plan as yellow dots), contrasted with the dense lines of forest rye, barley, spelt, buckwheat, and winter wheat (marked on the plan as green areas), echoing large-scale agriculture.

Adding aesthetic value to the garden (structuring, layering garden spaces, creating perspectives...), these cereals have also led us to consider important political issues of our time. Indeed, the vast majority of food crop seeds are genetically modified, patented, and rendered sterile, which means that each year they must be purchased anew. In light of this reality, groups like Via Campesina are fighting an epic battle. Prominent voices, like that of Vandana Shiva, rise against the privatization of Life and advocate for free access, mutual aid, and the preservation of millennia-old agricultural knowledge in the face of industrial agriculture that is becoming increasingly unsustainable both ecologically and energetically.

These plantings created a space for dialogue, where we invited agricultural professionals, farming and agri-food associations, and various collectives. Our conversations have been recorded and can be accessed via this QR code.

Tropicalia — Coloco

April 2022

Tropicalia is a series of botanical experiments conducted by Coloco and dedicated to the cultivation of tropical species in our temperate regions. We focused on their resilience and their interaction with native plants. As global warming progresses, it becomes increasingly important to reconsider our relationship with these tropical species that are becoming more established in Europe.

These so-called exogenous, exotic, or sometimes invasive plants bring to light our mixed feelings about foreignness. When plants like the horse chestnut, the plane tree, or the potato serve our needs, we easily adopt them, making them part of our heritage. But when some tree of heaven or Japanese knotweed happens to thrive in fringe areas, we violently express our xenophobia.

Whether we like it or not, global warming is driving species migration toward the poles, leaving more deserts behind them.

Which plants will best adapt to these changes and dominate our landscapes of tomorrow? And what if we think several centuries ahead, into the era of forest regeneration?

In the meantime, Tropicalia invites us to meet plants from the lands of samba, rumba, or even kathak.

← ©Emmanuel Gabily, Kevin Michels, Murielle Baticle
↗ Planting session — April 2022 — ©Emmanuel Gabily
→ Planting banana trees — April 2022 — ©Isabelle Siegel
→ Opuntia flower — June 2022 — ©Alexis Goncalves
↓ ©Yann Monel

Fig B.11
Criste marine, perce-pierre
Nom latin Crithmum maritimum
Famille Apiaceae
Habitat Bords de mer, creux des rochers,
rochers littoraux
Type biologique Vivace halophile
Usages Feuilles consommées crues ou cuites;
préparés au vinaigre comme des cornichons
Fig B.11

Fig B.12
Lyciet
Nom latin Lycium barbarum
Famille Solanaceae
Habitat Haies, bords de chemin,
Type biologique Petit arbuste
Usages Baies utilisées séchées sous
le nom de baies de goji
Fig B.13
Oxalis
Nom latin Oxalis articulata
Famille Oxalidaceae
Habitat Jardins
à tubercules
Usages Certains oxalis sont consommés,
mais plus généralement ils sont cultivés
pour l'ornementation
Fig B.12
Fig B.13

Object Growing — Miriam Josi, Stella Lee Prowse
May — July 2022

Myco–fabrication uses the growth of mycelium to create materials from organic waste. Experimental design studio Aléa is exploring this process by using soil as a mold to grow objects. This approach eliminates the steps and conditions typical of traditional myco–fabrication, such as sterilization, additional energy, and plastic molds, while focusing on the potential of mycelium to regenerate soil and enhance biodiversity.

After the initial proof of concept at the Domaine de Boisbuchet in September 2021, the Potager des Autres became an experimental site to test and develop this process in the open soil of the Île–de–France region.

Founded in Paris by Miriam Josi (CH) and Stella Lee Prowse (AU), Aléa transcends disciplinary boundaries and envisions new ways of creating for the benefit of both human and non–human systems.

"In the near future, we might grow our furniture while enriching the soil with mushrooms."

The three forms grown in the Potager des Autres

↗ Digging molds — May 2022
↗ Mold — May 2022
↗ Object ready to be unmolded — June 2022
→ Unmolded object — June 2022

SPORA — Francesca Borrelli, Roberto Dell'Orco, Charlotte Janis, Jérôme Legros

April — June 2022

In 2021, an association and collective called SPORA emerged from a desire to bring together a multidisciplinary community of experimenters involved in actions and research on fungi.

SPORA is building a network for growing edible mushrooms outdoors in community gardens and parks throughout Greater Paris. Seeking to develop an urban "brown corridor," SPORA cultivates in these locations an underground mycelial network, a true "internet" of mycorrhizae (fungal roots).

In open spaces, SPORA weaves a network of individuals around a schedule of educational workshops, lecture series, exhibitions, forest walks, and shared experiences in various urban areas. Through these research activities, SPORA aims to raise awareness, especially among young people, of various biodiversity-related themes such as:

— cultivating mushrooms and understanding their biological value;

— observing lichens (indicators of air quality and climate change);

— recycling organic matter and creating compost;

— exploring micro-interactions between plants and fungi, and the phenomenon of symbiosis.

For its mushroom biotope project at the Potager des Autres, SPORA invited mycologist and farmer Jérôme Legros, whose expertise has significantly increased our understanding of mycelium and its potential.

The installation of the SPORA garden was preceded by a mycological walk in the Versailles forest to find new strains for reproduction and to learn more about the ecological importance of fungi in forest ecosystems. Cloning workshops were then held with students and visitors.

↗ Harvesting oyster mushrooms on the forested hillsides of Versailles — © SPORA

↗ The SPORA garden in the potager des Autres — © Yann Monel, SPORA

→ Salvae Mundi: a strain of wild oyster mushrooms harvested in Versailles and cloned at a BAP workshop © JL@I2MSylvallia/MaisonsMARCON

UNE INVITATION MONDIALE POUR REPENSER LE VIVANT À TRAVERS UN PARTAGE DES ENGAGEMENTS POUR CRÉER DE NOUVEAUX IMAGINAIRES, ET DE NOUVELLES ACTIONS COLLECTIVES

24 HEURES POUR ET AVEC LE VIVANT. DE PROPOSITIONS ET DE CONVERSATIONS

17 AU 18 JUIN 2022

VIVANTS D'ABORD!

COLOCO
CIVIC CITY
GILLES CLEMENT

L'ÉVÉNEMENT PRENDRA LA FORME D'UNE CONVERSATION DE 24 HEURES, DANS LE CADRE DE LA BIENNALE D'ARCHITECTURE ET DE PAYSAGE, MODÉRÉE DEPUIS VERSAILLES ET DIFFUSÉE DANS LE MONDE ENTIER VIA VISIOCONFÉRENCE ENTRE LE 17 ET LE 18 JUIN 2022.

AVEC LES PLANTES DITES INVASIVES - QUI QUAND ON Y REGARDE DE PRÈS SONT AUSSI DES REMÈDES POUR LES MALADIES DE NOTRE TEMPS - C'EST UNE SORTE DE RENDEZ-VOUS QUE LE VIVANT NOUS DONNE

THIERRY THEVENIN

NOUS LES HAÏSSONS CAR ELLES NOUS MONTRENT LES LIMITES DE NOTRE POUVOIR. ALORS QUE QUELLES QU'ELLES SOIENT, LES PLANTES SONT TOUJOURS UNE NOUVELLE

Bap! Biennale d'architecture et de paysage · Île-de-France

coloco contemporary landscape creations

dix—milliards—humains

civic city

Memorizing the garden

During the Biennale, members of the Coloco team and visitors came up with different ways to memorize the garden.

The alphabetic guide of the Potager des Autres cataloged all living things identified on the site, carefully noting discoveries, beneficial associations between species, and the actions taken to observe and manage them.

Distillation preserved the garden's scents as essential oils. The tasting of edible flowers combined visual beauty with flavor, creating a Proustian memory of the garden.

An improvised vibraphone concert by Christopher Dell still lingers in our ears.

Dancing, a herbarium, and a painting workshop where participants used the vegetable inks made from garden flowers have further contributed to preserving these memories.

Seed harvest helped spread the Potager des Autres. We gave away many seeds and received others from fellow gardeners.

Finally, the 24–hour conference series "Vivants d'abord" (Life First), with Coloco, Civic City, and Gilles Clément, recorded live discussions on living things, featuring participants from many countries around the world: France, Spain, South Africa, the Maldives, Guatemala, Switzerland, Brazil, Bosnia and Herzegovina, China, Colombia, Venezuela, Chile, Canada, Thailand, Réunion, Italy, Romania, Japan, USA, Ghana, and Argentina.

↗ Alembic, distillation of roses and aromatic herbs – © Yann Monel
→ Vibraphone concert – © Alexis Goncalves
→ Botanical labels – © Yann Monel
→ Grains harvested from the PDA – © Emmanuel Gabily
← 24 hours of "Vivants d'abord" (Life First) © dix–milliards–humains and Civic city

4.

Engage with the living world

Here are five core concepts and tools for implementing them that have shaped the evolution of our professional practice so far. Interrelated with each other, they take you from a global vision to specific situations on the ground. Combined, these five ideas have led us to formulating Put Life First as a call on everyone to make it a guiding principle of any garden project.

Our invitation to take action comes in the form of ten questions shared at the end of this book. These questions will help direct your efforts as gardeners in the creative projects you are yet to begin.

The *Planetary Garden* r Earth as a garden and its gardeners.

There are three reasons for this:

The first reason is that humans are present everywhere on Earth, just as a gardener is present throughout their garden. Even where they don't set foot, they know what's going on.

The second reason is the mechanism of global migration. While it has always existed in its natural form through the dynamics of winds, animals, and ocean currents, global migration has been accelerated by humans. From the moment in history when the first garden was created, nomadic humans became sedentary. They built a protective enclosure where they placed the (mostly edible) species that they had previously gathered along their journey. Then they started "importing" species. As transportation evolved, garden plants began to arrive from increasingly distant locations, eventually crossing oceans.

The third reason relates to the definition of the word "garden," which means both "enclosure" and "paradise." While we cannot comment on the concept of paradise, the enclosure is a reality concerning "life" as we know it. Biosphere, the only known space where "life" is sustained, is a thin layer on our planet's surface, limited between the troposphere reaching approximately 11,000 meters above sea level, and the deepest ocean trenches at 11,000 meters below.

This concept was developed in 1997
→ The Domaine du Rayol, a Planetary Garden

efers to planet
to humanity as

The *Third Landscape* r areas where humans letting Life evolve fre spontaneously.

This may occur either through abandonment (wastelands) or due to the inconvenience of the location (e.g., steep slopes, marshes, or skeletal soils). The term "Third Landscape" emerged from a landscape analysis conducted in the region of Limousin, France, where observations revealed that managed spaces (primarily forests and pastures) were low in diversity, while those left untouched were rich in it. In binary landscapes, light dominates in grazed meadows and shadow in the undergrowth, while the Third Landscape would be one of diversity, composed of different landscape forms. The notion of "third" refers to Abbé Sieyès' pamphlet published in January 1789, shortly before the French Revolution, where he spoke of the "Third Estate," emphasizing that it refers to the majority of citizens.

Paraphrasing Sieyès, what has it done until now? Nothing; it lacks the means. What does it want to be? Something! It must, therefore, be given the means to do so.

If we consider biodiversity as a treasure upon which we depend, we must change the status of wastelands, viewing them as a valuable resource rather than something to be burned or built upon.

The Third Landscape is a refuge for the diversity expelled from everywhere else, a place where no one intervenes, and that unfolds its richness over time with no need for human presence.

This concept was developed in 2003
→ Sensitive mapping of the network of abandoned spaces in Montpellier, 2018 — ©Fabien David, Coloco

fers to all
do not interfere,
ely and

The *Garden in Motion* o gardening method tha not against, the living present on the terrain

This approach to gardening starts with observing and appreciating diversity, letting Life evolve according to its own dynamics. Rather than bending the landscape to our vision, we align ourselves with its natural flow. This practice observes, supports, protects, and enhances biodiversity.

The basic principle of "working with" the energies in place requires taking into account the behavioral diversity of the organisms in the garden. In the plant kingdom, there are a lot of species with short cycles, either annual or biennial. Having no vegetative systems to regenerate, they rely only on their seeds for survival. As for the seeds, they usually don't fall right at the foot of their parent plant, but tend to spread through the garden, carried by the wind and the animals. Each year, these plants show up in different places.

The term "Garden in Motion" reflects the garden's evolving spatial composition, which leads to new ways of creating paths and tending to the land, guided by respect for the physical movement of the plants. To preserve this diversity of wandering species, we need to accept that the shape of the garden will change every year.

This concept was developed in 1991
→ The Garden in Motion experiment at the Jules Rieffel High School (Lycée Jules Rieffel) in Saint-Herblain, France — © Lycée Jules Rieffel

riginates from a
works with, and
organisms

The *Map of Commons* i for the collaborative c of a landscape projec

The Map of Commons displays a network of stakeholders. It gathers comprehensive information and expertise on a given situation. It's a tool for both graphically representing and mobilizing expertise in uses, development, and management. This methodology helps build an understanding of the living environment and the ways in which the community cares for it.

In a single document, the Map of Commons correlates a cartographic representation with a temporal representation of a territory, laying out a shared vision and a sequence of localized actions. The actions are presented in the form of a score, which facilitates the coordination of efforts by creating collaborations around catalyst projects that can be implemented quickly. Tuning in to the connections between each level of decision and action is essential to optimizing resources and improving the quality of outcomes. This approach gives clear value and understandable meaning to actions that may seem modest but have global implications.

The Map of Commons is not static; it evolves according to the context. It has to be updated collectively every september, maintaining what works and discarding the rest to make room for newly prioritized actions and update the plantation calendar. This way of revising issues based on past experiences is a guarantee of balanced interventions. By incorporating feedback on uses and management, it offers a continuous improvement loop and remains open to future changes.

This tool was created in 2013

→ A map for the redevelopment of the Place de la Nation in Paris, 2017 — ©Coloco

s a tool
evelopment
within a territory.

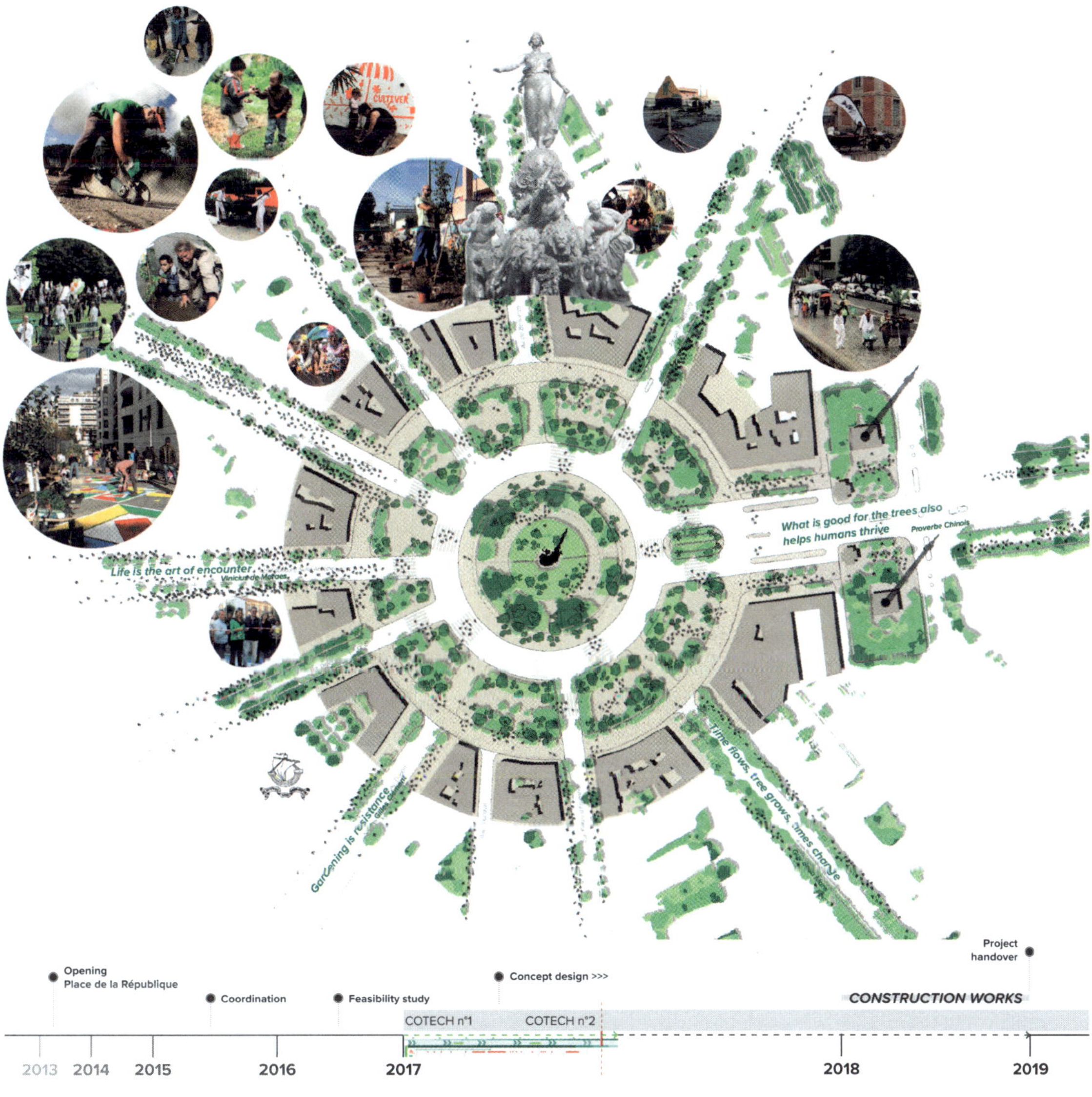

The *Call to Create* decl
will come to life here,
welcome to participat

In shared work, we need to let go of the idea of "control" and allow everyone's skills and responsibilities to come into play, starting with the professionals involved in these tasks. The Call to Create complements the spatial project with a human project.

It is initiated by a gardener or a collective that takes responsibility during the project's implementation phase and then organizes its handover. This collective creative process has no predetermined form; it is shaped by a combination of technical, scientific, and poetic exchanges and collaborations.

As the project progresses, the objectives are adjusted according to the strengths and skills of the group that organizes itself, follows emerging rules, and manages initiatives and disagreements. Sharing knowledge and learning how to care for the living world are key to this method: the aim is to become the gardeners of a project that we are building together. Depending on the context, different groups of people – residents, users, technical services staff, collectives, and engaged individuals – create specific setups.

The Call to Create fosters a shared attitude of care for the living world on the scale of a specific site. The transformation of the site entails changes in (non–)governance and (non–)management.

In this process, designers aim not to lead but to support a collective effort that connects living beings, both human and non–human. Here, we are invited to assume our role as Planetary gardeners.

This tool was created in 2004
→ Diventare giardino, Manifesta 2018 — revisiting the garden and planting two more trees in 2024 © Pablo Georgieff

res that a garden and that everyone is in its development.

10 questions **for starting a garden**

→ Tear this sheet out and use it as your guide to get started

The observer's standpoint has its elegance, but the world today demands action. Behind the decision to act is a vision of the Planetary Garden driving us to take charge of a small piece of the planet because we feel responsible.

The act of transforming a place changes our idea of what's possible. It moves us from 'there's nothing we can do' to 'when do we get started?' This optimistic stance comes complete with responsibility: you can no longer hide behind the 'yes–buts' like 'I have no budget' or 'I haven't got the tools.' There are no more excuses.

The ten questions that follow are designed to help you in starting and/or involving in a garden – or any space on its way to becoming one. Each of us can take the initiative.
Let's get in the game! It's our turn.

1. What's the potential for a garden here?

Every place can be a garden; we must explore its full potential by expanding our view. Immerse yourself in the logic of the place, look around to understand the geographical context in which this piece of land fits.

2. What kind of soil am I planting in?

Knowing the soil we are working on keeps us from hurting the land. We choose plants wisely; we don't mistreat the soil that hosts invaluable life, including countless seeds. We cover it, we mulch, we tend to it responsibly. We make sure we don't pollute it — because this is our shared treasure.

3. What water resources are available?

Water is a vital concern for the future; in the garden, saving water becomes imperative. Let's try to collect and retain it through infiltration, without ever leaving the soil bare. Understanding the water's path is crucial: where does it come from, and where does it flow? What level of permeability, what infiltration can I allow to nourish the soil?

4. What is the path of the sun?

Consider how light and shadow dynamics affect the spaces to understand whether to expose or shield them as plants grow. The sun can be both a benefactor and a threat — how can we adapt without being able to predict its moves?

5. Who is already living here?

Recognizing humans and non-humans that are present on the terrain as allies, preserving them, and welcoming the diversity of all living beings is key to a vibrant garden. A garden is a place for meeting, sharing, and learning above all. How do we make sure not to harm?

6. Who are the gardeners?

All living beings are or can be part of the interaction. Let's encourage the sharing of these rewarding experiences to amplify our strengths, but also to contemplate, unwind, and enjoy the silence...

7. Who are my partners in co-authoring the garden?

Embrace the principle of co-creation, acknowledging the garden's living beings as the co-authors of its development. Functioning as an ecosystem, a garden is a complex tapestry of interactions where a mindful gardener accepts, welcomes, and collaborates with all other organisms.

8. What's our gardening strategy?

What attitude do we adopt in shaping the world around us? Between letting nature take its course and actively crafting our own vision, all kinds of nuances exist; our task is to find the right balance that will evolve over time.

9. What's the timeline for our garden?

Think of time as a musical score, spanning from immediate action to long-term evolution. We are the interpreters of a story that is yet to be written. In this story, only harmony matters.

10. What are we hoping to achieve?

Weave a tale that unfolds over time, giving rise to new narratives. A garden never ends, its scenery is constantly changing — that's where the gardener enters as an artist. Aesthetic resolution seeks to inspire continual awe, consisting of small victories and great revelations.

Bibliography

A selection of texts to spark curiosity and enhance understanding

Manifeste du Tiers paysage
Gilles Clément, Sens et Tonka, 2014

Le jardin en mouvement
Gilles Clément, Sens et Tonka, 2017

Éloge des vagabondes
Gilles Clément, Robert Laffont, 2014

Le cri de Gaia
Sous la direction de Emanuele Coccia et Frédérique Aït–Touati, La Découverte, 2021

The Life of Plants: A Metaphysics of Mixture
Emanuele Coccia, Polity Press, 2018

Ré–ensauvageons la France :
Plaidoyer pour une nature sauvage et libre
Gilbert Cochet, Stéphane Durand, Actes Sud, 2018

Ethnographies des mondes à venir
Philippe Descola et Alessandro Pignocchi, Seuil, 2022

Éloge de la plante. Pour une nouvelle biologie
Francis Hallé, Points, 2014

Antidote au culte de la performance,
Olivier Hamant, Gallimard, 2023

Le grand traité du Jardin punk
Éric Lenoir, Terre Vivante, 2021

Le projet local
Alberto Magnaghi, Mardaga, 2003

Naviguer dans un jardin
Pablo Georgieff, Jean Michel Place, 2022

Microcosmos: Four Billion Years of Microbial Evolution
Lynn Margulis, Dorion Sagan, Wildproject, 2022

Raviver les braises du vivant
Baptiste Morizot, Actes Sud, 2020

Pour une écologie du sensible
Jacques Tassin, Odile Jacob, 2020

Terra Forma
Frédérique Aït–Touati, Alexandra Arènes, Axelle Grégoire, Editions B42, 2019

The Sea Around Us
Rachel Carson, Wildproject, 2019

The Death of Nature:
Women, Ecology, and the Scientific Revolution
Carolyn Merchant, Wildproject, 2021

Plutôt couler en beauté que flotter sans grâce
Corinne Morel–Darleux, Libertalia, 2019

Pour une écologie pirate :
Et nous serons libres
Fatima Ouassak, La Découverte, 2023

The Eye of the Crocodile
Val Plumwood, ANU E Press, 2012

Mémoires terrestres
Vandana Shiva, Wildproject, 2023

Les Plantes du Chaos
Thierry Thevenin, Vieilles racines & jeunes pousses, 2021

Les Carnets du paysage n°40 : Vivants d'abord
Collectif, Actes Sud, 2022

Acknowledgements

Thank you to all the authors
of the projects featured in this book for their involvement and dedication.

Thank you to the ENSP Versailles,
its directors Vincent Piveteau and Alexandra Bonnet, and all the faculty, and the staff at the Potager du Roi who made possible the exhibition and the Potager des Autres in 2022. Special appreciation to all the students, without whom this school would not be!

Thank you to l'Archipel and l'École de l'Anthropocène in Lyon

Thank you, Véronique Mure,
for sharing your love of all living beings

Thank you, Francis Hallé,
for scholarly and creative inspiration

Thank you, Sébastien Marot,
for visionary conversations

Thank you, Danilo Capasso,
Doctor in Colocology – soundcloud.com/dj–danylo

Thank you, Pierre-André Martin,
Fala Irmáo!

Thank you, Thierry Thévenin
for your botanical friendship

Thank you, Ruedi e Vera Baur, Susanna Cerri and the Civic city team

Thank you, Maren Hollman,
for your commitment and perseverance in designing this book

A huge thank you, Cécile Tourneboeuf,
for your flawless contribution throughout the entire project

Thank you, Delphine Longuet,
for your support, insightful advice, and surgical precision.

Last but not least, thank you to all those engaged with Coloco,
both long–term or temporarily. Over the past 25+ years, we have been thinking and acting together for the benefit of Life!

The authors express their gratitude to the Quartus Endowment Fund
for donating a hundred books to associations, schools, and centers for education and awareness.

Planetary Gardener – Life First

This book follows the exhibition *Putting Life First* (*La Préséance du vivant*), first presented from May 14 to July 13, 2022 at the École Nationale Supérieure de Paysage de Versailles as part of the 2nd edition of the Biennale of Architecture and Landscape of the Île-de-France region.

Exhibition commissioner : Région Île-de-France / Executive production : École Nationale Supérieure de Paysage de Versailles / Curators : Coloco and Gilles Clément / Coordination : Cécile Tourneboeuf / Exhibition design, graphic design and visual communication : Ruedi and Vera Baur and Integral designers (Maren Hollmann, Sulliane Bressoud) / Exhibition set-up : Atelier Médicis

Co-authors
Gilles Clément and Coloco –
Nicolas Bonnenfant, Miguel Georgieff, Pablo Georgieff
Coloco.org

Coordination
Cécile Tourneboeuf

Artistic direction and graphic design
Ruedi and Vera Baur, Maren Hollmann
Design support: Jakobina Tscholitsch, Gerrit Ludwig, Susanna Cerri

Proofreading
Delphine Longuet

Translation
Anna Yudina

Fonts
Self Modern, Lucas Bihan and
Aachen Bold, Alan Meeks

Cover photo
© Yann Monel

Published by
Lars Müller Publishers
Zurich, Switzerland
info@lars-muller.ch
www.lars-mueller-publishers.com
+41 44 274 37 40

Product safety
Producer: Lars Müller Publishers GmbH
Pfingstweidstrasse 6, 8005 Zurich, Switzerland
Responsible person in accordance with EU Regulation 2023/988 (GPSR):
Michael Klein, sales representative,
Hub 1, DE-84149 Velden
+49 8742 964 552 2, gpsr@lars-muller.ch
–
Civic city, civic-city.org
F–93100 Montreuil
Printed in March 2025
Printed in Poland
ISBN 978-3-03778-775-5
Legal deposit: June 2024

Distributed in North America, Latin America and the Caribbean by ARTBOOK | D.A.P.
www.artbook.com